Uncommon Allies

Uncommon Allies

AMERICAN JEWS AND CHRISTIANS
UNITING AGAINST HITLER, 1933–1945

Alan M. Shore

Syracuse University Press

Copyright © 2024 by Syracuse University Press
Syracuse, New York 13244-5290

All Rights Reserved

First Edition 2024

24 25 26 27 28 29   6 5 4 3 2 1

∞ The paper used in this publication meets the minimum requirements of the American National Standard for Information Sciences—Permanence of Paper for Printed Library Materials, ANSI Z39.48-1992.

For a listing of books published and distributed by Syracuse University Press, visit https://press.syr.edu.

ISBN: 9780815638438 (paperback)
9780815657125 (e-book)

Library of Congress Cataloging-in-Publication Data

Names: Shore, Alan M., author.
Title: Uncommon allies : American Jews and Christians uniting against Hitler, 1933–1945 / Alan M. Shore.
Description: First edition. | Syracuse, NY : Syracuse University Press, [2024] | Includes bibliographical references and index.
Identifiers: LCCN 2024005168 (print) | LCCN 2024005169 (ebook) | ISBN 9780815638438 (paperback) | ISBN 9780815638445 (hardback) | ISBN 9780815657125 (ebook)
Subjects: LCSH: Judaism—Relations—Christianity | Christianity and other religions—Judaism.
Classification: LCC BM535 .S4635 2024 (print) | LCC BM535 (ebook) | DDC 940.53/1—dc23/eng/20240509
LC record available at https://lccn.loc.gov/2024005168
LC ebook record available at https://lccn.loc.gov/2024005169

Manufactured in the United States of America

To my beloved Kirsten, whose love, companionship, and encouragement mean the world to me and more.

Contents

List of Illustrations   *ix*

Acknowledgments   *xi*

Introduction
*Reframing Twentieth-Century
American Jewish-Christian Discourse*   1

1. Setting the Stage
*Cooperative Efforts among Jews
and Christians at the Start of the Nazi Era*   15

2. Broadening the Jewish-Christian Alliance
against Nazi Germany   67

3. Differing Jewish Responses to the Final Solution
in 1943 and Their Effects   115

4. Jewish and Christian Zionists
Uncommon Allies in a Common Cause   161

Conclusion
*Madison Square Garden and the Staging
of Judeo-Christian Values*   200

Notes   215

Bibliography   243

Index   253

Illustrations

1. Rabbi Stephen Wise speaks out at Madison Square Garden, 1933   57
2. *New York Times*, front page, March 28, 1933   58
3. *New York Times*, inside coverage, March 28, 1933   59
4. *Time* cover, "Gov. Al Smith, 'Happy Warrior of the Political Battlefield,'" July 13, 1925   60
5. Photo journalism from the Yiddish press, *Forverts*, March 28, 1933   61
6. Widely distributed American Jewish Committee pamphlet "The Voice of Religion"   62
7. Front-page headlines, *Forverts*, March 8, 1934   63
8. "Hitler Guilty of Mass Murder," *Forverts*, March 8, 1934   64
9. *New York Times* notice, "Amusements" section, "The Case of Civilization against Hitlerism"   65
10. The historian and suffragette Mary Ritter Beard   66
11. New York Mayor Fiorello LaGuardia, vociferous advocate for the Jewish cause   151
12. William T. Manning, Episcopal Bishop of New York   152
13. John Haynes Holmes, Unitarian minister   153
14. Michael Williams, the founding editor of the Catholic weekly *Commonweal*   154
15. Ben Hecht, the A-list Hollywood screenwriter and committed Zionist   155

16. The creative artists Kurt Weill and Lotte Lenya   156

17. "We Will Never Die" program cover,
Tears of Rage, by Arthur Syzk   157

18. The Oscar-winning composer and conductor
Franz Waxman at the Hollywood Bowl, July 21, 1943   158

19. The French Catholic theologian Jacques Maritain   159

20. "Jews for Sale," Hecht's bitter plea
in *The New York Times*, February 16, 1943   160

Acknowledgments

The task of acknowledging help for bringing a published work into existence is a hazardous undertaking. Will I be haunted by some glaring omission or another? If so, I can only hope that no one will hold it against me.

I think it may be best to work backward. It is a significant honor to find a publisher of the caliber of Syracuse University Press. My thanks go out to Deborah Manion, the acquisitions editor who saw enough in my approach to shepherd me through the process from proposal to acceptance, and to Kelly Balenske, who seamlessly followed her in that same capacity. Kudos to Jackson Adams, SUP's promotion and publicity coordinator, who has skillfully positioned my work to be seen and considered as both an academic work and an accessible history for the general reading public. I would be remiss if at this point I did not mention Kim Surasky, a friend and editor of uncommon skill who serendipitously appeared at just the right moment when it came time to prepare the manuscript, track down permissions, and attend to whatever else was needed once the book had been accepted.

This is putting the cart before the horse, however, because the genesis of this book began over a decade ago during my time at the Center for Jewish Studies at the Graduate Theological Union in Berkeley, where I greatly benefitted from the guidance of Naomi Seidman and Dan Joslyn-Siemiatkoski, now director of the Center for Christian-Jewish Learning at Boston College. Deena Aranoff at the Center for Jewish Studies and Randi Walker, now retired from the Pacific School of Religion at the Graduate Theological Union, provided indispensable learning opportunities as well. I am particularly indebted to Yaakov Ariel of the University of North Carolina at Chapel Hill, whose even-handed and insightful treatment of the fraught terrain of Jewish-Christian relations provided such a fine standard to which to aspire. Finally, a grateful *sheynem dank* (thank you very much) to Yael Chaver, with whom I studied Yiddish at UC Berkeley. I am convinced that a more patient and forbearing teacher does not exist.

Finally, enduring gratitude to those too numerous to name who acted as my mentors, even if they were not aware they were doing so.

Uncommon Allies

Introduction

*Reframing Twentieth-Century
American Jewish-Christian Discourse*

Almost a decade ago, while on a summer stroll in Manhattan down Broadway, my wife, Kirsten, and I stopped on impulse for a moment just north of 72nd Street at an outdoor used-book stall. For some reason, our eyes were simultaneously drawn to a slim volume wedged among the thicker books. I withdrew it and we were greeted with the title *One Destiny: An Epistle to the Christians*, by Sholem Asch. I vaguely recognized the name as a Jewish writer who in an earlier day had achieved a measure of stature in public consciousness.

I knew nothing of the controversy that had swirled around him in Jewish literary circles due to what many considered his inordinate flirtation with the followers of Jesus and the New Testament. The title intrigued me, and upon opening the book, I discovered that it had been published in 1945. I wondered why he, a Jew, was writing to Christians and what he wanted to tell them at the moment of the conclusion of World War II when the crushing loss of European Jewish life was becoming known to the fullest extent possible. I also wondered what Asch was up to by calling his work "an epistle," as though he were appropriating an apostolic authority normally associated with New Testament writers.

I paid two dollars for the book, and for that price of admission I entered an utterly unexpected chapter in midlife that has culminated in the production of this book. Asch's essay turned out to be an extended cri de coeur for the convoluted history of Jewish-Christian relations, a topic to which I was already drawn. Although the merits of his argument to square the circle of Jewish-Christian differences were questionable, I was intrigued by his interest in and approach to Christianity and, most particularly, by his determination to reclaim Jesus as a figure whose importance to Christians could not be considered apart from his Jewishness. My initial interest in Asch proved to be the portal through which I entered the field of modern Jewish history and culture.

As I pursued this course of study, the world that I entered provided the context for a far deeper understanding of the complexity of the Jewish-Christian encounter in modernity. As I continued, I sought a previously underexplored area that could unite my interests in the Jewish-Christian encounter and the Yiddish language, culture, and literature that I had begun to learn and love. I also found the argument that is the basis of this book. It was that the conventional wisdom that placed the real beginning of meaningful Jewish-Christian relations in America in the years following World War II was misguided.

That position is succinctly stated by Dr. Michael Wyschogrod in his paper "Orthodox Judaism and Jewish-Christian Dialogue" delivered on January 28, 1986, at a conference of the Rabbinical Council of America:

> For several decades now, Jews have participated in Jewish-Christian dialogue. Prior to World War II, this was hardly an issue. There simply was not anywhere in the world organized and sustained contact between the Jewish community and church bodies. Here and there, individual Jews may have had personal contact with a minister, a priest, or some church personality. But this was strictly personal rather than organizational. One can only wonder whether the outcome would have been different if Jewish-Christian relations had been more developed before the Nazi period . . . Be that as it may, the fact is that after World War II, a process of reassessment of Jews and Judaism began to make itself felt in the churches.[1]

It is undeniable that the viewpoint Wyschogrod sums up prevails. For proof of its wide acceptance one need look no further than the multitude of books, symposiums, and congresses over the past decades that have stressed a post-Holocaust perspective in Jewish and Christian self-assessment and its effects on Jewish-Christian relationships. One such gathering, "Religion in a Post-Holocaust World," organized by a Holocaust scholar, Abraham J. Peck, was held at Hebrew Union College in 1980 and attracted over twelve hundred attendees drawn from Jewish, Protestant, and Catholic seminaries. Shortly thereafter, Peck edited and published symposium essays under the title *Jews and Christians after the Holocaust*, with a foreword by Elie Wiesel.[2] Another related volume, featuring a collection of essays with a post-Holocaust emphasis in Jewish-Christian relations, *From the Unthinkable to the Unavoidable: American Christian and Jewish Scholars Encounter the Holocaust*, edited by Carol Rittner and John K. Roth, was published in 1997.[3] *The Holocaust and Its Religious Impact: A Critical Assessment and Annotated Bibliography*, edited by Jack R. Fischel and Susan M. Ortmann, which appeared in 2004, directs the reader to dozens of other similar works.[4] These are only a few examples within a vast sea of literature on the subject that all assume that Jewish-Christian dialogue begins as a result of the Holocaust.

Valuable as they and others of their kind may be, they have nonetheless produced an unfortunate side effect. The narrative this postwar perspective advances is that the possibility of a Jewish-Christian dialogue respectful of Jews developed largely as a result of Christian shame, at the very least for their indifference to six million Jewish deaths in Europe, and at worst, for specific instances of their active collaboration with the Nazis. As a result of this construction of events, instances of interreligious exchange and cooperation occurring during the years leading up to and including World War II have been widely ignored by religious and secular scholars alike.

This book overturns the assumption that a new era of constructive Jewish-Christian relationships occurred only after the conclusion of World War II, and then mainly as a result of Christian contrition over its failure to adequately address the plight of European Jewry. Not only was there far more than casual contact "here and there" between individual, well-meaning Christians and Jews, but the organizational relationships that Dr. Wyschogrod and those who share his view dismiss out of existence until after the war's conclusion were well under development not only during the war, but from the first days of the Hitler regime and even earlier. This omission from the historical record has allowed a false account of American Jewish-Christian relations to become entrenched when the facts point in quite the opposite direction.

Although the efforts of American Jews and Christians to exert pressure on the United States and other world governments on behalf of European Jewry were largely ineffective and may even have been counterproductive at times, the significant although largely forgotten instances of organized Jewish-Christian cooperation that began only weeks after Hitler took power laid the groundwork for interfaith dialogue opportunities that did indeed develop in the postwar years. Yet even the term "Jewish-Christian dialogue" is misleading, as though this dialogue was merely bi-vocal. It was not. Think of a multiplicity of voices arising from either side of the hyphen, sometimes in unison but also attempting to stridently rise above the others.

In short, it is not necessary to wait for the end of the war, as has been commonly thought, to locate the beginning of a new era for Jewish-Christian relations in America. Stimulated by the persecution of the Jews of Europe under the Nazis, new forms of encounter between Jews and Christians emerged concurrently with the rise of Hitler. These early, coordinated efforts to create a rationale that could convince Americans that the European Jews were worth saving is where the genesis of the transformation of Jewish-Christian relations in America should be relocated.

This book tells the story of how American Jews and Christians responded, separately and through coordinated efforts, to the challenges set forth by the rise of Nazi Germany not only behind closed doors but in full view of the public and press at Madison Square

Garden, the premier venue for American sports and other, more ideological, contests. Thrust into new proximity and pitted against a common opponent, Jews and Christians had an opportunity to inspect one another and themselves more closely than they had ever done. In so doing, they achieved a relative closeness that had previously been absent in their relations in the midst of the existing social order.

This social order bore the stamp of the American Protestant establishment that in past decades had sought to impose its authority on American religious and civic society. As William Hutchison points out, at the start of the twentieth century, a symbiotic relationship between the wielders of political and economic power and mainline Protestant churches began to exert a grip on American society.[5] This mutual reinforcement rendered by the Protestant Church establishment and the upper echelons of the rich and the powerful created an alliance whose goal was to establish and reinforce a hegemony intending to define normative American identity and to shape public morals. This determination to occupy center stage had a profound effect on minority Protestant traditions, Catholics, and of course Jews, all of whom were relegated to a marginalized status. The rise of Hitler, however, triggered a response among elements of Jewish and Christian communities that broadened and reconfigured the scope of their relations, leading to a new foundation for mutual recognition.

In *Discourse and the Construction of Society*, Bruce Lincoln posits that while social structures and hierarchies may tend to be self-replicating, the possibility for disrupting the existing order of things occurs when groups or individuals "employ thought and discourse, including even such modes as myth and ritual, as effective instruments of struggle."[6] He measures the success of such "disruptive discourse" on whether it gains a hearing, is persuasive, gathers a following, and "whether a discourse elicits those sentiments out of which new social forms can be constructed."[7]

The relevant "disruptive discourse" here consists of a redefinition and an elevation of the status of Jews in relationship to the dominant Protestant culture in America. Speaking in concrete terms, the alarming reports generated by Nazi persecution in Germany galvanized concerned American Jews to find ways to persuade Christians that they had enough commonality between them to warrant combined concern and interest. On the one hand, in order to accomplish that aim, Jewish leaders had to discover the key to unlock the mentality of their Christian counterparts. On the other hand, Christians had to acknowledge why they were becoming involved with Jewish concerns and, in doing so, embracing them as they had never done before. The practical application of these conditions would be underscored by examples where cooperating Jews and Christians overcame existing social taxonomies in order to succeed in winning sympathy for persecuted European Jewry and in garnering popular support for intervention on their behalf. But do such examples exist?

As I searched for instances where public sympathy could be measured and where examples of Lincoln's disruptive discourse could be found, I unearthed evidence of a mainly forgotten public event that offered what I sought: a mass meeting at Madison Square Garden in New York City on March 27, 1933, organized in protest of the ill treatment of Jews in Germany by the recently installed Hitler regime. What intrigued me most about this event was that while it was orchestrated in large part by Rabbi Stephen Wise, much of the center stage was occupied by non-Jews, particularly highly reputable Christian clergy, who appeared to have been thrust into the spotlight to construct a credible case for public outrage on behalf of German Jewry. Surely these Christian advocates did not materialize overnight out of nowhere. Their presence indicates that there was a history of prior relationship, at least with Wise, if not also with other Jewish leaders, that was worth probing further.

As an added bonus, I learned that the press coverage of the meeting was extensive, conveying a sense of immediacy and drama available nowhere else. Journalism also provided a treasure trove of primary materials in English and Yiddish about the event and extensive quotes from the texts of both Christian and Jewish speechmakers in both languages. In addition, English- and Yiddish-language media coverage offered some striking contrasts, most notably between how

Jewish figures presented themselves publicly and how they spoke privately among themselves.

As I delved deeper into this topic, I made another serendipitous discovery. The 1933 event was not the only one of its kind. Over the next years, Madison Square Garden would become the chief venue where other similar protests, some orchestrated by Wise and some not, would take place. I have charted the course of the Madison Square Garden rallies, including their background, content, reception, and impact as they unfolded over the course of the Nazi era, and analyzed how they aimed to fashion a new, more sympathetic perception of Jews among the dominant Christians culture during this time.

I make extensive use of archival and other primary sources in order to find historical contexts from both Jewish and Christian life that framed the mass meetings around which this work is organized. These include meeting minutes, official and personal correspondence, personal papers and resources from communication outlets, books, pamphlets, periodicals, journals, and newspapers. This extensive variety of material reconstructs an account of the shifting dynamics of the Jewish-Christian encounter and its effects during the rise of National Socialism, World War II, and the immediate aftermath of the war.

Building on the work of worthy scholars in the field, this research closely examines the relationships between agencies and individuals and the complexity of religious, political, and cultural factors in play in those relationships. Each of the protest meetings marks a pivotal moment during the Nazi era when influential Jewish and Christian advocates combined their efforts in an attempt to foment public outrage against the increasingly brutal persecution of Jews by the Nazis, first in Germany and later throughout Europe. Each showcases the broad range of participation by Jews and non-Jews who often played their parts in this movement for vastly different reasons.[8] The differing motivations of the various actors provide valuable insights not only into the development of Jewish-Christian conversation but also into the passionate discussions and urgent struggles that were taking place at the time. Together they comprise a historical record that is compelling and colorful.

Beginning with the event or the events precipitating the organization of these meetings, this research recounts how each meeting was conceived and arranged, who the organizers were, how the speakers were recruited, and what was done to maximize public notice both before and after the meeting. The account of the communications that occurred and the relationships that were formed sheds much light on what motivated Jews and Christians to join forces in this new and urgent way. This background information is deeply revealing, providing profound insights not only into the progression of Jewish and Christian rapprochement throughout the era but also offering instances of internecine strife that shaped the character of the meetings and their ramifications.

This work surveys the background of the speechmakers, with an eye toward understanding the constituencies they represented, and provides in-depth analysis of the content of their speeches, noting changes in rhetoric over the years and in the midst of a worsening situation for European Jews, particularly with the onset of the war. Press coverage here was enormously helpful. In a number of instances, media publications printed the full texts of speeches that would have been otherwise unavailable.

Without a doubt, expressions of mutual Jewish-Christian appreciation entered the public record at the time through statements issued from both sides in a manner not previously known. However, this work also evaluates what, if any, short- or long-term aftereffects were generated by these statements and rallies. Did the joint efforts of Jewish and Christian leaders strengthen the ties between them and their organizations in such a way as to enable them to build on past accomplishments in order to shape a shared future? Did Jews and Christians learn to act more effectively in concert as a direct result of what they perceived to be the successful outcomes of the Madison Square Garden rallies and their cumulative effects?

Each chapter of this book provides the context of the events that precipitated each of the Madison Square Garden mass meetings that began in protest of the treatment of German Jewry beginning in 1933 and grew in intensity in the following years as the circumstances of European Jewry deteriorated and became increasingly dire.

The first chapter covers the planning, execution, and results of the rally held at Madison Square Garden on March 27, 1933, scarcely two months after Hitler took power. Beginning with an overview of the various Jewish organizations that were jockeying for influence and their already existing ideological differences and methods, this account highlights how Stephen Wise, through his various leadership capacities, not only addressed opposition to public protest within the Jewish community but also critiqued those who felt he did not go far enough to express the indignation of fellow Jews to Nazi depredations.

Despite opposition, some of which emanated from Jewish community representatives in Germany, with the help of other Jewish community leaders and representatives of the Yiddish press, Wise was able to assemble a program and to secure the venue in only nine days. In addition, the rally's sponsors prioritized the recruitment of an array of non-Jewish representatives from the political arena and Christian institutional life to share the platform with Jewish speechmakers, shrewdly deploying them to build the case for Jewish advocacy. Careful analysis of the speeches of the Jewish and Christian speakers reveals how the first flush of awareness of the persecution of Jews in Germany pushed both sides to articulate why Jewish suffering in Europe should be a matter of national importance in America.

As a result of the press coverage this hugely successful mass meeting received in both English- and Yiddish-language media, it experienced a dynamic afterlife through similar events orchestrated in other major American cities. Beyond that, the continued protest of progressive Christians and other forms of activism provided a foundation for growing cooperation between Jews and Christians and their representative bodies in the ensuing years. These concrete expressions of shifting attitudes in Jewish-Christian relations exemplify a trend that continued to develop over the next dozen years and beyond.

The second chapter investigates how, after the March 1933 mass meeting, Jewish and Christian communities expanded their collaborative efforts, building on the foundation of alliances that had actually been laid some years previously. Providing an overview of the neglected area of Jewish-Christian relations in America prior to the 1930s, I trace the genesis of the institutional ties between American Jews and Christians initiated through the efforts of Reform Rabbi Isaac Landman and representatives of the Federal Council of Churches (FCC), as well as the Permanent Commission for Better Understanding between Protestants, Catholics, and Jews in the late 1920s. I also probe the reasons for opposition to closer Jewish-Christian relations generated from elements on both sides.

The almost immediate impact of the Nazis' growing threat to German Jewry that was the impetus for the March 1933 protest rally further stimulated Jewish leaders to continue to seek allies among the sympathetic Christians they had already encountered on an organizational level. I analyze how influential Jewish organizations employed sometimes contrasting strategies that were grounded in the differing ideological bases and the internal culture of the institutions under examination. Covering developments in the ensuing months that followed the 1933 rally, I devote considerable attention to the American Jewish Committee's behind-the-scenes cultivation of Christian support, which culminated in two important publications that year: *The Jews in Nazi Germany: The Factual Record of Their Persecution by the National Socialists* and *The Voice of Religion: The Views of Christian Leaders on the Persecution of the Jews in Germany by the National Socialists*.

The former, a record of numerous anti-Jewish decrees already implemented by the Nazis by the spring of 1933, also contains extensive editorial quotes from mainstream American press deploring the situation. The latter is a compilation of quotes protesting Germany's actions culled from Christian journals and prominent Christian representatives, not only from liberal denominations but also from more conservative, little-known sources. I track the reception history of both publications, and in particular, consider how the American

Jewish Committee reversed its long-standing attitude against involvement with Christians to develop an active search for their support, contrasting the more self-effacing approach of the American Jewish Committee with that of Stephen Wise and the American Jewish Congress, the driving force behind of the second Madison Square Garden event.

Staged as a courtroom drama by the American Jewish Congress on March 8, 1934, *The Case of Civilization against Hitlerism* was timed to closely coincide with the first anniversary of the March 5, 1933, German election that placed Hitler on the road to his unbridled dictatorial power. Beginning with an account of the planning and execution of the drama, I go on to assess the arguments it presents on behalf of the Jews and evaluate the press coverage and the aftereffects of the event. As I show, stimulated by growing indignation, the Christian case for Jewish sympathy and inclusion continued to be more fully articulated.

The third chapter examines the differing Jewish and Christian responses to the Final Solution in 1943 and their effects. As the war unfolded and the position of European Jewry became increasingly desperate, the American Jewish Congress, under the guidance of Stephen Wise, was widely perceived to have failed to deliver measurable results in terms of saving Jewish lives. As a result, it lost some of the grip Wise had sought to maintain as Judaism's authorized representative to the wider world. An increasingly vocal element of the Jewish community, impatient with what they felt was the obsequious approach of the Jewish establishment to advance their cause, sought and found a more assertive voice with which to define the Jewish presence.

As a result, activists of other stripes added their voices to express their outrage not only toward Hitler but toward indifference on the part of the Allied nations to Europe's Jews and their suffering. I analyze two events held at Madison Square Garden on consecutive Mondays in March 1943, which emerged as a result of public revelation of the plan for the extermination of European Jewry known as "the Final Solution." The first, on March 1, 1943, was sponsored by the Zionist Organization of America. Called "Stop Hitler Now," it consisted mainly of speechmaking designed to promote Jewish-Christian solidarity in the context of wartime patriotism and featured additional Christian involvement. The second, *We Will Never Die*, was sponsored by adherents of the rival Zionist revisionist faction on March 8. Bolstered by a cast of Hollywood celebrities, it took the form of the highly popular genre of theatrical pageant. It went a step further by blending solemn ritual and extravagant spectacle to elicit an emotional response as a means to alter public perception of Jews and to gain sympathy for them.

I explore and analyze the background, the planning, the execution, the content, the press coverage, and the aftermath of both events, particularly as they relate to each other, paying special attention to the contrasting styles and the pronouncements of the revisionists and the more mainstream Zionist Organization of America, and how each sought to employ religious language in its rhetoric. I discuss how mutual understanding and expanding Jewish-Christian relations were further shaped by the progression of the war, noting some of the more assertive actions that Christian groups took to protest Germany's heinous acts, and emphasizing the ways in which Christians sought to further empathize with Jewish persecution. In doing so, Christian spokespersons attempted to make tangible a connection between the suffering of European Jewry and the suffering of a Jewish Jesus.

I also discuss the neglected enduring relationship between Jewish and Christian Zionists. Their mutual recognition and respect not only predated World War II but was already well established even prior to the beginning of the twentieth century through the common ground they shared in their determined efforts to create a Jewish homeland in Palestine. The combined efforts of Jewish and Christian Zionists were intensified during the Nazi era by the unfriendly stance of Great Britain toward Jewish refugees who, shunned by Allied governments, were desperate to enter Palestine as their only remaining recourse.

After a brief summary of the early cooperation between Jewish and Christian Zionists in America, I go on to uncover the renewed efforts of Jewish Zionists who, through the efforts of Emanuel Neumann and the American Zionist Emergency Committee (later Council), sought partnership among Christian Zionists. Neumann's efforts were rewarded with the formation of the American Palestine Committee and the Christian Council on Palestine, the activities and the publications of which come under detailed examination. Another element taken into consideration is the change that occurred within American Protestantism in the decades leading up to the Nazi era that led Jewish leaders to turn from the evangelical Christian base of support it had accessed in the past to the more theologically liberal Zionist supporters whom they later sought to cultivate.

Finally, the fourth chapter turns to the last mass meeting (within the time frame of this work), held at Madison Square Garden on September 30, 1945. This occurred along with a series of related protests in response to England's announcement that it would continue the policy of the 1939 White Paper, which restricted Jewish immigration to Palestine. In the moment encompassing the immediate aftermath of the cessation of military conflict, when thousands of displaced Jewish survivors were struggling to find even basic necessities, this statement galvanized a response that not only filled the Garden once more to overflowing but also reported an overall crowd of as many as seventy thousand. I scrutinize the background and the publicity leading up to the event, the content of the speeches, Yiddish- and English-language press coverage, and the aftereffects of the event, including the controversy it incited with non-Zionist Jewish leadership.

This multifaceted assessment of American Jewish-Christian relations during the Nazi era is a contribution to the history of Jewish-Christian relations in the United States and the separate, unfolding stories of both traditions. Thrown together as they were in response to the dire threat of Nazism in Europe, American Christians and Jews were forced not only to evaluate one another but also to undertake a degree of self-examination that enabled each group to encounter the other in a spirit of new possibilities.

In conclusion, I examine the aftereffects of this newly articulated language of interfaith dialogue as it played out in the decades after the war. In those ensuing years, as the emerging concept of "Judeo-Christian values" became more deeply imbedded in American civil and religious discourse, this development continued to shape not only American self-awareness but also its attitude and stance toward the wider world.

1

Setting the Stage

*Cooperative Efforts among Jews
and Christians at the Start of the Nazi Era*

On March 28, 1933, readers who turned to *The New York Times* for news of an increasingly anxious moment in European affairs were greeted by a series of blaring headlines and lengthy reports about an event that had taken place the previous evening. For *Times* readers, the headline "Crowd Overflowing the Garden Hears Leaders Assail Persecution" would have been considered nothing terribly out of the ordinary. For decades in its various incarnations around town, Madison Square Garden, the venue of the demonstration, had been the setting not only of celebrated sporting exhibitions but also of a wide variety of political and cultural events in the public square of New York City's dynamic civil discourse. No stranger to spectacles, throughout the 1930s it would play host to other demonstrations sponsored by civic, religious, and other groups that vigorously and publicly promoted the agendas of constituencies drawn from a broad representation of interests, including Jewish causes, as well as Labor, Socialist, Communist, and even the openly Nazi German-American Bund.[1]

The largest headline proclaimed, "55,000 HERE STAGE PROTEST HITLER ATTACKS ON JEWS." The meeting, the *Times* reported, which had taken place the previous evening, was large even by New York standards. It reflected the timeliness of the topic that inspired the gathering, which was a series of disturbing depredations directed toward Germany's Jewish populace by the newly formed

National Socialist government under the leadership of Adolf Hitler. It was natural that the Jewish community should respond, the *Times* reader might muse, under what was portrayed as the guiding hand of Rabbi Stephen Wise. Wise, in his twin capacities as honorary president of the American Jewish Congress and as Reform rabbi of the Free Synagogue in New York City, which he founded in 1907, was a generally respected Jewish leader and no stranger to readers of the English-language press, who regarded him as a reliable spokesman for the Jewish community. It was also natural that New York politicians, mindful of the influence of their Jewish constituents, would lend their support to an event unfolding at the epicenter of Jewish life in America.

Alongside the expected politicians, Wise and other Jewish leaders, whose speeches were quoted at great length, an additional element was present that would have been less familiar to the general public. Placed under the subheading "Other Faiths Join In," this angle of the story went on to describe how an assembly of well-respected Christian clergy was also present that evening to lend their voices to the message that Hitler's treatment of the German Jews must not be countenanced by the silence of Christian America. The public utterances of Christian speechmakers that evening went even further, turning the spotlight on antisemitism in America, the importance of which had been suddenly amplified by Germany's shameful treatment of its Jewish citizens.

Here, at the beginning of what would prove to be over a decade of unimaginable agony and death for Europe's Jews, something was coming to life in America. Although amicable Jewish-Christian relations had by no means been unknown before that moment, they were about to take significant strides forward. Stimulated by the persecution of the Jews of Europe, a new form of discourse between Jews and Christians in the United States would begin to emerge, the ramifications of which would become manifest during the war years and beyond.

Beginning in 1933, the mass meeting would become a highly visible, well-publicized expression of solidarity between Jews and Christians in the Nazi era in the United States. The concerted effort of

Jewish and Christian leadership to promote a public image of shared indignation took the form of numerous well-attended and highly publicized demonstrations against Nazism in New York City as well as in dozens of other localities around the country. These events not only articulated the argument *against* Hitler but also had another, indirect effect, to argue *for* the inclusion of the Jews in mainstream American life.

The hidden, behind-the-scenes maneuvering that brought about these events sheds light on not only the state of Jewish-Christian relations in each of these historical moments but also the ideological conflicts that shaped the manner in which each approached the other. The development of Jewish-Christian relations during this era cannot be meaningfully assessed without a close look at the internal forces at work within each group at each given moment. These intense expressions of public outrage, coordinated at the highest levels of Jewish leadership, and which included the participation of some of the most influential Christian leaders of the day, provide a glimpse into both Jewish and Christian responses to rapidly developing events in Germany as they were occurring.

Equally, if not more important, the archival material that pertains to them in speeches, press reports, and interpersonal communications provides valuable background and perspective regarding the critical issues of how Jews aspired to be understood by Christians and the various ways in which different Christians responded to the challenge posed to them by Jewish people suffering under Nazi persecution. The participation by sympathetic elected officials also throws into sharp relief some of the long-held perceptions of the Jewish place in American civil life and the political strategies through which concern for Jews could be "sold" to a general public. These views were deeply informed by the values of the Protestant establishment, which, paradoxically, also exhibited a significant and growing antagonism toward the presence of Jews in American society.[2]

The March 27, 1933, anti-Nazi protest in New York City was sparked by a rapid and sharp rise in anti-Jewish rhetoric and persecutory actions in Germany. The electoral triumph of the Nazi Party and the breakneck speed with which Adolf Hitler seized the levers of political power in Germany at the beginning of 1933 had a profound and an almost immediate effect on the security of Germany's Jewish citizens. At once, alarming reports began to leak out of Germany about the mistreatment of Jewish citizens ranging from physical abuse to the destruction of Jewish businesses and property.

Jewish leaders in America, out of their own concern and that of the constituencies they represented, felt pressed to formulate a response that would prompt action by the newly created Roosevelt administration to deter Germany's harsh policies against their people. Their sense of urgency was, however, tempered with the knowledge that Jews in America were not widely popular as a group and with the fear that their protests would appear to be self-serving or likely fall on deaf ears. They needed allies, and the most natural place to turn was other influential non-Jewish fellow Americans with whom they had already cultivated a degree of rapport and the various political and religious constituencies and institutions they represented.

New York City was the natural staging ground for such an action. Not only did it contain the largest Jewish population of any city in the United States by far, but it also hosted the headquarters of the American Jewish Congress and was where Rabbi Stephen Wise, its leading light, presided over the Free Synagogue that met at Carnegie Hall.[3] New York was also home to other important Jewish institutions and influential organizations, including the rival American Jewish Committee.[4] In addition, New York City was a hotbed of progressive Christianity, among whose proponents the event's Jewish organizers were most likely to find sympathetic participants.

Such support drawn from Christian America could by no means be taken for granted given the number of adversarial forces that were already at play. Large swaths of an increasingly isolationist post–World War I American society were not likely to be inclined to intervene on behalf of foreigners of any ilk, nor to extend hospitality to them.[5] Any proposal to remove Jews from the mounting danger would inevitably raise the issue of where they might go to find more permanent shelter. The prospect of allowing for an increase in the threshold of Jewish immigration to America in light of the intensifying persecution they were facing in Germany, and in time throughout Europe, would become the focus of continuous contention until the end of the war.[6]

Another formidable obstacle was the rise of antisemitism in America in the 1930s. Jewish advocates were operating in an American environment that was deeply affected by the unfriendly influences of nativism, with a prevailing anti-immigration sentiment, and the Red Scare, which cast increased suspicion on Jews in general because of their supposed communist leanings. Many citizens were too willing to accept the stereotypical specter of "the international Jew" that Henry Ford and his ilk had raised in the popular mind in the previous decades.[7]

Despite these obstacles, the goal of the March 27 Garden rally to raise the alarm on behalf of Germany's Jews succeeded spectacularly both in terms of publicity and attendance. Its organizers created a roster of speakers that included not only illustrious representatives of the Jewish community but also important politicians and well-known Christian clergy who stepped forward with a powerful collective voice and will. According to multiple press reports, the rally not only filled the twenty-thousand-seat arena but also attracted an additional thirty-five-to-forty-thousand attendees who could not gain admittance but heard the speeches broadcast over loudspeakers.[8] In addition to the main event in New York City, other protests were timed to take place simultaneously in Chicago, Boston, Philadelphia, Baltimore, Cleveland, and dozens of other smaller cities.[9]

However, as successful as the New York City protest proved to be, it had been far from easy to arrange. The obstacles that preceded these hastily organized demonstrations is instructive when understood in the context of the events unfolding in the United States and Germany at this time. The urgency of the matter at hand did not make the already existing ideological differences and power struggles among Jewish leaders and their organizations disappear as if by magic. Even before common cause with Christians could be attempted, the first order of business was to address the lack of harmony that hampered Jewish efforts to achieve a united front from the outset.

The clash of perspectives among Jewish leaders was made manifest by sharp disagreement about the best alternatives to respond to reports of the worsening situation for Jews in Germany that had begun to circulate near the beginning of 1933. Sensing the need to plot a united and prudent course, Alfred M. Cohen, president of B'nai B'rith, called a meeting on February 22. The objective of that meeting was twofold: first, to form a Joint Conference Committee of the mainstream Jewish organizations, including B'nai B'rith, the American Jewish Committee, and the American Jewish Congress, that would speak on behalf of the Jewish community, and second, to manage, and if necessary suppress, the responses of some other Jewish organizations deemed to be out of line. Although these three organizations, each of which represented large and significant constituencies, had their differences, they agreed that a united front that could most persuasively present the Jewish situation to the American public was the most desirable course to take.

Unity, however, proved to be an unattainable goal. Although they agreed that they should reach out to the newly elected Roosevelt administration, their amity lasted only three weeks. It foundered over the American Jewish Congress's decision to proceed with public protest meetings that the American Jewish Committee in particular vehemently objected to on the grounds that they would do more harm than good. This disagreement was compounded by the failure of the American Jewish Committee and the American Jewish Congress to curb their long-standing rivalry over which organization could best represent Jewish interests in America and elsewhere.

If ideological differences over issues such as the validity of Zionism, the advantages or disadvantages of public visibility, and other conflicts about how best to promote Jewish causes frustrated the possibility of creating lasting and effective cooperation, other factors also complicated the task of finding a common stance and of articulating a unified message. Jewish leadership, especially that of the American Jewish Committee, was disinclined to criticize the German government and felt compelled to soft-pedal Jewish grievances over the plight of foreign Jews. The American Jewish Committee was particularly reluctant to take bold steps, given its habitual preference for behind-the-scenes persuasion and an aversion to publicity. Besides, the entrenched culture of the Committee was largely informed by the background of its elite German-Jewish leaders, who were enamored with a Germany that represented to them the epitome of European civilization. They were, at that point, simply unwilling to view Hitler as anything other than a grotesque anomaly that the Germans themselves would soon have the good sense to reject.[10]

There were also other forces at work to suppress a fuller expression of the sense of alarm felt by American Jews who were following the situation and to deflect their impulse to protest the actions of Hitler's newly formed government. Jewish groups in Germany were frightened by the unintended consequences American intervention might have, which might provoke fearful repercussions for thousands of German Jews. To complicate matters, as indicated above, the American Jewish Committee, the American Jewish Congress, and B'nai B'rith were not the only active Jewish groups in America at the time. A broad spectrum of Jewish constituencies, both religious and secular, was also on the scene, including potentially disruptive outliers such as the Socialists and the Communists, who were well represented by vocal leaders of their own, had a lively press, were far less beholden to established authorities, and could therefore afford to be as outspoken as they chose.

Another reason for more mainstream groups, such as the American Jewish Committee and American Jewish Congress, to calibrate their public response more carefully was that the Roosevelt administration, having just barely grasped the reins of office, was particularly concerned to promote amicable relations with Germany. As Shlomo Shafir puts it, "Moreover, because of the priority of the big domestic issues, he would refrain from antagonizing the new German government in spite of his hatred for Hitler and the Nazis. Thus there was not much room for American governmental intercession except the protection of the rights, life, and property of American citizens."[11]

Jewish leaders seeking to gain purchase with the new administration felt it behooved them to curb statements that would supply fodder to Germany against the new administration. They felt the administration had given them reason to hope for sympathetic action but was as yet uncertain about how to approach it, especially in light of its cautious approach to Hitler's government. The new State Department's careful diplomacy toward Germany was borne out. As one report from Berlin indicates, "The United States Embassy made plain today that it had not protested to the German Foreign Office against anti-Semitic attacks, but had merely received instructions from the State Department to place special emphasis in its regular reports to Washington upon the matter of persecutions of Jews in Germany."[12]

Apart from this limp reaction, further evidence concerning the new US administration's reluctance to take Germany to task appears in a telegram sent a few days later on March 27, the day of the protests, from Secretary of State Cordell Hull to Cyrus Adler, president of the American Jewish Committee, Stephen S. Wise, honorary president of the American Jewish Congress, and Bernard S. Deutsch, president of the American Jewish Congress, which was made public in time for a response by speakers at Madison Square Garden. While paying lip service to Jewish concerns, Hull's telegram clearly communicates the reluctance on the part of the State Department to take anything more than a wait-and-see position:

> [Whereas] there was for a short time considerable physical mistreatment of Jews, this phase may be considered virtually terminated. There also was some picketing of Jewish merchandising stores and instances of professional discrimination.
>
> These manifestations were viewed with serious concern by the German government . . . I feel hopeful in view of the reported attitude of high German officials and the evidences of amelioration already indicated, that the situation, which has caused such widespread concern throughout this country, will soon revert to normal. Meanwhile I shall continue to watch the situation closely, with a sympathetic interest and with a desire to be helpful in whatever way possible.[13]

If Hull's telegram was intended to lull American Jewish leaders into inactivity, it had precisely the opposite effect. Together with other reports, which directly contradicted Hull's sanguine assessment of the situation, mounting concern finally overcame the paralysis that seemed to grip Jewish leadership regarding a response to the rapidly developing situation for Jews in Germany. The rising intensity of Jewish concern, the determination of other Jewish groups to push ahead, and the increasing level of press coverage made it impossible for Jewish leaders in America to remain passive. A report sent from Paris dated March 19, which appeared the next morning in *The New York Times*, made public what Wise and others either already knew or otherwise suspected. Headlined "GERMAN FUGITIVES TELL OF ATROCITIES AT HANDS OF NAZIS," the opening paragraph reads:

> Americans arriving here from Germany are expressing more and more concern over the course of events in that country. Neither the full truth about them nor the implications arising therefrom are reaching the outside world these Americans say nor can the truth come out except gradually and by stealth for excellent reasons.[14]

The article proceeds to describe the Nazi stranglehold on the German press, other forms of censorship, the suppression of political dissent, and eyewitness accounts of attacks on Jews that were either ignored or abetted by the police. A report from the Jewish Telegraphic Agency on March 24 carried the account of a London physician who witnessed what he described as the smashing of windows at Jewish stores and personal assaults against Jews that included tearing off their beards and burning their hair. Another account described five armed Nazis breaking into a home and bludgeoning the male inhabitant with the cry, "Death to the Jews." Another described the actions of a Nazi mob that formed outside a restaurant known to be frequented by Jewish clientele:

> The Nazis formed a double line to the restaurant door. As the boy called out a name, a stalwart Brown Shirt seized the respectable

businessman bearing it and propelled him toward the gauntlet. As he passed through it every man first on one side and then on the other smashed him in the face and kicked him with heavy boots until finally the last in the line knocked him into the street.[15]

In response to mounting pressure to act, Wise convened an emotionally charged meeting at New York City's Hotel Astor on March 19 that drew about fifteen hundred attendees and brought into the open the different opinions concerning how to proceed. The clash of viewpoints extended for more than four hours. In particular, two specific proposed courses of action aroused heated debate: the first was whether public protest was an advisable step in the first place, and the second was Wise's rebuke of the former course of action. A telegram from Irving Lehman, a judge on the New York Court of Appeals and vice president of the American Jewish Committee, that counseled against mass protest met with angry opposition from representatives of six hundred Jewish organizations in New York City and ten national organizations who were present.[16] Lehman's views were echoed by other members of the American Jewish Committee leadership, including James Rosenberg and Joseph Proskauer, who, fearful of German reaction, implored the gathering, "In the name of humanity, don't let anger pass a resolution which will kill Jews in Germany."[17]

Determined to formulate a strong public response, Wise responded in sharp disagreement. His rebuke to the American Jewish Committee brought into the open the ongoing antagonism and rivalry existing between these important Jewish organizations that so often sought influence at the expense of the other. As the *Times* reported the following day, "Dr. Wise praised Mr. Proskauer and Mr. Rosenberg, but remarked that 'they should not have waited all these years to attend a meeting under the auspices of the American Jewish Congress.'"[18]

The other more controversial issue was a call, spearheaded by the Jewish War Veterans, for an economic boycott against Germany in retaliation for its hostile acts. This set off alarms among mainstream

Jewish organizations, which were unwilling to support such a course of action at that time. Despite significant pro-boycott sentiment among their representatives, Deutsch and Wise were able to prevail against an amendment proposed by J. George Fredman, the commander in chief of the Jewish War Veterans, to implement a boycott of German products.[19] Even so, against the strenuous objection of the American Jewish Committee, a decision was taken to coordinate anti-Nazi rallies that took place on March 27, 1933. In the end, Wise seemed to have gotten the protests that he wanted, over the objections of the American Jewish Committee, and to have quashed the more controversial boycott proposal advocated by the Fredman faction.

Still, unfolding events were not wholly under Wise's control. The week that passed between the meeting at the Hotel Astor and the protests saw an escalation of tension and rhetoric, with representatives of the American and the German Jewish communities issuing sometimes conflicting statements. On March 23, at a meeting convened at Yeshiva College in Upper Manhattan, representatives of the Union of Orthodox Jewish Congregations passed a resolution to protest against the persecution of German Jews and called on its membership to turn out in force for the March 27 Madison Square Garden rally. They also sent a telegram to Secretary Hull, urging him to open America's doors to imperiled German Jewry, a step that Wise, fearful of being perceived as too importuning, declined to take. Other Orthodox Jewish organizations joined in, including the National Federation of Orthodox Congregations and the Independent Order of B'rith Abraham. In addition, three rabbinical associations—the Union of Orthodox Rabbis, the Council of Orthodox Rabbis, and the American Board of Rabbis—called for a day of prayer and fasting on the day of the rally.[20]

Wise's determination to guide events was also frustrated on another front. Despite the decision taken at the Astor to forego the boycott, Fredman was unwilling to abandon the idea. He decided, instead, to attract political support for it through a march from Cooper Square to City Hall. On March 23, he and the Jewish War

Veterans were joined by members of the American Legion, the National War Veterans, the Veterans of Foreign Wars, and various other religious, civic, and fraternal organizations in a parade of two thousand, cheered on by a crowd of ten thousand, which swelled to twice its original number by the time the demonstration arrived at its destination.[21]

Mayor John Patrick O'Brien met with leaders inside City Hall and, as the *Times* reported, "received a set of resolutions calling on all citizens to boycott German goods and services and to urge the United States government to address a direct diplomatic protest to Germany."[22] Promising to say more in his speech at the Garden, O'Brian commented, "I can sum up what I want to say in these words. Any regime that has for its basis religious or racial intolerance or persecution is bound to meet the moral opposition of the entire world."[23] Although no comment was elicited from Stephen Wise or other representatives of the American Jewish Congress regarding the parade, it should be noted that Fredman was not among the speakers invited to address the crowd at the Madison Square Garden event that was now only three days away.

As stories of German brutalities multiplied, the threat of boycotting German goods, which had already manifested informally through actions of individual merchants, now appeared to be serious.[24] Hitler's government bristled and complained sharply through the German press. The *Berlin Localanzeiger* editorialized, "The government must point out to several foreign governments that agitation against Germany must come to an end. This is especially true in the case of the United States."[25] The Roosevelt administration sought to temporize, making it clear that it would issue no official protest of Germany's activity. Even as reports trickled out of Germany citing beatings and the destruction of property, the German Foreign Office pleaded innocent to wrongdoing, accusing American correspondents with spreading baseless "atrocity propaganda."[26] One German spokesman noted with pride that "despite extraordinarily strong anti-Semitic feeling among the German people, there had not been a single pogrom."[27]

Given the pressure that the German government was exerting on the Jewish community and the degree of terror being inflicted, the reaction of German Jewish leadership was difficult to assess fully. Given the intensifying danger, the placating tone of some of the Jewish leadership's public statements to the German government was not surprising. The German Council of Rabbis proclaimed its patriotism, issuing this statement: "Our history is ample proof of the spirit that lives within us. We know what the German fatherland means to us. Since time immemorial our religion has taught us loyalty to the State."[28]

Plans for the Garden rally and the other protests throughout the country proceeded. However, on the day the event was scheduled to take place, the *Times* reported that Ernest Wallace, vice president of the Central Association of German Citizens of Jewish Faith, had forwarded a telegram from Julius Prodnitz, the organization's president in Berlin, to Stephen Wise and some of the other scheduled speakers urging Wise to cancel the meeting. The telegram read:

> We earnestly urge you to do all in your power that Monday's mass meeting be called off, or if such should, against our sincere hopes, not prove possible, to prevail upon the speakers of the evening to refrain from stirring the emotions of their audience against Germany. We can assure them that the German government is permanently and successfully engaged in assuring peace and order to all citizens without discrimination.[29]

Wise's response, issued from his pulpit to a crowd that filled and overflowed Carnegie Hall, was an unequivocal repudiation of the Central Association's request. Perhaps the telegram struck a nerve with Wise, since its plea seemed to lend weight to the arguments of his adversaries. In any case, such a course of action, which appeared to be in direct conflict with the stated wishes of so important a representative of Germany's Jews as the Central Association, certainly called for a reaction, particularly since it had been leaked to the public. Wise denied that the American Jewish Congress was responsible for exciting public opinion, but rather had "merely sought to channelize the high indignation and the solemn protest of America into ways that shall be orderly and effective."[30]

A statement issued by the American Jewish Congress that Bernard Deutsch read went further. Calling the Association's statement "pitifully unconvincing," Deutsch cited the testimony of American Jews who had been brutalized in Germany and asked, "If these American citizens . . . felt constrained to sign exculpating statements for their Nazi torturers under duress, how can we now credit any denial emanating from the terrorized Jews of Germany . . . ?"[31]

Wise further rationalized his actions in his Garden speech, where he was openly critical of German Jewish leadership:

> Some of their leaders are under the impact of panic and compulsion, in any event the compulsion of a great fear if not actual coercion. Do they appeal to the Nazi government to bring about a cessation of its anti-Jewish campaign as they have appealed to us to end our protest? We have no quarrel with our Jewish brothers in Germany and their leaders, but their policy of uncomplaining assent and of super-cautious silence has borne evil fruit. They who have been virtually silent through the years of anti-Jewish propaganda cannot be followed by us as the wisest of counselors.[32]

On the face of it, Wise's open criticism of German Jewish leadership is questionable, and even insolent, considering his position of safety in America. It would also have been shocking to those who held the much-cherished maxim that Jews ought not to air their internal differences for public consumption. In his frustration, Wise may have been conflating his feelings about the Jewish leadership in Germany with his perception of the complacent approach of the American Jewish Committee, with which he had so recently come into conflict.[33] Perhaps his indignation is more fully understandable in light of his recollection of events. He later wrote in his autobiography that private letters had been smuggled to him from Germany urging him not to take the reassuring public statements of German

Jewish organizations at face value. These missives also contained torture accounts, including the cutting of swastikas into Jewish flesh, which doubtlessly influenced Wise's decision to move forward.[34]

The early difficulties Jewish leadership encountered in finding enough common ground to act in concert would persist. The religious and ideological spectrum along which Judaism and the Jewish community existed was simply too great to accommodate all viewpoints. For the moment, however, Wise held the reins. Despite objections raised toward his leadership from both left and right, his failure to completely control the message that he sought to convey to the Roosevelt administration, and the defiant acts of the Jewish War Veterans, he succeeded in gathering enough of a coalition to organize and to execute the first of the Madison Square Garden demonstrations. In so doing, he also positioned himself as the most visible spokesperson of the Jewish community, at least in the eyes of the English-language press.

Despite their friction, one aspect of the Jewish response that the American Jewish Congress, the American Jewish Committee, and B'nai B'rith were able to agree on was its desire for Christian cooperation in opposition to German policy.[35] The rise of antisemitism was certainly not news. Over a year earlier, Wise had expressed the necessity of enlisting Christian sympathy on behalf of imperiled Jews.[36] Seeking to raise the alarm about dangers that he felt were not being taken as seriously as they ought to have been, in February 1932 he expressed this view in his article "Germany at the Crossroads" in the Jewish magazine *Opinion* that "world opinion—shall we not say the opinion of Christendom—must be invoked lest a monstrous wrong be inflicted upon Israel and Germany suffer unspeakable and uncancellable shame."[37] Wise continued to press this agenda from his pulpit at the Free Synagogue in New York, where he dwelt on the growing Nazi threat. In a deft play on Jesus's words from the cross, Wise exhorted:

We must forgive them though they know that which they do . . . Non-Jews as well as Jews must forgive them. I turn to the Christian churches of America, to Cardinal, Bishop, priest and minister, and I say "gain for them forgiveness by moving them to a change of heart, to a consciousness of the sin they are committing. Prepare the way for God's forgiveness by moving them to penitence and a sense of shame."[38]

Some Christian leaders were already mobilizing and offering more than vague platitudes. They were not only roundly condemning the German government from their pulpits but also making pointed recommendations to the United States government, joining Jewish leaders in urging the Roosevelt administration to speak out unambiguously on behalf of endangered German Jews. Moreover, the press was taking notice in a flurry of reports published during the week leading up to the rally.

On March 23, the *Times* reported that Theodore A. Green, pastor of the First Church of Christ in New Britain, Connecticut, had composed a protest letter on behalf of sympathetic colleagues that was sent to Secretary Cordell Hull and Stephen Wise to be read at the protest on March 27. The same article reported that Edward Lodge Curran, president of the International Catholic Truth Society, had also written to the State Department, "I wish to add my protest and the protest of the society to the many that should be pouring into the State Department against the unjust, un-Christian and barbarous anti-Semitic activities of the Hitler regime."[39] Curran went on to add, "A protest from the United States Government may be the means of awakening the great bulk of the German people to the folly of being represented by a former Austrian citizen whose path has already been marked by blood."[40]

That same day, the *Herald Tribune* reported that after conferring with former governor Alfred E. Smith, representatives of The Greater New York Federation of Churches (Protestant) and the Interfaith Committee (Protestant and Catholic) issued a statement drafted by William B. Millar, executive director of the Federation, and Charles Tuttle of the Interfaith Committee. These important Christian leaders, on behalf of their organizations, publicly prioritized "a protest on behalf of American Christians against the persecution of Jews in Germany under the reign of Chancellor Hitler." The article noted that Smith, Bishop William T. Manning, and other Christians planned to join "Rabbi Stephen Wise and other Jews" at the Madison Square Garden meeting.[41]

Meanwhile, the agenda was shaping up under the guidance of Samuel Margoshes, editor of the Yiddish-language daily *Der Tog*. On the day of the event, *Der Tog* proclaimed on its front page: "Today is the day of our great outcry. Let's shout together and let our loud thunder be heard over the whole world. Tonight, we all have one goal in mind, one point where we have to go—Madison Square Garden! Are you Jewish? Do you speak Yiddish? Do you know what you have to do? Go to Madison Square Garden."[42]

One advantage in bringing in well-respected voices from the Protestant establishment was that they could make demands for action in the politically sensitive area of immigration policy, which Wise and the Jewish leaders in his camp felt they must avoid, given their inhibitions about placing Roosevelt at a disadvantage with his enemies on the right. For instance, Rev. C. Everett Wagner, pastor of Union Methodist Church in Manhattan, had no such reluctance. He issued a pointed challenge to the politically powerful that if taken seriously would have posed truly vexing problems for the newly elected president: "The United States Government should lift the bars of immigration to allow the persecuted Jews and others who are discriminated against to enter this country."[43] Such support, emanating from influential Christian quarters, did not go unnoticed by Jewish leadership. On the day of the protest, the Central Conference of American Rabbis issued a statement that expressed "appreciation and gratification for the protests made by our Christian neighbors in America."[44]

Two things are evident from the extent of press coverage prior to the event. The first is that in these early days of the Hitler regime, the disclosure of the persecution of German Jews and the response of Jewish and Christian leadership were considered highly newsworthy. The second is that a variety of Jewish and Christian leaders and organizations felt compelled to respond publicly, and the lengths to which Christian leadership was willing to forthrightly speak out were considerable. As Jewish and Christian leadership became more conscious of each other, the common cause they found against German policy beginning in the early 1930s would become the basis on which a new dimension of Jewish-Christian mutual awareness in America would emerge.

The significant buildup that the Madison Square Garden program received in the New York press in the days preceding the event and the strong statements emanating from a variety of pulpits throughout the city produced a crowd whose attendance far surpassed the capacity of the Garden arena. The Garden was the logical choice for this particular meeting, as it was already a familiar venue for Jewish activists. As early as 1917, an estimated fifteen thousand people attended a joyous gathering of Jewish immigrants on March 20 at the Garden's earlier site at the intersection of Broadway and Fifth Avenue at 23rd St. The rally was organized by various Jewish organizations with socialist leanings to celebrate the overthrow of Czar Nicolas II.[45] No longer located on Madison Square, the third incarnation of this venerable New York arena that was the site of the 1933 protest opened in 1925 between 49th and 50th Streets on Eighth Avenue.

As Wise hoped, the agenda was carefully structured to include as many non-Jews as possible. He understood that styling the situation in Germany as a simple plea by American Jews to enlist American sympathy and help for Jews on foreign soil was the wrong approach. While Jewish voices must be heard and their grievances aired, the protest could not be viewed solely as an effort to support the narrow interests of the Jewish community against the Nazi mistreatment of German Jews. It must be understood as a patriotic American protest against the fundamentally un-American and unchristian values of the Nazis.

The prominent positioning of the significant number of politicians who gave speeches was meant to underscore the civic dimension of American indignation against Hitler and to create an image of wide public approval for the Jewish cause. In choosing to adopt the tactic of promoting higher visibility for non-Jewish representatives to plead their case, Jewish leaders were able to channel the condemnation of the Nazis into the larger language of religious precept and humanism. This strategy was flexible enough to not only stress the injustices perpetuated against the Jews but to also provide the cover needed by presenting the Nazis' depredations as crimes against a more general notion of civilization that could include even Germany, whose civilized society, it was fervently hoped, would soon come to its senses.

The 1933 protest speeches offer a number of perspectives about how Americans ought to respond to Nazi persecution of the German Jews. Equally important, they provide a glimpse into the values that informed these perspectives, as well as how Christians perceived Jews and how Jews wanted to be perceived by Christians. The non-Jewish voices that asserted their authority to speak for American culture were well-represented by political figures and Christian leaders who, one by one, took the podium to denounce the Nazis' policy toward Germany's Jewish minority. Yet the reasoning they employed in castigating Germany's actions reveals much about their own thinking toward the Jewish minority in America. That is, these speeches are important because they provide concrete examples of how Jews were seen and evaluated by the segment of dominant Christian culture represented that evening.

If the speeches themselves provide insight into this significant moment of Jewish-Christian concord, the type of press coverage the event received is also an indispensable historical element to consider. The degree of attention the rally received and the manner in which it was reported, in New York City and elsewhere, is a valuable measure of the extent of its impact. From the standpoint of publicity, the 1933 Madison Square Garden protest and those that took place concurrently around the country were an all-out success.

The rallies received nationwide coverage in major newspapers including the *Herald Tribune* and other New York dailies, the *Chicago Tribune*, *The Boston Globe*, the *Detroit Free Press*, and *The Christian*

Science Monitor, among others, with *The New York Times* account providing the most comprehensive descriptions.[46] Headlines splashed across its front page and numerous stories were meticulously reported with the complete text or extended excerpts of speeches. Moreover, the nature of journalism provides insight into not only what occurred but also how it was meant to be understood by readers. The *Times* articles and others that appeared the day after the event not only reported what was said but also interpreted the meaning. As such, they may actually be considered a part of the event itself.[47]

The press reported the rally and the circumstances surrounding it, such as the logistical difficulties the large crowd presented. Articles about the participants included lengthy quotes from some of the speakers as well as audience responses. One story described the challenge of managing the roughly thirty-five thousand people who were unable to enter the auditorium to join the twenty thousand who were fortunate enough to gain admittance. They crammed the surrounding streets, jamming the subways and creating a traffic nightmare. About three thousand people gathered several blocks away at Columbus Circle for an impromptu meeting, where they were addressed by a series of speakers, including representatives of the American Jewish Committee and Rabbi Lewis Newman of the Upper West Side Congregation Rodelph Sholom, who was quoted as saying, "It is not the German Jew who is under attack, but all Christianity. Surely Christendom has acted rightly in condemning Nazi cruelties as un-Christian and barbarous."[48] Additional front-page stories pointedly emphasized the substance of the protest. "BAN ON JEWS SPREADS," subheaded "Hitler's Party Prepares Boycott in Revenge for 'Atrocity Tales,'" consisted of the official Nazi response to the highly public and embarrassing American criticism of its policies. In addition to vigorous denials of wrongdoing, this story announced the German government's threat to intensify its boycott of Jewish businesses and restrict the admission of Jews to "certain academic professions and public institutions."[49]

The *Times* reporting, whether consciously or unconsciously, fulfilled the strategic priorities of the protest organizers to condemn

Nazism itself and not merely the Nazi treatment of the Jews. The anti-Jewish policies of the Nazis were subjected to a criticism that, while acknowledging antisemitism, gave additional reasons to condemn Germany's actions. The opening paragraphs of the lead story on March 28, which feature a summary of the remarks of Al Smith, a well-known and popular politician known for his humble beginnings and common touch, offer a succinct statement of the recurring themes of the other featured speakers:

> Hitlerism with its anti-Semitic propaganda and the persecution of Jews must be dragged out of the open and given the same treatment "we gave the Ku Klux Klan," former governor Al Smith told a cheering audience of more than 20,000 Jews assembled in Madison Square Garden last night to protest against Hitler's treatment of the Jews in Germany.
> In a speech lasting about twenty minutes, the former Governor brought the otherwise solemn audience to its feet as he denounced racial and religious bigotry and suppression of civil liberties and appealed to the German people to remember the principles of human love and brotherhood. Mr. Smith absolved the German people from any wrongdoing or sympathy with antisemitism, but laid these at the door of those whom he denounced as demagogues and enemies of the German people.[50]

By conflating the Nazis with the Ku Klux Klan, Smith shrewdly provided his audience with an object of scorn that was presumably better known to them and closer to home than the German Nazis. In making this connection with a well-known domestic hate group that would have been unpopular with his listeners, he was able to further stigmatize the home-grown variety of antisemitism. In addition, by attempting to drive a wedge between Hitler and the German people, Smith and speakers who followed him created a narrative that Hitler's rise to power had somehow come about behind the backs of the German people, whose qualities of decency he and others enlarged on repeatedly in their speeches. Smith forthrightly defended the Jews and lauded their contribution as "a God-fearing, a peace-living class of citizenship that have been helpful to every country where they have been found."[51] In reference to Cordell Hull's telegram, he expressed a mixture of hope that the worst was over and skepticism that Hull's report was an accurate assessment of the situation.

Although Smith, whose Catholicism had in part derailed his presidential aspirations in 1924 and 1928, understood the lash of religious prejudice from personal experience, he displayed a certain tone-deafness to Jewish difference, for it was to the values of Christianity that Smith finally appealed to validate his plea on behalf of the Jews. In his speech, as if to put the finishing touches on his argument, Smith appealed to the divine guidance of Christianity to remind Germany of its better self and to bring about a happy resolution to this painful chapter. He concluded his speech by saying to the full house consisting largely of Jews, "We all subscribe to that Christmas hymn, 'Glory to God on High and on earth Peace to Men of Goodwill.'"[52] In so doing, he seemed to invite his largely Jewish audience to share not only in the values of Americanism but also in Christian civilization's purported religious beliefs now being publicly deployed to stand over and against Nazism.

Smith was not the only prominent politician to air his views that night. Under the headline "HUMAN TOLERANCE, NOT JUDAISM, IS THE ISSUE, WAGNER DECLARES," Senator Robert F. Wagner joined the chorus of those who spoke glowingly of Germany. He depicted the Nazi government as an aberration, saying, "I have not come here to condemn Germany. I come to awaken her, to arouse her to a realization that a few of her children are bringing shame upon her name."[53] Wagner's message resonated with much of what was expressed by his fellow civil servants. He reminded his listeners of another cardinal point that was developed throughout the evening, the more universal issues encompassing the Jewish persecution: "Our concern is not limited by the common kinship of our Jewish citizens with the Jews of Germany. Our interest and anxiety are in response to the universal call of humanity."[54]

Fulfilling his promise to the Jewish War Veterans, Mayor O'Brian expanded on Wagner's remarks, although the substance of his speech was curiously tentative and somewhat at odds with the other addresses. Expressing disbelief that Germany could be guilty of such bad behavior, he seemed to mean just that; he did not believe that it was possible for Germans to act in so guilty a manner. Not only did he hasten to absolve the German people of antisemitic sentiments, but he went so far as to take Cordell Hull's reassurances of the benign will of the Nazi government at face value. O'Brien went so far as to say, "They [the actions of the Nazis] could not be sanctioned by the government in Germany."[55] Even so, he took the opportunity to express solidarity with those protesting "any outrages or excesses that may have taken place," in the hope that "no such abuses of the fundamental rights of human beings will be permitted in that great country to take place again."[56]

The one Jewish politician whose speech was quoted extensively in the *Times* was New York Governor Herbert Lehman. Unable or unwilling to appear in New York City that evening, Lehman spoke from an assembled rally in Albany, stressing the contribution of Jews in Germany:[57]

> In science, in literature, in music and art, in every form of spiritual, moral and intellectual activity, only those steeped in ignorance and prejudiced deny an honored place to Germans of Jewish faith. In peace they contributed to Germany's well-being; in war they laid down their lives for Germany's greatness.[58]

Forthrightly asserting his own heritage as a German Jew, Lehman added a distinctly personal touch to his call for Germany to remember and to reclaim what he and his co-presenters characterized as the higher ground at the heart of German culture. At the conclusion of his speech, Lehman declared:

> My parents and their ancestors for many generations were born and lived in Germany. As a boy and as a man I have spent many happy months there. I know and believe I understand its people. No country can boast a more sturdy, loyal or more idealistic population than that represented by the average man and woman in

Germany. In the past they have striven for the principles of civil and religious liberty. I am confident they will do so again and will refuse to be deluded by falsehood and misrepresentations.

The truth must in time allay the passions aroused by appeals to bigotry. All right-thinking people, regardless of race, creed or nationality, must unite in the effort to hasten that time.[59]

Despite some discrepancies and differences in style, the speeches of the politicians repeatedly strike many of the same chords: The Jews are being unfairly treated but the German people as a whole are not responsible. Nazi policy is a betrayal of the tradition of German civilization. Right-thinking people everywhere should condemn antisemitism. Persecution of the Jews is not only wrong in itself but is also an affront to the human values of an enlightened age.

But the stage belonged not only to politicians that evening. Jewish and Christian clergy and other influential figures also took their turn. The reported remarks of the Jewish speakers, beginning with the introductory remarks of Bernard S. Deutsch, president of the American Jewish Congress, faithfully toed the line to carefully distinguished the German people as a whole from the aberrant Nazi regime. Deutsch disavowed "any feeling of unfriendliness or ill will toward the German nation"[60] and couched his indignation in the language of a larger concern for human rights. His carefully crafted presentation of Jewish grievance pressed the case for all minorities: "The time has come when the civilized nations of the world should be concerned not only for the safety and protection of their nationals abroad, but should be keenly interested in the preservation of human rights of all minorities wherever they may be."[61]

One striking element of the *Times* reportage is that many highly influential Jewish speakers who shared the platform received no coverage at all, apart from a brief mention of their presence in the concluding paragraph of the lead story "55,000 Here Stage Protest" on page twelve. Among them were Dr. Joseph Tenenbaum, chairman of the executive committee of the American Jewish Congress; the *Der Tog* editor Dr. Samuel Margoshes, who had been so instrumental in organizing the meeting; Morris Rothenberg, president of the Zionist Organization of America; Rebecca Kohut, president of the World Congress of Jewish Women; Alexander Kahn, president of the People's Relief; and Abraham Cahan, editor of *Forverts*, who was arguably the most prominent Jewish journalistic voice in the United States.

In the *Times* press coverage of the Jewish speakers that evening, the spotlight belonged most fully to Stephen Wise; the full text of his remarks appeared under the heading "'WE ASK ONLY FOR THE RIGHT,' SAYS WISE" in the center of page twelve under a large photograph of the crowd gathered in the arena. As others had done, Wise lauded the German people and culture, its "monumental, indeed eternal contributions to human well-being in the domain of religion, literature and the arts," and stressed the ecumenical makeup of the gathering.[62] He disclaimed any sentiment of enmity, declaring:

> We are the friends of and believers in Germany—Germany at its highest, Germany at its truest, the German nation at its noblest. Because we are the friends of Germany, because we have inextinguishable faith in the basic love for righteousness of the German people, we appeal to Germany, representing, as this meeting does, Protestants, Catholics, Jews, in the name of America, which has been stirred as rarely before against wrongs perpetrated upon German Jews.[63]

Wise also answered critics who had publicly rejected his decision to move forward with the protests, and he sternly criticized German Jewish leadership: "Their policy of uncomplaining assent and of super-cautious silence has born evil fruit."[64] Articulating both hope and resignation, Wise stressed:

> And if things are to be worse because of our protest, if there are to be new penalties and reprisals in Germany, which I cannot bring myself to believe, then humbly and sorrowfully we bow our heads in the presence of the tragic fate that threatens, and once again appeal to the public opinion of mankind and the conscience of Christendom to save civilization from the shame that may be imminent.[65]

Like other presenters, Wise framed his call for a public condemnation of Germany's treatment of its Jews in the wider context of universal values:

> The conscience of humanity has made a world-problem of the present situation of the Jews in Germany. We lay down no conditions tonight, we make no stipulation, we do not even urge demands. But we do affirm certain elementary axioms of civilization. The Jews of the world, no more than the Jews of Germany, do not demand exceptional treatment or privileged position or favored status for themselves. We do not even ask for rights. We ask only for the right. We demand the right.[66]

Specifically, Wise called for "the immediate cessation of anti-Semitic activities and propaganda in Germany, including an end to the policy of racial discrimination against and of economic exclusion of Jews from the life of Germany" and the protection of Jewish life and property.[67] At the conclusion of the evening's program, the resolution "empowering the congress to appoint a committee to raise a large fund to combat antisemitism and protect Jews throughout the world was adopted unanimously by standing vote."[68]

Jewish leaders and their organizations were not the only groups considering the growing dangers besetting German Jewry. Christian clergies were also mobilizing at the same moment. On March 22, the Jewish Telegraphic Agency reported:

> Clerical and lay leaders of the Greater New York Federation of Churches have been in conference with former Governor Alfred E. Smith; Bishop William T. Manning; Rev. Dr. William B. Millar, Executive Secretary of the Federation of Churches, a Protestant Organization, and Charles H. Tuttle, Chairman of the Interfaith Committee, which comprises Catholics and Protestants, have prepared the draft of a protest which will be submitted for signature to prominent Christians, who will sign it, after which it will be made public.[69]

Although nowhere is it mentioned, in light of this report it is reasonable to suppose that Smith, who was acting as the middleman between the Jewish leadership and the above-mentioned Christian organizations, must have garnered the additional support of William T. Manning, bishop of the Episcopal Diocese of New York, and Charles H. Tuttle to be added to the roster of speakers that night. Wise and Smith had enjoyed a fruitful friendship since their first meeting in 1911 and a political alliance that brought them mutual benefits. Wise supported Smith's first presidential run in 1924 and campaigned for him for governor in 1926 and again in his presidential bid two years later.[70] In return for this fealty, Smith responded to Wise's political counsel. In 1926, at Wise's urging, Smith, in spite of possible political risk, appointed the distinguished Jewish jurist Benjamin Cardozo to the seat of chief justice of the New York Court of Appeals.[71]

Manning and Tuttle were both prominent voices, active in the nascent movement toward closer official Jewish-Christian relations, which began in 1923 as the Commission on International Justice and Goodwill, a subcommittee of the Federal Council of Churches that was created to address the issue of religious bigotry, and which later developed into the National Conference of Jews and Christians in 1928, then renamed itself the National Conference of Christians and Jews ten years later.. Manning and Tuttle continued to play a role in Jewish-Christian relations in years to come, particularly Manning, who was a constant and vociferous opponent of the Nazis throughout the war.[72]

As other speakers had done, they characterized the persecution of the Jews as an affront to civilization. As liberal Christian clergy, they added an additional moral and ethical dimension to the protests. Beginning with Manning, they interpreted the Nazi actions as an offense against the ecumenical spirit that he and his colleagues represented. As he noted:

We are here to assert together the great basic truth that God has made of one blood all nations of men on the whole earth, and that, because we have one Divine Creator and Father, we are all brothers . . . Upon the fact of the common Divine Fatherhood, we base the truth of our common brotherhood, our common humanity, the quality of all in the sight of God, the equal right of every human being to justice, to liberty and to life.[73]

Like others, Manning was careful to distinguish between the Nazi government and the rest of Germany. He declared, "We feel confident that the real Germany is as deeply opposed to acts of racial or religious persecution as any of us are."[74] No friend of the Soviet Union, Manning also took the opportunity to warn the audience, "[We] must not forget the tyrannical and cruel persecution carried on against those representatives of all religious faiths and the brutal attempt to stamp out all religion, which still continues under the Soviet Government in Russia."[75] In conclusion, Manning offered an outspoken appeal on behalf of what he interpreted as true Christian principles:

> The Christian religion calls upon men not only for justice, but for brotherliness toward all, and in these days of world crisis we see clearly that we must sweep out the spirit of hate and fear and banish war and draw all nations together in brotherhood and fellowship if civilization is to be saved.[76]

Charles Tuttle was also quoted extensively as a representative of the Christian community. A well-known US attorney in the Coolidge administration, he had earned a reputation as an anticorruption crusader. Touted to run for higher state office, Tuttle was the 1930 Republican gubernatorial candidate. Although personally a nondrinker, his position favoring the repeal of prohibition cost him the support of his constituency and he lost to FDR that year by what was at that time the largest margin of defeat in the history of New York State. Taking up private legal practice, he involved himself in religious affairs and, like fellow Episcopalian William Manning, took a greater interest in ecumenical issues.

Speaking on behalf of the Interfaith Committee, Tuttle reinforced the points Manning made, asserting that "the laws of humanity and of God are the foundations of all other laws, and that if and when these fundamentals laws are violated, then the whole commonwealth of man instantly acquires a right and a duty to speak out loud."[77] It is also worth noting that where Mayor O'Brien had cited Cordell Hull's telegram in an attempt to defuse protest, Tuttle quoted it to support the seriousness of the allegations:

> We do indeed earnestly hope that the acts of aggression and violence are less widespread than the current reports have led us to believe; but we are bound to note that our own Secretary of State, after a full investigation, has reported that there has been considerable physical mistreatment of Jews, picketing of Jewish stores and professional discrimination.[78]

Appealing to the religious sensibilities of his listeners, Tuttle stated that it was "the sacred duty of every member of the human family and every adherent of the Christian faith to counteract this subversive, un-Christian and inhuman propaganda which is abroad in the world and has lately so painfully manifested itself in Germany." Referring to Germany's "present hardships of unrevised treaties" and its "right to demand of us and the world justice and cooperation," he concluded, "But those who seek justice must extend justice. Those who seek freedom for themselves must preserve the freedom of others. Those who complain of international discrimination should not allow racial and religious discrimination within their own borders."[79]

A third influential Christian voice to urge that Germany should be held accountable in the court of public opinion for its behavior was that of Methodist Bishop Francis John O'Connell. A committed reformer, O'Connell was deeply involved with the Social Gospel movement not only within his own denomination but also through the Federal Council of Churches, the presidency of which he had assumed in 1928.[80] Calling for a continuation of public protest against antisemitism in Germany even in the event of the cessation of overt acts of persecution, he declared:

> We must come to a crystallization of public sentiment. We shall always have something to say as to the conduct of our neighbors. If we can create the kind of sentiment that holds up to a nation the errors of its course and stop that nation before it is too late, we can work then for the best kind of peace in the world. It does not mean a sitting down in quietude in the presence of injustice. It does not mean that. It means the springing out for humanity always.[81]

Despite his indignation on behalf of Germany's Jewish people, O'Connell's alarm occurs primarily in the broader context of humanitarian concern typified by the ideology of the Federal Council of Churches. The Christian speakers, drawn from the liberal end of the denominational spectrum, were able to defend the Jews most comfortably on the basis of general humanitarian values and Jewish contributions to Western culture. Yet they seemed to be at something of a loss in considering the merit of the Jews as a religious community. Steering clear of religious differences, O'Connell could only project on them his own universalist sentiments: "The Jewish race, above all, have thought that there is something inalienable and sacred about humanity wherever it is found. For that truth I stand, and in that spirit I come to give what little support I have to this meeting tonight."[82]

This broad-minded approach, eloquent and reasonable as it may be, was limited in that it was certainly not representative of American Christianity as a whole. Alliances among even the like-minded involved embracing a more expansive, less particularized set of religious values that came at the expense of religious difference. The dominant presence of the theologically liberal Christian representatives that evening excluded other voices, some of whom would later emerge as surprising allies. This may not have been consciously planned. It may simply have been a case of like calling out to like, for these were the kind of Christians whom Wise would have found to be the most congenial company and with whom he had cultivated friendships for many years.

Among them, John Haynes Holmes, whose friendship with Wise had flourished for almost twenty years, also took the platform. Holmes, a widely respected Unitarian minister, was a deeply committed pacifist.[83] Nonetheless, his abhorrence of war did not prevent him from condemning Hitler in scathing terms and rebuking those who sought to minimize the destructive intent of his government. With startling foresight, he declared:

> When Hitler straightaway destroyed the Republic and made himself dictator, we were told that responsibility would temper his spirit and that he would do nothing he had threatened . . . Do not be deceived. If the reign of terror has been momentarily stayed in Germany it means that Hitler's emissaries have been withdrawn in perfect order and under as precise direction and control as they were released in the beginning for their dreadful work. But it does not mean that this work is ended . . . For be not deceived, whatever Hitler is doing or not doing at this moment, it is the will of this new Danton to destroy the Israel that for a thousand years has given the genius of its life to Germany.[84]

Not all influential Christian voices whose support may have been expected stepped forward. One notable exception, Bishop John J. Dunn of the Catholic Archdiocese of New York, had originally agreed to be one of the evening's speakers but withdrew at the last moment. Offering Cordell Hull's reassuring telegram as the reason, Bishop Dunn explained in a telephone interview reported in the *Times*: "Therefore, it seemed to me that there was nothing to protest against at the meeting. I have no control over the meeting, but I have control over my own actions, so I withdrew . . . now it doesn't seem that further protests are necessary."[85]

Bishop Dunn's withdrawal notwithstanding, the speeches offered by non-Jewish speakers were all that Wise could have hoped for. They made the case that enlightened thinking in general was on the side of the Jewish people. In particular, Christian brotherhood toward Jews, as warmly emphasized by Bishops Manning and O'Connell, stood against the policies of Hitler and the Nazi government.

Of course, Christian imagery regarding the Jews could be turned to more than one purpose. Threatening to extend the one-day boycott that Hitler called for in retaliation for criticism from foreign powers, Joseph Goebbels declared at a rally attended by eighty thousand persons in Berlin on March 31: "I prophesy to you that the day is at hand when humanity will at last be freed from the eternal Jew, who for thousands of years has wandered through the Continent as mass murderer and murderer of Christ. Golgotha shall be avenged, and the Jew himself is on the way to Golgotha."[86]

The Madison Square Garden protest and others around the country also earned front-page treatment in the Jewish press. Not surprisingly, it emphasized the Jewish voices heard that night and their aspirations for the support of the wider American public. The coverage of three influential Yiddish-language newspapers, *Forverts*, *Der Tog*, and *Morgn Frayhayt*, not only reveal differing perspectives driven by ideological disparity but also provide a measure of internal dialogue that was lacking in the English-language reporting. Among the dozens of Yiddish-language newspapers that serviced the seemingly insatiable Jewish appetite for print, *Der Tog*, *Forverts*, and *Morgn Frayhayt* were the three that over time wielded the greatest influence and demonstrated the most staying power.

In contrast to the avowedly nonpartisan *Der Tog*, *Forverts* and *Morgn Frayhayt* were both closely associated with political ideologies and parties: *Forverts* with the Socialist Labor Party and *Morgn Frayhayt* with the Communist Party. As such, they represented significant constituencies within the Jewish community that were often sharply at odds with one another. *Forverts* and *Morgn Frayhayt* were both beholden to political apparatuses with competing visions of a just world and the means through which it might be achieved. Their respective editorial policies were guided by the parties whose views they reflected, although in the case of *Forverts*, the editor Abraham Cahan was able to break free of the yoke that his overseers sought to impose on him, largely because of his powerful persona and the stupendous success that *Forverts* was able to achieve in circulation and profitability.

Forverts came into existence as an indirect result of a dispute between the anarchist and social-democrat factions in the Socialist Labor Party. After a contentious split in 1890, Social Democrats decided to start the weekly newspaper *Di Arbiter Tsaytung* (The Workers' Newspaper) and a publishing association that would manage the newspaper, appoint its staff, and guide its editorial policy. Under the editorial leadership of Philip Krants, a Socialist from London, the paper began to thrive, with Cahan as a frequent contributor second only to Krants.[87] Four years later, the publishing association started the first-ever Yiddish socialist daily, *Dos Abend Blat* (The Evening Paper), also edited by Krants, whose circulation quickly climbed to thirty-six thousand.[88]

Soon after, however, power struggles erupted within the publishing association. Cahan and some colleagues accused Krants and his cohorts of high-handedness and repressive attitudes toward dissenting opinions. In January 1897, Cahan and about fifty others broke away to form another publishing association and another Yiddish newspaper, *Forverts*. Although it maintained its socialist bent under Cahan's editorial direction, it also sought to cultivate a broader readership through offering a variety of features with some of the finest literary talent of the day, including Sholem Asch, Jonah Rosenfeld, and the Singer brothers, Israel Joshua and Isaac Bashevis.[89] By the 1920s, its circulation reached about a quarter of a million and was by far the most widely read Yiddish newspaper in the world in the years leading up to and including World War II.

On March 28, 1933, *Forverts*' bold front-page headline proclaimed "HUGE PROTEST MEETING AGAINST HITLER— FURIOUS STORM IN ALL AMERICA," with the subheading "Famous Christians Condemn Antisemitism as World Peril." Directly beneath was a photograph of Bishop O'Connell and the aged Rabbi Moses Z. Margolies of the Union of Orthodox Rabbis, who delivered the evening's invocation, standing together. The photo was captioned

"Christian and Jewish Unity—Rabbi and Priest Together in Protest of the Hitler Persecution of the Jews." While the speeches of the politicians and the Christian clergy were duly reported, there was far more space devoted to the Jewish speakers to whom the *Times* had given short shrift, beginning with the *Forverts* editor Cahan, whose editorial "What's Happening with the Hitler Plague in Germany Right Now?" dominated front-page center.

Another striking feature of *Forverts'* coverage is the diminished role of Rabbi Wise. While a brief excerpt of Wise's remarks is included, it appears alongside other speeches, in proportional length with the others and without the fanfare the *Times* had accorded him or even an accompanying photograph. While Wise seems to have been the darling of the *Times*, such was not the case with *Forverts*. Cahan's editorial policy would have been sharply at odds with Wise's more conservative political views. *Forverts'* perception was that Wise had traded his independence for access to the political establishment. In addition to this, it was well understood that no one's stature surpassed that of Cahan at *Forverts*.

With less political capital to lose among the upper echelons of power, Cahan could afford to be less inhibited and more frank in his remarks, as his denunciation of the attitudes of the German people as a whole reveals. Perhaps this is why his speech, at variance with Wise's and others' attempts to exonerate Germany society and culture, was left unreported by the more mainstream *Times*. The *Times'* omission of even a brief summary of Cahan's speech is doubly shocking in that in addition to being the editor of the most widely read Yiddish daily in the country, he had been known for decades as one of the most popular and compelling lecturers in the New York Yiddish-speaking community.[90]

Cahan's speech was a forthright condemnation of "the brutality and savagery of the storm troopers against the German Jewish citizens." He also had sharp words for "those who are foolish and naïve enough to believe that the Hitler government intended to protect Jewish businesses from the attacks of the brown shirts." He concluded his address with the impassioned declaration, "We protest here this evening against the anti-Semitic wave that has flooded Germany, the German tyranny and despotism that tramples underfoot Jewish feeling, Jewish pride and destroys Jewish property and possessions."[91]

Close by the coverage of Wise's remarks and on more than equal footing with them are those of Rebecca Kohut, another speaker whom the *Times* had neglected. Kohut, president of the World Congress of Jewish Women, whose importance was accentuated by an accompanying photograph, was portrayed as "a Jewish woman to the women of Germany" speaking "in the name of Jewish mothers in America to Christian mothers in Germany." She exhorts:

> As a woman I appeal to German women, the mothers and daughters, that they should help make an end to the dishonorable barbarism that rules now in their country. That they should help cleanse the pestilence of Jew hatred and race hatred that has taken hold in Germany. Mother Rachel's heart is grieving . . . she sees her children in pain, destroyed.[92]

Another noted voice from the Yiddish press whose speech was omitted from the *Times* was that of Samuel Margoshes, who had worked behind the scenes to bring the rally to fruition. He was only briefly quoted in *Forverts*, saying that Hitler's assurances of Jewish safety in Germany were "not worth a damn."[93] As editor of *Der Tog*, Margoshes had much more to say for himself in the paper whose pages bore the imprint of his personality.

Der Tog was established in 1914 by a group of public-spirited Jewish activists, including David Schapiro, Dr. Judah L. Magnes, and Herman Bernstein.[94] Although it could not boast nearly as large a circulation as *Forverts*, *Der Tog* sought to carve out a niche as a highbrow publication for a discriminating readership, its masthead proclaiming "*Der Tog* is the newspaper for the Jewish intelligentsia."[95] Less interested in promoting Jewish literature, it concentrated on recruiting top-drawer columnists and critics, such as Shmuel Niger and Chaim Zhitlovsky.[96]

Just as Cahan had done, Margoshes used his editorial license to highlight his role in the evening's proceedings, as the March 28 issue of *Der Tog* demonstrates. In the front-page article "The Father of the Idea," his photo is printed on the bottom right-hand corner of the front page with the caption "Dr. S. Margoshes, editor of *Tog*, who first proposed a resolution calling for a protest demonstration against Hitlerism."[97] The front page also carried more of his speech, which concluded, "We have formulated our demands to Hitler and to his Nazi government. We stand by them. And until he will accept them and accept them in full we will not cease our protest and our struggle. We swear this solemnly before God and humanity."[98]

Like *Forverts*, *Der Tog* emphasized in its headline the perception of American solidarity with the Jewish cause: "ALL AMERICA SUPPORTS JEWS IN PROTEST AGAINST HITLER." The subheading lists the non-Jewish speakers, describes the packed house and the streets that were "black with people," and reports that governors from many states had sent messages of sympathy and support. The inside coverage contains more of the same, with brief summaries of the speeches given by both Jewish and non-Jewish speakers.

The headline on the top of page 3, "ANGER AGAINST THE GERMAN INQUISITION FIRES ECHOED YESTERDAY LOUD AND STRONG TO THE WHOLE WORLD," draws on another dark chapter that lived in Jewish memory. *Der Tog*'s coverage of the program itself included a section titled "The American Christian Religious World Lets Its Voice of Protest Be Heard." The opening sentence reads, "There thundered from the platform the deep protest of the Christian religious world in America," and follows with an account of the Christian participants and brief summaries of their remarks.[99] The paper also carried reports of well-attended protest meetings in Jackson, Mississippi; Cleveland, Ohio; and Oakland, California, emphasizing the participation of both Jews and Christians. Inside coverage included a lengthy excerpt of Rebecca Kohut's speech and the article "Jewish Women Protest," describing in colorful terms the large number and variety of women who turned out: "old and young, homey grandmothers in wigs, young American women with platinum blond bobbed hair, West Side society matrons and East Side storekeepers."[100]

Not everything in *Der Tog* about the meeting was as reverential as the reportage seen elsewhere. Ben-Zion Goldberg, the son-in-law of the beloved Sholem Aleichem and the successor of Margoshes as editor in 1937, wrote a lengthy, somewhat sarcastic piece that actually lampooned the program and some of its speakers.[101] Among his first observations is that it was a "great wonder" that, somehow, not only do the Yiddish speakers understand the English speeches, and vice versa, but they are also all able to applaud in the right places.[102] In a humorous tone, Goldberg singled out Mayor O'Brien's stumbles, attributing them, somewhat tongue-in-cheek, to typographical errors on the part of his secretary. These included unfortunate mispronunciations of the names Albert Einstein as Albert Weinstein and Heinrich Heine as Henry Hein. Even so, Goldberg did give O'Brien credit for a surprising degree of erudition regarding German Jewish culture: "Go know the surprising places a little Torah will turn up."[103]

He also criticized the program itself, how lengthy it was, how the important Senator Wagner had been held back for too long, and how, when he finally arrived, he stood too far away from the microphone to be properly heard. Goldberg noted with some amusement the number of non-Jews present on the platform, remarking, "What a delight it was to be a goy on the platform" and to be able "to take a swipe at what the world was up to." He singled out Wise's great friend John Haynes Holmes, whom he identified as the "Jewish priest who seemed to have brought the larger part of his congregation with him," conceding, however, that Holmes's speech delivered a powerful punch and that he clearly took Hitler to task in no uncertain terms.[104]

In sharp contrast to the stories published by *Forverts* and *Der Tog* were those of *Morgn Frayhayt*, which by 1933 had been the organ of the American Communist Party for a decade. Its history provides another example of the labyrinthine nature of the various left-leaning political organizations among which members of the

Jewish working class could choose. Founded in 1922, *Morgn Frayhayt* was birthed in the milieu of internal strife among the warring factions of the multifaceted Jewish leftist political scene, as was the case with *Forverts*. Only in this case, *Morgn Frayhayt* originated as an indirect result of dissatisfaction on the part of certain Socialist Party members who were unhappy with the lack of party supervision over the powerful Forverts Association and the even more powerful Cahan.

Cahan's detractors were also disgusted by what they perceived to be *Forverts'* sensational journalism and inferior content.[105] This coterie, which included the Bundist Russian émigrés Ben-Tsien Hofman, Shakhne Epshteyn, Yankev Salutski, and a number of other activists, sought and in the end failed to bring the Forverts Association and Cahan to heel. This ultimately led to the creation of *Morgn Frayhayt*, a newspaper that could at last, they hoped, displace *Forverts* as the true voice of the Jewish working class. They faced formidable obstacles. Tony Michels notes, "Whereas *Forverts* attracted the large number of immigrants who were sympathetic to socialism but not necessarily party members, *Frayhayt* appealed to a small number of ideologically committed radicals."[106] After a short time, unable to achieve financial independence, it fell under Communist control and its editorial board functioned as the servant of the Communist Party.[107]

In light of this background, it is reasonable to expect a different slant in *Frayhayt's* front-page coverage of the protest on March 28, particularly since representatives of the Communist Party that the paper championed had been carefully shut out of visible participation in the event itself. Not surprisingly, the evening's program was cast in a dismissive light with only cursory mention of the lineup of speechmakers. One headline reads, "SPEAKERS AT GARDEN MEETING FROM 'JEWISH CONGRESS' SPEAK VAGUE PHRASES." It reads, in part:

> Ten thousand people were disappointed not to hear heated words of protest and sharp condemnation, but rather the speakers from

the "Jewish Congress" and the other self-contained, Jewish community cliques came up with entreaties, with submissive and vague appeals "to the conscience of the German people."[108]

In keeping with Communist doctrine that sought at that time to deemphasize what it perceived to be the parochial concerns of special interest groups, *Morgn Frayhayt* downplayed the German persecution of Jewish citizens, laying much more emphasis on the imperiled state of Communists in Nazi Germany than on the plight of the Jews.[109]

To summarize, while *Frayhayt* remained aloof, the reports of *Forverts* and *Der Tog* both mirror the extensive emphasis of the *Times* on what was indisputably a large outpouring of public concern driven by alarm over rapidly developing events in Germany. However, the Yiddish press's interpretation of the importance of the protests and the tone of its reporting far more closely reflects the more specific concerns of the Jewish community. While Wise was busy lining up Christians to plead the Jewish case to the wider world, the Yiddish press, unconcerned with non-Yiddish readers, found its own voice to speak to its own constituents.

Forverts and *Der Tog* were clearly united in their gratitude for the public outcry on behalf of Germany's persecuted Jews, particularly among participating Christians. It affirmed what they hoped could be their own rising status in the eyes of Christian America. But the differing perspectives that the Yiddish press brought to the reporting on the Madison Square Garden protest meeting of 1933 are also an apt reminder of the multifaceted nature of the Jewish community and the divisions within it that, if anything, deepened in the years leading up to and including the war.

Sensational as the turnout for the Garden rally and its attendant publicity had been, there was no guarantee that it would prove to be anything more than another soon-forgotten item of yesterday's news. However, such was not the case. The rally found an afterlife not only in New York City but in regions throughout the country as Christian organizations, denominational leadership, and the religious press became responsive to the threat posed by Germany's increasingly draconian policies.

The day after the meeting, the New York City Board of Aldermen unanimously adopted a resolution calling the persecutions "a most cowardly, inhuman and un-Christian assault upon every precept of civilized living." It also urged the Roosevelt administration to "make vigorous and proper representations to the German government to put an immediate stop to these barbaric persecutions and to restore to German Jewry its civil and religious rights and the protection of the Laws of the Reich."[110] However, as for a stiffened tone from the State Department toward Germany, little came of it.

Likewise, the widespread protests and the press coverage they received in America did little in terms of positive results for Jews in Germany. In fact, the opposite was the case. Germany, under Hitler's orders, implemented a boycott of Jewish businesses, physicians, and attorneys on April 1, for which the American Jewish Committee bitterly blamed the March 27 protests. Conditions in Germany continued to deteriorate for German Jews in 1933, culminating with the enactment of the Nuremburg Laws in September of that year. Concrete action by the Roosevelt administration, which fended off the importuning efforts of the American Jewish Committee and the American Jewish Congress with vague assurances, failed to materialize.

Regardless, swift follow-through from Christian churches and organizations was forthcoming in further public expressions of support, which resulted in a strengthening of relations between the Jewish and Christian representatives who had participated in the March 27 protests or were otherwise sympathetic with their aims. On May 26 the *Times* carried a petition composed by Harry Emerson Fosdick of the Riverside Church in Manhattan, which was signed by approximately twelve hundred Protestant ministers. The primary recipients were leaders of about a dozen Protestant denominations in Germany. The petition reads in part:

> We, a group of Christian ministers, are profoundly disturbed by the plight of our Jewish brethren in Germany. That no doubt may

exist anywhere concerning our Christian conscience in the matter, we are constrained, alike with sorrow and indignation to voice our protests against the present ruthless persecution of the Jews under Herr Hitler's regime ... Systematically they are prosecuting a "cold pogrom" of inconceivable cruelty against our Jewish brethren, driving them from positions of trust and leadership, depriving them of civil and economic rights, deliberately condemning them, if they survive at all, to survive as an outlawed and excommunicated people and threatening Jews with massacre if they so much as protest ... We deplore the consequences which must fall upon the Jews, upon Christendom, which permits this ruthless persecution, and in particular against Germany itself. For, protesting thus against Herr Hitler's antisemitism, we conceive ourselves to be speaking as sincere friends of the German nation.[111]

This petition must have been tremendously affirming for Wise, who for decades had planted the seeds of interreligious cooperation among like-minded Christian clergy beginning with his first rabbinate in Portland, Oregon, in 1900. Now it seemed his efforts were coming to fruition. Some American Christians were publicly expressing united opposition to not only the deteriorating situation of the German Jews but to antisemitism itself.

Also important, Jewish and Christian leaders were becoming more fully aware of one another. The cast of players that took the stage at Madison Square Garden that night in 1933 would expand in the years that followed. Over the next decade to the end of the war, some of these same Jewish and Christian figures would reprise their roles from 1933. Others would add their voices.

Wise's mission resembles that of another, earlier Jewish rabbi who sought to be a guardian of his people, the Maharal of Prague, with whom the legend of the golem has become most closely associated. This tale, which has found an enduring place in literature, the stage, and film, tells of how, in a moment of intense danger to the Jewish community, the rabbi fashioned a powerful figure from river clay and brought it to life to protect his people. Animated by the word *emeth* (truth) engraved on its forehead, the golem was controlled by a *shem*, a magical formula placed in its mouth. Thus, although unpredictable, the golem could be programmed to follow simple instructions. It was, however, prone to erratic behavior.

In drawing together the reliable voices of Christian clergy and other non-Jewish worthies, Stephen Wise attempted to fashion a golem from the clay of our national culture and place a set of instructions in its mouth. He was determined to amplify his intentions by deploying the power of the American Christian establishment on behalf of his vulnerable co-religionists abroad. Wise is deemed a failure by his detractors with regard to the fate of European Jewry. If that is true, perhaps it is partly because his golem's behavior proved in the end to be as unreliable as that of its predecessor in Prague.

1. Rabbi Stephen Wise speaks out at Madison Square Garden, 1933. United States Holocaust Memorial Museum, courtesy of National Archives and Records Administration, College Park, MD.

55,000 HERE STAGE PROTEST ON HITLER ATTACKS ON JEWS; NAZIS ORDER A NEW BOYCOTT

BAN ON JEWS SPREADS

Hitler's Party Prepares Boycott in Revenge for 'Atrocity Tales.'

VAST PROPAGANDA OPENS

Religious Leaders Send Cables to Clergymen Here Denying Persecution Reports.

STEEL HELMETMEN SEIZED

Leaders of Veterans' Society, Which Has a Cabinet Post, Accused of Plot.

By FREDERICK T. BIRCHALL.
Special Cable to THE NEW YORK TIMES.

BERLIN, March 27.—The National Socialist party announced tonight that it would conduct a counter-boycott against Jewish business concerns in Germany if Jews in the United States and England continued their boycott and atrocity propaganda.

That the boycott campaign has the support of Chancellor Hitler was indicated in the official announcement that Herr Hitler had a long conversation Sunday with Dr. Paul Joseph Goebbels, his Min...

Braun Cabinet of Prussia Out; Lost Its Power Last Summer

Special Cable to THE NEW YORK TIMES.
BERLIN, March 27.—The Prussian Socialist-Centrist Cabinet, which was headed by Otto Braun, a Socialist, resigned today.

This Cabinet lost most of its power last Summer, when former Chancellor von Papen seized Prussia through a Presidential decree. Since then the Cabinet has fought for the lost powers in the courts. The resignation had been long anticipated and received only two-line items on the back pages of Berlin newspapers.

35,000 JAM STREETS OUTSIDE THE GARDEN

Solid Lines of Police Hard Pressed to Keep Overflow Crowds From Hall.

AREA BARRED TO TRAFFIC

Mulrooney Takes Command to Avoid Roughness—3,000 at Columbus Circle Meeting.

More than 35,000 men and women who came from the five boroughs and near-by communities to attend the protest meeting at Madison Square Garden last night were un...

OTHER FAITHS JOIN IN

Crowd Overflowing the Garden Hears Leaders Assail Persecution.

CHEERS PLEA BY SMITH

He Likens Hitlerism to Klan, Calls Upon German People in Name of Humanity.

NO ATTACK ON COUNTRY

Manning, Wise, McConnell and Green Denounce Bigotry— 1,000,000 Meet in Nation.

Hitlerism with its anti-Semitic propaganda and persecution of Jews must be dragged out into the open and given the same treatment "we gave the Ku Klux Klan," former Governor Smith told a cheering audience of more than 20,000 Jews assembled in Madison Square Garden last night to protest against Hitler's treatment of the Jews in Germany.

In a speech lasting about twenty minutes, the former Governor brought the otherwise solemn audience to its feet as he denounced

2. *New York Times*, front page, March 28, 1933. © 1933 The New York Times Company. All rights reserved. Used under license.

THE NEW YORK TIMES, TUESDAY, MARCH 28, 1933.

Faiths Voice Indignation at Anti-Semitism

PART OF THE GREAT CROWD GATHERED IN MADISON SQUARE GARDEN.

View of the Meeting Last Night to Protest the Treatment of Jews in Germany.

55,000 IN PROTEST ON HITLER ATTACKS

Continued from Page One.

sistant Chief Inspector John Sullivan.

At none of the meetings were there any attacks directed against Germany and the German people. The denunciations were concerned with the anti-Semitic propaganda of the Hitler régime and the Hitler government was warned that the attacks on the Jews must stop. Appeals were addressed to the German people to have the persecutions stopped in the name of humanity and Christian principles.

Scoffs at "Pussyfooting."

In his address Mr. Smith revealed that pressure had been brought upon him not to appear at the meeting, but he scoffed at what he termed the pussyfooting that sought to prevent the protest. He declared that he had never appeared at any public gathering with greater satisfaction than at the Garden rally to protest against the persecution of Jews. He came, also, he said, to raise his voice "against intolerance, against bigotry, against the suppression of freedom of speech, against the suppression of the freedom of the press, and against any infringement of the right of public assembly."

And he would do this, he declared, whether the wrongs committed were in Germany, Russia, the United States or any other country.

"Now there is no denying the fact that there has been a kind of council of pussyfooting about whether we should have this meeting or not," Mr. Smith said. "There was a great cross-fire and current of opinion that was in conflict. I got all kinds of telegrams and all kinds of cablegrams telling me there wasn't any reason for a meeting, that nothing had taken place, that we wanted to avoid the possibility of hysteria at a time like this.

"Well, all I can say about this is that where there is a good deal of smoke there must be fire. And the only thing to do with it, not only in

We appeal here cessation everyw of right, of hun ligion."

Wagner Sees

Senator Wagn spoke as "a frie people, as one loves the land of cherishes her his of her accomplis "I have not c demn Germany." come to awaken to a realization children are brin her name. Are v version to medie centre of civiliza."

The Senator a with "horror an read "reports o in Germany that this meeting, of of intolerance ar He declared that of intolerance, sensics, laden heavy with discr ening the darkn manity has been fort to reach th day."

"The emergenc tive spirit is of to the Jewish pe is a menace not man people; unl it threatens to b pect of progress. springs of our c Saying that ne the form of go many were the but that "human man cooperation Senator Wagner Germany nor the can recover "as vision, dissensio tions are gnawir humanity."

All Faiths

Mr. Tuttle sai Committee, of v dent, "is a sym which this gr gathered." Spea of the committ Catholics, Prote Mr. Tuttle sai Semitic outbrea concerned all ideals." He decl man people had termine their fo

'We Ask Only for the Right,' Says Wise

The speech of Rabbi Wise last night at Madison Square Garden follows:

The American Jewish Congress has called but not caused this protest meeting of tonight. The American Jewish Congress has not aroused this protest against

before against wrongs perpetrated upon German Jews. This meeting was called because of the acts of the enemies of Germany. We meet tonight as the friends of Germany.

We know that it is not easy to cancel the Nazi program of thirteen years and still we know that it can be done. A dictatorship is omnipotent and above all

privileged position or favored status for themselves. We do not even ask for rights. We ask only for the right. We demand the right.

What are these elementary maxims of civilization, as we call them? The immediate cessation of anti-Semitic activities and propaganda in Germany, including as an end to the policy of racial

3. *New York Times*, inside coverage, March 28, 1933. © 1933 The New York Times Company. All rights reserved. Used under license.

4. *Time* cover, "Gov. Al Smith, 'Happy Warrior of the Political Battlefield,'" July 13, 1925. Wikimedia Commons.

5. Photo journalism from the Yiddish press, *Forverts*, March 28, 1933. *The Forward*, National Library of Israel.

The Voice of Religion

The Views of Christian Religious Leaders on the Persecution of the Jews in Germany by the National Socialists

> And one of the scribes came, and heard them questioning together, and knowing that he had answered them well, asked him, What commandment is the first of all? Jesus answered, The first is, Hear, O Israel; The Lord our God, the Lord is one; and thou shalt love the Lord thy God with all thy heart, and with all thy soul, and with all thy mind, and with all thy strength. The second is this, Thou shalt love thy neighbor as thyself.
>
> —Mark 12:28-31.

Second Printing

New York
The American Jewish Committee
1933

6. Widely distributed American Jewish Committee pamphlet "The Voice of Religion." Courtesy of the American Jewish Committee (AJC) Archives and Records Center.

7. Front-page headlines, *Forverts*, March 8, 1934. *The Forward*, National Library of Israel.

8. "Hitler Guilty of Mass Murder," *Forverts*, March 8, 1934. *The Forward*, National Library of Israel.

9. *New York Times* notice, "Amusements" section, "The Case of Civilization against Hitlerism." Used by permission of the American Jewish Historical Society.

10. The historian and suffragette Mary Ritter Beard. Library of Congress, Prints and Photographs Division, LC-USZ62-68955.

2

Broadening the Jewish-Christian Alliance against Nazi Germany

The year that elapsed between the first and the second Madison Square Garden gathering was a period of intensifying persecution for German Jewry and increasing consternation for American Jewish leadership. Seeking a way to halt the escalating violence of the Nazi government and its mounting social and economic pressure on the German Jewish community, American Jewish leaders continued to seek allies to pressure the US government to take concrete steps to deter the Nazis. The protest meetings of 1933 demonstrated most dramatically that there was significant Christian sympathy for Germany's Jews.

As the situation in Germany worsened, Jewish leadership began to pay serious attention to discovering the scope of support it could hope to find to engage the American public with its concerns. Heartened by the positive response they found among Christians to the protests of 1933, in the months that followed they sought to widen their network of non-Jewish supporters. During this time, they achieved notable success in locating them among Christian representatives who were sympathetic to their cause. The resulting more fully articulated arguments on behalf of the Jews that the speech-makers had begun to advance in 1933 came to fruition in the carefully crafted program of the March 7, 1934, Garden rally, "The Case of Civilization against Hitlerism," which also bore the imprint of Wise's leadership and organizational abilities. But by then there were also more players in the arena.

Although the efforts of Jews and Christians to form a united home front accelerated greatly at this time and found new dimensions, this pivotal moment in the Jewish-Christian encounter owed its existence to far more than just Stephen Wise's patiently built-up network of Christian connections. The Jewish-Christian alliance that Jews urgently sought did not have to be manufactured out of whole cloth. As Jews and Christians increased their efforts to find unity in response to the Nazi threat in the prewar years, they found themselves continuing to negotiate a delicate pact of mutual recognition that had already begun to take shape. To evaluate their efforts properly, it is necessary to supply the context of the state of Jewish-Christian relations prior to the 1930s.

With the notable exception of the achievements of Jewish and Christian Zionists, which I will address at a later point, interfaith relations did not exist in the lexicon of American religious thought before the 1920s. Prior to that time, there were no official movements specifically constituted for the purpose of fostering positive interreligious relations between Jews and Christians on the basis of mutual religious esteem. One of the most important side effects that the ascendance of Nazi power had on Jewish and Christian leadership in America was that it challenged it not only to respond to the brutalities being visited on Jews in Europe but also to break new ground in forming closer, more respectful relationships. Yet up until that time, the language of mutual religious recognition had not yet truly developed a vocabulary.

The groundwork, however, had already been laid. As early as 1919, Alfred Williams Anthony, chairman of the Federal Council of Churches, in a letter to Reform Rabbi Leo Franklin, president of the Central Conference of American Rabbis, expressed the desire for Jews and Christians to foster relations on a footing of greater reciprocity.[1] As well, early efforts to promote positive interreligious relations were not initiated solely by Christians. Throughout the 1920s, Reform Rabbi Isaac Landman, editor of the influential *American Hebrew*, advocated not only interreligious cooperation but also a vision of a universal, blended, religious faith that would emerge when Jews and

Christians agreed to set aside their differences in favor of progressive principles that Landman believed were the essence of the message of the biblical prophets.²

Spring 1927 seemed a propitious time for him to advance his agenda. That year, Easter and the first day of Passover fell on the same day, April 17. In honor of the occasion, Landman convened a meeting composed of nine distinguished representatives from Jewish, Protestant, and Catholic faiths. These included Henry Morgenthau, a distinguished public servant and former American Ambassador to the Ottoman Empire; Judge Irving Lehman; and Rabbi Stephen Wise, all of whom joined Landman from the Jewish side. Protestants were represented by an array of highly respected, well-known mainline ministers, including Rev. Dr. S. Parkes Cadman, president of the Federal Council of Churches (FCC); Dr. W. H. P. Faunce, president of Brown University; and Dr. Roscoe Pound, dean of the Harvard Law School. The Catholic contingent was composed of Justice Victor Dowling of the Supreme Court of the State of New York; Father Francis Duffy; and Martin Conboy, an attorney who was also the Knight Commander of the Order of St. Gregory the Great.

Together, they formed the Permanent Commission for Better Understanding between Protestants, Catholics, and Jews. Conceived as an ad hoc committee that would meet only to address specific complaints of religious bigotry, Landman nonetheless envisioned an enormous role for his zealous band of willing Christians and Jews. Writing for the *American Hebrew*, he declared:

> It will determine for itself whether a protest from a particular group comes within its purview. But when it has investigated painstakingly, and when it has spoken after careful and unbiased deliberation, the whole nation will listen and accept its pronouncement as the enlightened voice of the Protestant, Catholic, and Jewish population on the broad grounds of American humanity.³

The Permanent Commission was not called into action until autumn 1928 when, shortly before the Day of Atonement, a blood-libel accusation arose in the upstate New York town of Massena after the disappearance of a young girl. Fortunately, the girl was discovered unharmed and appropriate apologies were extended.[4] But by this time, although it issued a public statement, the Permanent Commission's influence had all but vanished, overshadowed by the newly-formed National Conference of Jews and Christians. Content to let the Permanent Commission die a natural death, Rabbi Landman enthusiastically supported the National Conference and directed his efforts toward furthering its goals.

It was evident that new openness from both sides was afoot. The Protestant establishment, specifically from the impetus generated by the growing influence of the Federal Council of Churches, matched Jewish efforts to further interreligious relations. Propelled by the participation of Christian luminaries such as Bishop Francis J. McConnell of the Methodist Episcopal Church and the theologian Reinhold Niebuhr, the FCC's prestige was enhanced further by the endorsement of Theodore Roosevelt, Charles Evans Hughes, and other prominent public figures who numbered in its ranks, some of whom were also active supporters of the Christian Zionist movement. The energetic efforts of the FCC resulted in the 1924 formation of its Committee on Good Will between Jews and Christians. Heartened by the Committee's avowed commitment to the improvement of Jewish-Christian relations, B'nai B'rith contributed $6,000 to its annual budget.[5]

Early attempts at interfaith amity did not prove to be entirely smooth sailing. Not only did many Jews and Christians regard one another with a measure of caution, suspicion, or outright hostility, but factions within each group were divided about the aims of such an enterprise or its desirability in the first place. One measure of how touchy the topic of Jesus was in some sectors of religious Jewry was the outraged response to Stephen Wise's sermon "A Jew's View of Jesus," delivered at the Free Synagogue meeting in Carnegie Hall on December 20, 1925. In his message, Wise expressed views that were aligned with those of Joseph Klausner, whose *Jesus of Nazareth: His Life, Times, and Teaching* had appeared recently in English translation. Along with other, earlier Jewish New Testament scholars, Klausner noted Jesus's Jewish identity and offered an assessment of his life and ministry uncoupled from his role as Christian savior. Following in this vein, Wise asserted that although Jesus was not God incarnate, Jews could nonetheless embrace him as a Jew, even if Christians had failed to appreciate or to follow his essentially Jewish teachings.[6]

These views could hardly be said to be revolutionary in the world of Jewish scholarship at this time. Yet Wise's favorable utterances from his prestigious pulpit regarding the Jewish Jesus's stature and teaching set off a firestorm of indignation, spearheaded by the religious contingent of the Zionist movement, which led to his forced resignation as chairman of the United Palestine Appeal.[7] Wise was vilified further by the Yiddish press. *Morgn Zhurnal*, informed by Orthodox perspectives, accused Wise of betraying Judaism in its front-page editorial, and *Tageblatt*, another upholder of the faith, charged Wise with leading "the younger generation to the baptismal font."[8] These somewhat overheated charges point to a major source of discomfort among some Jews about even the smallest breach of the boundaries separating Judaism and Christianity.

If Wise's flattering remarks about Jesus were so unsettling, the concerning matter of Christian proselytizing was far more serious. It was well known to Jewish leaders that the FCC supported missionary efforts directed toward their people, which had in recent decades escalated as a result of the massive migration of over two million Jews to America from Eastern Europe, beginning around 1880. By 1910, there were forty-five Christian evangelical missionary organizations in the United States whose focus was to evangelize Jewish people, many of whom were immigrants, by employing the tools of publications, public meetings, and practical aid.[9]

Conscious of these pressures, Jewish leaders were adamant in their demand that if goodwill was truly the goal of a Christian approach to their community, then Jewish participation in any form of interreligious dialogue was contingent on the understanding that proselytizing was off the table.[10] Despite repeated assurances, some

Jewish leaders continued to be skeptical of the FCC's motives and remained aloof. Men such as Joseph Proskauer of the American Jewish Committee, who would be at the forefront of outreach to Christians in the following decade, took the tack that the goal of goodwill between Jews and Christians would be better served without the aid of organizations and meetings as each concentrated on learning to become better adherents of their own traditions.[11]

The matter of Christian evangelism toward Jews and the obstacle it presented to Jewish-Christian relations was also a bone of contention among Protestant churches, albeit for a different reason. While Jews were naturally suspicious of hidden missionary agendas in the goodwill movement, some of the more conservative figures under the umbrella of the more generally theologically liberal FCC were deeply troubled by the implication that the ground rules for interreligious dialogue required Christians to lay down their tracts and cease to carry out what they perceived as their religious duty to bring Jewish people (among others in general) to faith in the claims of the Gospels. Conrad Hoffman, director of the FCC's International Missionary Council's Committee on the Christian Approach to the Jews, and others like him, viewed such a move as a portent that would not only undermine Jewish evangelism but would also have a greater unwholesome effect on the church's commitment to world evangelism generally.[12]

Hoffman was a highly influential figure. Widely recognized as both an able executive and a committed missionary, he had worked under the auspices of the YMCA during World War I, first with German prisoners of war in England and later in Germany as an advocate for Allied prisoners. Maintaining his European contacts after the war, Hoffman would later work tirelessly in the 1930s to rally support to help Christians of Jewish background leave Germany.[13] Serving at the same time as secretary of the Presbyterian Board of National Missions, Hoffman also oversaw that denomination's work among the Jewish community.[14]

Hoffman was also painfully conscious of the harmful effects of Christian antisemitism on his evangelistic goals. In his pamphlet

"The Jews Today: A Call to Christian Action," published in 1941, he writes, "Antisemitism . . . is largely a problem for the Christians rather than the Jews, for it is the Christians who discriminate . . . the Christian who tolerates or aids antisemitism is morally responsible and guilty."[15] Speaking from the more evangelical wing of the FCC, Hoffman makes the case against antisemitism from three directions.

First, he condemns it as being antithetical to authentic Christian teachings. He cites a statement unanimously accepted by a gathering of church leaders and missionaries in Vienna in 1937 under the auspices of the International Missionary Council: "Realizing that enmity to the Jews has now become a cloak for the forces of anti-Christ and conceals hatred for Christ and his gospel, the church must reject antisemitism with complete conviction."[16] Next, Hoffman relays what he characterizes as the underlying kinship that exists between Christianity and Judaism, noting Christianity's dependence on the Hebrew scriptures, as well as the fact of Jesus's Jewish identity and that of his early followers. Quoting, among others, Sholem Asch's recently published *What I Believe* to bolster his case for the Jewish foundation of Christian faith, he concludes, "The Christian approach to the Jew must embody full respect and gratitude for Judaism."[17]

Finally, most important from his standpoint, Hoffman urges Christians to reject antisemitism because it impedes Jewish evangelism. For him, the most pernicious effect of Christian antisemitism is that it causes Jews to turn a deaf ear to the Gospels. Deeply ashamed of the history of Christian coercion, Hoffman was also well aware of the antipathy that Christian evangelism created. Yet, despite the ill feeling he knew his views were bound to stir up, he believed that to exclude the Jews from the church's Great Commission was itself a form of antisemitism.[18] As he wrote, "To exclude him (the Jew) from the church's universal missionary responsibility would be discrimination. Moreover, it would virtually mean that Judaism is good enough and adequate for the Jew, and therefore apparently he has no need for Jesus Christ."[19]

This last remark cuts to the heart of the matter. Christian missionaries of Hoffman's stripe, believing themselves to be well intentioned, viewed Judaism as a faith awaiting completion through belief in the messianic credentials of Jesus. As such, they were unwanted in most Jewish quarters. Active Christian evangelists to the Jewish people, some of whom were Jewish themselves, placed leading Christian figures in the goodwill movement in a dilemma. If they were perceived to be abandoning their commitment to evangelism, they would be accused of breaking faith with much of the rank-and-file membership they represented. In the end, they prioritized placing Jewish-Christian relations on what they believed to be more productive footing. Whatever their convictions may have been regarding the Great Commission, they were clear-eyed enough to see that if they were to make any progress at all with their Jewish counterparts, they would have to convince them that as for establishing interreligious cooperation, their goals lay where they said they did.

On this issue, the rifts between progressives and conservatives in the FCC only widened. At last, weary of struggling with more conservative elements in its own coalition that were suspicious of the goodwill enterprise in any event, leading members of the Committee on Good Will decided in 1927 to act independently of the FCC to join forces with willing Jewish leaders to form the National Conference of Jews and Christians, which superseded Rabbi Landman's Permanent Commission. This exodus of FCC progressives is a vivid illustration of the widening chasm between evangelicals and more theologically liberal Christians.

The leadership of the National Conference of Jews and Christians (NCJC) consisted of three co-chairs: Judge Newton D. Baker, a Protestant who had served as secretary of war; Columbia University professor Carlton J. H. Hayes, a Roman Catholic historian; and Roger Williams Straus. Straus, a member of one of the wealthiest Jewish families in America, went on in 1945 to co-found Farrar Straus and Co., a highly respected publishing house, which eventually expanded to become Farrar Straus & Giroux. Straus's membership in the upper echelons of the American Jewish Committee made him a valuable liaison for the American Jewish Committee with prominent Christians in the years to come.

The NCJC leadership was supported by an executive committee consisting of a number of Jewish leaders, including Rabbis Stephen Wise and Mordechai Kaplan, Justice Benjamin Cardozo, and influential Christians who were already active in the goodwill movement, such as Henry Sloan Coffin and Reinhold Niebuhr. Others, including Samuel McCrea Cavert and S. Parkes Cadman, became prominent advocates of the Jewish cause in later years. Everett Clinchy, who continued as secretary of the FCC's Committee on Good Will, became the first president and served in this capacity for the next thirty years. Through their combined service in this newly formed organization, Clinchy cultivated close ties with Roger Straus and, through him, with the American Jewish Committee.

Growing interfaith connections begun in the 1920s provided a foundation for Jews and Christians to build on in the following decades. As Jewish leaders began to know their Christian co-workers more closely, they also became more conversant with the chorus of voices that informed the broad range of American Christian beliefs and perspectives regarding Jews and Judaism. Jewish leaders interpreted the rousing public response to the rallies of March 1933 and the outpouring of support from Christian clergy across the country who signed the petition of protest to the German churches as encouraging signs. These positive results also seemed to validate Stephen Wise's strategy to gain more widespread support by presenting the German Jewish plight as not merely a Jewish cause célèbre but an affront to the universal principles of Western civilization and, specifically, to Christian values.

Wise and the American Jewish Congress were not the only ones actively looking for support from the American body politic beyond the Jewish community. Others were also turning toward Christian representatives in their quest to develop concrete measures to counteract the increasingly draconian measures of the Nazi government against German Jews. Although they had strenuously opposed the Garden and other such public demonstrations, the American Jewish Committee had certainly awakened to the necessity of employing vigorous countermeasures against pro-Nazi activities. In keeping with their characteristic reticence and carefully reasoned approach, they concentrated on creating and distributing well-prepared publications designed to counter Nazi propaganda.[20] As early as 1931, it formed a subsection tasked to keep track of pro-Nazi publications, and in 1933 it created, under the leadership of the attorney Wolfgang Schwabacher, a group called the "Information and Service Associates," whose function was to expose pro-Nazi organizations and individuals active in the United States and to "immunize the American people against the virus of antisemitism."[21]

While continuing to eschew a high public profile, the American Jewish Committee sought nonetheless to enlist the support of the non-Jewish public and formulated its own tactics on behalf of the German Jews. Employing its traditional emphasis on educational material, the Committee published and distributed two pamphlets in the latter months of 1933. The first was *The Jews in Nazi Germany: The Factual Record of Their Persecution by the National Socialists*. Its purpose was to publicize the intensifying difficulties of German Jewry and to demonstrate widespread support for the Jewish cause emanating from numerous sectors of American society. In so doing, it would, it was hoped, raise an increasingly sympathetic public response to pressure Germany to reverse its course and also have a measurable effect on the actions of the United States government to achieve that goal.

The Jews in Nazi Germany first appeared in June 1933. It came about as a result of discussions held by the American Jewish Committee that began shortly after the Garden protest the previous March. Minutes of its executive committee meetings that spring reveal a significant rise in interest among the leadership, which had been previously lukewarm, toward forming a relationship with the non-Jewish world as a result of the escalating troubles in Germany. At an April 9 Committee meeting held with the leaders of B'nai B'rith, Joseph Proskauer said, "The situation in Germany now warrants a more fundamental and more comprehensive attack" and "the group sponsoring such a movement should consist, if not entirely of non-Jews, certainly predominantly of non-Jews."[22] Proskauer raised the name of Nicolas Murray Butler, president of Columbia University, as a possible leader of such a group, not only because of his distinguished public profile but also because of his close ties to the Committee member Judge Herbert Lehman.[23]

The record of the April 9 meeting also brings into focus a willingness to formulate more cooperative efforts among the American Jewish Committee, B'nai B'rith, and the Federal Council of Churches. Board member Roger W. Straus, who was co-chair of the National Conference of Jews and Christians and had close ties with likeminded Christians, reported that the FCC "was elaborating a plan to secure the use of radio church hours throughout the country for the promotion of a favorable and discreet propaganda" on behalf of the Jewish cause.[24] The Committee agreed to help to defray expenses and that it should "be consulted in connection with the program for such radio propaganda."[25] It also agreed "that a pamphlet be issued . . . containing a full review of the development of Hitlerism from the beginning to the present moment, as far as possible based upon original German sources, including a full translation of the Nazi program."[26] This was the genesis of *The Jews in Nazi Germany*, also nicknamed the "White Book."

Two months later, at its June 5 meeting, the executive committee reported that *The Jews in Nazi Germany* was ready for publication.[27] The suggestion that fifty thousand copies be ordered was duly approved. Another item worth noting in the minutes of this meeting is some discussion of a letter that Justice Proskauer received from Michael Williams, the editor of the Catholic weekly *Commonweal*, regarding the possibility of organizing relief efforts to help Jews and converted Jews or Christian descendants of Jews to leave Germany.[28] This evidence of ongoing communication between Williams and the American Jewish Committee makes more fully comprehensible the pamphlet's emphasis of Williams' experiences in Europe and its willingness to publish his forthrightly expressed opinions in both *The Jews in Nazi Germany* and the second pamphlet, *The Voice of Religion*.[29]

The stated purpose of *The Jews in Nazi Germany* was to submit the facts of German's oppressive policy and actions "to the judgment of the public of the United States in the light of traditional American principles of justice and fair play."[30] In a published statement, Cyrus Adler, the president of the Committee, declared, "In the preparation and publication of this book, the American Jewish Committee has endeavored to assemble material bearing upon the situation of the Jews in Germany only from official and authoritative sources. The record speaks for itself and requires no interpretation."[31] Of course, by making such a statement, Adler led the book's readership to only one interpretation: Germany was guilty of horrendous behavior and should bear the brunt of disapprobation from all right-thinking, civilized public opinion and that of the governments that represented them.

The Jews in Nazi Germany consists of four sections: (1) a detailed record of the numerous decrees already promulgated by the Nazi government throughout the spring of 1933 to deprive Jews of their livelihoods and civil rights, and the impact of these policies on the Jewish population; (2) specific, corroborated acts of violence perpetrated on German Jewish citizens; (3) a description of the Nazi anti-Jewish campaign; and (4) a sampling of editorial and other expressions of indignation by the mainstream American press across the country. The last section also contains numerous resolutions from a variety of legal, medical, and academic associations conveying their condemnation of Nazi policies, as well as a reprint of the clergy's May 1933 petition of protest to the German churches.[32]

The sheer scope of official Nazi decrees and measures against the Jews, as was catalogued by the American Jewish Committee, and their swift implementation in a mere matter of weeks is staggering. The description of their effects on the Jewish community is particularly grim. As an example, one sobering section deals with the sharp increase of suicides among German Jews and the attempts of the German government to obscure these statistics by listing the deaths as accidental, by altering cemetery records, or by suppressing death notices.[33]

The Jews in Nazi Germany also warned against the effects of Nazi propaganda among Americans. It warned, "The apologists for the Hitler regime in Germany have been sedulously endeavoring to assure the American public that the position of the Jews in Germany is safe."³⁴ Offering a direct rebuttal to this bald lie, the American Jewish Committee quoted at length from an appeal to the League of Nations penned by Michael Williams. Having recently returned from a fact-finding tour of Germany, Williams wrote:

> The situation of the Jews in Germany is deplorable beyond words. Israel in Germany is perishing under a yoke only comparable to that under which its forefathers groaned in Babylon and Egypt.
>
> Don't be deceived by false denials concerning the persecutions of Jews under Hitler's regime; guard against its paid and voluntary propaganda. Pay no heed to certain journalists who seem to learn only what the dictatorship desires them to believe.³⁵

Williams concluded his appeal to the League of Nations with a challenge to the world powers to make a stark choice, "Either harden your hearts and let the worst crime in our age proceed in the deliberate extinction of nearly 1,000,000 men, women and children, or come quickly and strongly to the rescue."³⁶ Williams not only wrote forcefully on behalf of the Jewish cause as *Commonweal's* editor and in connection with the American Jewish Committee but was also featured prominently as a speaker at the next Madison Square Garden event.

From the outset, it is clear that non-Jews were the intended audience for *The Jews in Nazi Germany*. In a letter from the American Jewish Committee secretary Morris Waldman to the executive committee dated June 12, members were informed of the availability of advance copies, and he noted, "it will be extremely helpful if some of these advance copies are brought to the attention of outstanding non-Jews accompanied by a request for their comments, which might serve for publicity."³⁷ The letter asked Committee members to compose a list of ten names that they were willing to write to personally for that purpose.

In a "Confidential Bulletin" issued later that month, Committee members were informed that the book "made its appearance on

June 19, and secured wide publicity and editorial comment in leading newspapers."[38] The Bulletin followed, stating:

> The offices of the Committee have received and are receiving numerous requests for copies and the Committee has made certain that this document shall reach the hands of every responsible professional and business leader, newspaper publisher, editor, and editorial writer and every other person who aids the formation and guidance of public opinion.[39]

Positive reviews for *The Jews in Nazi Germany*, gathered by the Committee for their additional publicity value, appeared immediately across the country upon publication. *The Literary Digest* review stated: "[The] White Book, published by the American Jewish Committee, explodes as myths the reasons of the persecutions of less than one percent of the German population" and made a mockery of the Nazis' "extravagant arguments" about Jews, especially those drawn from the *Protocols of the Elders of Zion*, which it characterized as "hoary frauds."[40] It went on to approvingly cite the book's refutations of German calumnies, especially with regard to the record of Jewish soldiers during World War I.

The New York City press, as well as a number of other newspapers from across the country, weighed in with positive comments. *The New York Herald Tribune* found it "a heavily documented review of the Nazi effort to convert the German Jews into a pariah caste. It deserves close reading by all Americans who are still in doubt about either the reality or the injustice of such an effort."[41] *The New York Times* followed suit in vindicating the findings of the American Jewish Committee, particularly with regard to the brutalization of German Jews: "The calm presentation of facts by the American Jewish Committee makes two opinions on the subject impossible. Private letters, press reports, and word-of-mouth testimony establish that many Jews were slain and many more were tortured."[42] William Randolph Hearst's *New York Evening Journal* praised it as "the most impressive indictment of the Hitler regime yet published . . .

After reading it no fair-minded American can doubt the gravity of the plight of the Jews in Germany."[43]

Elsewhere, newspapers including the Massachusetts *Lowell Courier-Citizen*, *The Nashville Tennessean*, *The Saginaw Daily News*, *The Tampa Morning Tribune*, and the *Capital Journal* of Salem, Oregon, all published uniformly positive reviews, each one heaping ridicule and condemnation on the Nazis and praising the thoroughness of the American Jewish Committee's research, its systematic presentation, and its calm and collected tone. The *Lowell Courier-Citizen* was particularly disdainful, scoffing at the Nazis' "utterly absurd anthropology" and asserting, "The perverted book learning of pedant Germany of the middle of the 19th century is considerably responsible for a God-awful mess in the ignorant and superemotional Reich of today."[44] The *Tennessean* was fervent in its praise and hopeful about the impression the book might have on the public, stating that it "stands as a rock of truth answering heated propaganda with documented facts. It might well be the instrument which will cause a freer generation of Germans to repudiate the campaign of atrocity which carried Hitler to his day in the sun."[45]

The American Jewish Committee leadership was enormously pleased with the reception of *The Jews in Nazi Germany*. The executive committee minutes of November 1 record:

> Eighty thousand copies of the White Book, "The Jews in Nazi Germany," have been distributed and have elicited favorable editorials and news stories from the secular and religious periodicals reaching many millions of readers. This booklet has come to be regarded as a standard text on the recent events affecting the Jews in Germany.[46]

The Committee's leadership was becoming increasingly aware of the untapped potential of Christian cooperation and was applying itself to the task of finding a language with which to reach Christian religious awareness. It found a way with the release of its second pamphlet, *The Voice of Religion: The Views of Christian Leaders on the Persecution of the Jews in Germany by the National Socialists*, published later in 1933.

The executive committee minutes of November 1933 record that *The Voice of Religion* was the brainchild of committee member James N. Rosenberg. With the committee's approval, an original ten thousand copies were distributed "to those people and organizations where they are most effectively helpful in obtaining sympathy and support of the American people."[47] This project represented a marked change from the organization's official policy in prior decades, when its leadership deemed the cultivation of Christian support unimportant. Prior to the 1930s, Cyrus Adler, an American Jewish Committee founding member, had actively discouraged the possibility of interfaith cooperation, unwilling or unable to see "what possible advantage can come from making the Christian clergymen and the Christian religious press acquainted with the organization of our Committee."[48]

Adler's views notwithstanding, even prior to 1933 a trend began to develop among American Jewish Committee activists toward creating greater visibility among Christians, particularly with regard to mainline Protestants. Straus was already serving as co-chair of the NCJC. Proskauer, in a reversal of his earlier apprehensions about organizations and conferences, had, along with Felix Warburg, already participated in a series of goodwill conferences held under the auspices of the NCJC toward the end of 1930. Their speeches, introduced by Everett Clinchy, appeared in *The Christian Century* in the January 21, 1931, issue, which was devoted to a collection of NCJC conference addresses. That *Century* issue also carried addresses by other conferees, including the FCC general secretary, Samuel McCrea Cavert, and other prominent activists, such as the Unitarian minister John Haynes Holmes, Wise's old friend who had spoken at the Garden protest, as well as the theologian Reinhold Niebuhr. The growing familiarity of these prominent representatives of Jewish and Christian worlds led to other opportunities for interaction at a variety of venues in the following years.

The Voice of Religion, a thirty-one-page pamphlet, featured an artistically presented cover that prominently displayed Jesus's citation of the Hebrew scriptures recorded in Mark 12:28–31, "Hear O Israel, the Lord our God the Lord is One . . . and thou shalt love thy neighbor as thyself." Such use of New Testament scriptures and the pointed identification of its central figure with the Shema, the best-known prayer of Judaism, represented a dramatic step away from the habitual wariness characterizing the conventional Jewish attitude toward the dominant American Christian culture. For the American Jewish Committee, at any rate, the taboo attached to Jesus had been brushed aside. Instead, it found the flexibility to explore previously unthought-of strategies to gain recognition and alliance with Christians affiliated with a variety of American Protestant denominations.

In addition to publishing yet another reprint of the American clergy petition of protest, *The Voice of Religion* contained articles from twenty-seven publications by the American Christian press that were drawn from a far broader spectrum of denominational participation than had yet been represented in the coterie of Wise's contacts who had represented Christianity at the Garden Rally. These included not only the expected liberal Christian publications, such as the mainline Protestant *Christian Century*, with whom the American Jewish Committee was already familiar, and other publications advocating progressive positions, but also those of more conservative groups, including mission-minded Presbyterians and others representing fundamentalist leanings.

The survey of viewpoints assembled by the American Jewish Committee in *The Voice of Religion* was gleaned from a far greater assortment of American Protestant faith publications. While *The Voice of Religion* included a sampling from previously named liberal voices, these are by no means the only ones who displayed a willingness to publicly denounce Nazi tactics. The wide range of sources the editors so diligently assembled paints a deeply revealing portrait of the variety of denominational organs that existed along the spectrum of American Protestants at that time and their attitudes toward Jewish people and Jewish faith.

The most prestigious voice of mainline Protestant Christianity was that of *The Christian Century*, to which the American Jewish

Committee was no stranger.⁴⁹ Providing a platform for some of the most influential Protestant voices of the day, its roster of writers included Reinhold Niebuhr, Henry Sloan Coffin, Samuel McCrea Cavert, and S. Parkes Cadman, along with others whose views formed liberal Protestant opinion toward the Jews throughout this era. An additional mention of the May clergy petition in the *Century's* article "Christian Ministers Protest Anti-Jewish Campaign," sets forth a strong if somewhat self-congratulatory condemnation of Nazi policy:

> [It] was a significant pronouncement by a group whose judgment has weight not only because of their numbers but because of their standing. The statement breathes no holier-than-thou air. It acknowledges with humility our own shortcomings in tolerance and justice. But it challenges the principle by which the Nazis and their leaders have openly avowed and denounces the inhuman program by which that policy has been put into practice. The facts cannot be waved aside by any general statements about the probability of exaggeration and the impertinence of criticizing the internal policies of a distant government.⁵⁰

Assuring as these words may have been to the editors of *The Voice of Religion*, *The Christian Century* would over time prove to be an uncertain ally. In the years up to and including the war, it displayed an unmistakable inconsistency in its views concerning the Jewish plight that often downplayed the seriousness of their situation.⁵¹ Identified with mainline Protestant religion and culture, its views both shaped and were shaped by a deeply rooted ambivalence toward the American Jewish presence.

Another well-established Christian periodical known for its affinity with liberal Christian theology and social activism was *The Congregationalist and Herald of Gospel Liberty*, founded in 1808.⁵² Although its article "The Jews in Germany" professed a strong condemnation of Germany's actions against the Jews, it viewed those actions as part of a more complex set of injustices that ought to be addressed. In declaring that "Hitlerism, whatever it may possibly offer for Germany in other directions, stands condemned for its encouragement of the spirit of hate and for its uncivilized attitude toward a group within the state," it refrained from portraying Jewish suffering as neither more or less important than the suffering of other oppressed peoples.[53] The article went on to report:

> The suppression of the rights and liberties and the endangering of the lives in Germany, of Negroes in America, or of any group in any land is subversive to the world's hope of peace and prosperity . . . We hope that the League of Nations will face squarely the facts of racial discrimination and terrorism as they are related not only in relation to the Jews in Germany, but to similar groups in other countries.[54]

By contrast, the Southern Baptists were powerful among the Christian traditions opposed to the progressive positions with which the American Jewish Committee had the most immediate affinity. *The Baptist Courier*, founded in 1869, was a highly influential publication among its readership. After a brief summary of Germany's known offenses in an article titled "The Jews in Nazi Germany," the *Courier* issued an unambiguous condemnation of the Nazi government: "What the Jews in Germany have suffered has not only not been exaggerated, it has not been fully revealed. The Nazis are a persecuting party."[55] Not only did the *Courier* express concern for Germany's Jewish population, but it also spoke quite warmly of American Jews, and in particular, the American Jewish Committee's efforts:

> The American Jews, who have been profoundly sympathetic with their people in Germany, have made a thorough investigation and have published the facts in a pamphlet entitled "The Jews in Nazi Germany." It can be had from the American Jewish Committee, New York. One might think that a defense of the Jews by Jews would be partial. But he will not think this after reading the pamphlet. Those who prepared the pamphlet, with its body of facts,

were aware that they would have to be careful and reserved. They were both.[56]

This level of praise shows that not only were leaders of the American Jewish Committee paying close attention to what Christians were publishing, but that the reverse was also true, at least in this case. The editors of *The Baptist Courier* had taken notice of the American Jewish Committee. Moreover, they were also willing to endorse the Committee's efforts and commend them to their readership. Certainly, such friendliness emanating from what might have seemed an unlikely source must have been gratifying to the Committee.

Another publication boasting a considerable circulation was *The Christian Advocate*, which was issued by the Methodist Episcopal denomination, a precursor of the United Methodist Church. In condemning Nazi persecution, it hearkened to biblical images, such as those of the Jewish "wanderer" and "Israel scattered abroad." In alluding to Genesis 12:3, "And I will bless them that bless thee, and him that curseth thee will I curse," the *Advocate* admonished:

> If Herr Hitler's four-year lease of power (with possible extensions) fails to rebuild German unity and to re-establish the influence of the Jewish state in world affairs, it is not unlikely that the ultimate cause of such failure will date from his hostility to the sons of Abraham, who are as the sands of the sea in number, and who, even though disbursed on every shore, are everywhere Israel still: assertive, acquisitive, forceful, and bound together by a vital racial consciousness intensified by twenty centuries of persecution. The tyrant who regards them as men without a country is liable to find many countries ready to come to their defense.[57]

The Christian Advocate's use of biblical imagery to anchor the Christian response to German Jewish suffering is revealing. It indicates a view of Jewry that is deeply embedded in a hermeneutical principle that interprets the significance of Jews not merely as one people among a multitude but as the Israel of scripture. Yet the qualities for which the *Advocate* praises the Jewish people are drawn from stereotypes for which they are vilified in other quarters. As for the assertion that many countries would potentially rise to defend beleaguered Jews, the content of such early, confident predictions would soon be called into gravest question.

The Epworth League, a religious society for young adults formed in 1889 under the auspices of the Methodist Episcopal denomination, conceived its mission to be a "more thorough enlistment of young Christians in Christ's work."[58] Its publication, *The Epworth Herald*, attributed the persecution of the Jews and other groups to insufficient Christian commitment. The article "Jew and Gentile" stated:

> There is a real danger that nominal followers of Him who was done to death by the narrowness and bigotry of men shall themselves become guilty of the same narrowness and bigotry . . . but wherever men mistreat their fellow men, whether because of national, racial, and religious differences, they do violence to the spirit of Christ, and cannot claim to be Christian.[59]

Viewing the problem of oppression in primarily spiritual terms, the article continued to exhort, "Before we can become Christian at this particular point we must go through the old-fashioned formula of confession, repentance, and restitution. And it is only in Jesus Christ himself that we can find the remedy for this plague of intolerance."[60] Turning to the specific attitude with which Christians ought to regard the position of the Jews vis-à-vis the Christian faith, the article declared:

> It will help us to realize that Jesus was a Jew. Perhaps we ought to have a ritual in our churches which would make us declare along with the Apostles' Creed the fact that Jesus was born of a Jewish mother, raised in a Jewish home, went to a Jewish Synagogue, and worshipped the God of Abraham, Isaac, and Jacob . . . A proper reading of the New Testament, the Old Testament, and of history would make it easier for us to give to the Jewish people the honor they deserve.[61]

The *Herald* grounds its attitude of tolerance and respect for Jewish people in the Christian Bible and in a Christian reading of history. In so doing, it indicts Christian cultures that failed not only to value a Jewish presence but also to practice the religious values they professed, as demonstrated in their treatment of victims of oppression. The article stresses the universality of the Gospel message of love and justice toward all, while at the same time preserving the privileged position into which it elevated the Jews on account of Jesus. In proposing a more pronounced liturgical recognition for the Jewishness of Jesus, the *Herald* offered, for its time, a startling blurring of borders from the Christian side.

The Jewishness of Jesus had posed no such difficulty for missionaries to the Jewish people; for many, it was their chief calling card. By the 1930s, a number of well-established nondenominational or interdenominational mission organizations, such as the American Board of Missions to the Jews in New York City and the Chicago Hebrew Mission, had prioritized the evangelization of Jewish people. The largest denominational commitment to Jewish evangelism during this period came from the Presbyterian Church (USA) through its Department of Jewish Evangelization, organized by the Board of Home Missions of the Presbyterian Church in 1920, which operated under the guiding hand of Conrad Hoffman.[62] By 1932, this department staffed centers in major Jewish communities in Brooklyn, the Lower East Side, Newark, Philadelphia, Chicago, St. Louis, San Francisco, Los Angeles, and other Jewish-population centers.[63]

It is therefore not surprising that its publication *The United Presbyterian* would be shaped to a large extent by its evangelistic program. What is surprising is that despite this, the American Jewish Committee chose to include the article "Christian and Jew" in *The Voice of Religion*. In keeping with the adamant belief in the eventual turning of Jews to the Gospels, "Christian and Jew" even detected a silver lining in the cloud of Nazi persecution in the form of improved Jewish-Christian relations:

One of the best things that has come out of the affair is the centering of attention upon the relation of Christian and Jew . . . The present attention given to the relations between Christian and Jew will lead to its improvement. The fundamental position of each is radically different, but there is a great deal in common. The conversion of the Jew to the Christian faith is not progressing as rapidly as we desire, but even so there ought to be and there will be a growing mutual appreciation between Christian and Jew in building moral values into the life of the world.[64]

The above examples of editorial opinion collected by the American Jewish Committee for *The Voice of Religion* demonstrate that there was wide agreement among Christians of differing traditions in condemning the Nazi oppression of German Jews. However, this sampling also reveals sharp differences in theological and political outlook that fall into two basic categories.

The writings derived from the more liberal traditions, as seen, for example, in *The Christian Century* and *The Congregationalist and Herald of Gospel Liberty*, base their objections to Jewish persecution on an assumed set of universal values that condemns injustice enacted on any group. In contrast, for more theologically conservative periodicals, such as *The Baptist Courier, The Christian Advocate, The Epworth Herald,* and *The United Presbyterian,* the meaning of Jewish suffering is grounded in a worldview that is informed by more than an exposition of Christian ethics. It is also fueled by a perspective that views modern Jews as a special case inextricably linked to the Israel of the scriptures, where, according to their viewpoint, Jewish destiny is indelibly written.

In addition to press clippings, *The Voice of Religion* included lengthy quotes collected from the published statements of prominent American and British Christian leaders, including William Thomas Manning, the Episcopal Bishop of New York, whose speech at the Garden was reprinted; the archbishops of Canterbury and York; and, surprisingly, Hilaire Belloc (1870–1953), the widely read author, activist, and Catholic apologist whose previous writings were certainly less than sympathetic to the Jewish people.[65] Belloc's earlier book, *The Jews*, published in 1922, draws on the deeply ingrained characterization of Jewish people as a "foreign body" to be dealt with by "elimination or segregation." Belloc asserted that "the continued presence of the Jewish nation . . . presents a permanent problem of the gravest character: that the wholly different culture, tradition, race, and religion of Europe makes Europe a permanent antagonist to Israel."[66]

S. Parkes Cadman, a minister of the Central Congregational Church in Brooklyn, was also quoted at length. A pioneer of religious radio broadcasting, author of a widely read syndicated column in *The New York Herald Tribune*, and past president of the Federal Council of Churches, Cadman was one of the best-known Christian voices in America. His words, based on lofty enlightened values and democratic principles, echo other progressive expressions denouncing Hitler and his policies:

> Antisemitism in Germany will die when the citizens of that splendid nation awaken to the new democracy. Civilization has passed through the day of homogeneous tribal states. Thoughtful leaders of mankind now prize diversity of cultural groups . . . The present movement, as all anti-Semitic agitation in the past, can hardly be judged by intellectual and sympathetic critics as other than a shame and a disgrace to Germany, a blot on German culture, a danger to German unity, and a flagrant injustice to Jews themselves.[67]

As co-founder of the National Conference of Jews and Christians, Cadman maintained close ties with American Jewish leaders until his death in 1936. His statement is a fine example of the developing critique that deployed civilized, progressive democracy against what were characterized as outmoded values of tribalism and its attendant antisemitism.

As with *The Jews in Nazi Germany*, *The Voice of Religion* sought to create an impression of widespread sympathy for Jewish suffering, this time culled from a broad cross-section of the American Christian press. Its introduction claims, "These views express the verdict of the religious conscience of the Christian, English speaking peoples on the persecution of hundreds of thousands of Germans who have adhered, or whose ancestors adhered, to the Jewish faith."[68] It is evident that *The Voice of Religion* is the product of a close reading of a remarkable variety of Christian publications, some of them relatively obscure. All convey disapprobation of Germany's mistreatment of its Jewish citizens, many of them in terms that seem like echoes of the speeches from the previous year's protests.

Beyond that, this digest of the commentary is valuable for more than simply its presentation of the Christian condemnation of the Nazis. It also calls into question Christian perceptions of Jews and Judaism, as well as their theological bases. The crisis facing German Jews not only caused American Jewish leaders to reconsider their relationship with Christian institutions and leadership but also prodded Christians to take a stand regarding Jews both in Germany and closer to home. In searching for a suitable response to Nazi persecution, Christians were forced to search themselves and come to grips with the dubious attitudes they had already formed toward Jews.

Christian representatives joined forces to support the Jewish cause, but traveled toward that destination via differing pathways. The sometimes contrasting viewpoints in *The Voice of Religion* are rooted not only in the prevailing ethos of Protestant culture and Christian interpretation of the New Testament but also in Christian usage of the Hebrew scriptures. They are expressions of movements born in the larger contexts of American Christianity's differing religious worldviews and expectations.

The publications of the American Jewish Committee in 1933 aimed to create the impression that the Jews had at long last gained the imprimatur of the Christian establishment. Stimulated by the rise of the Nazis, the nascent desire for mutual Jewish-Christian relations that began with the goodwill movement in the 1920s made visible strides in the prewar years. More positive pronouncements about Jews by Christians came not only on the printed page preferred by the American Jewish Committee but also through the medium of public performance favored by the American Jewish Congress.

A year later to the month after the 1933 protest meeting, Madison Square Garden was once again the scene of an event sponsored by the American Jewish Congress that brought the elements of self-examination and indignant protest among Christians on display in *The Voice of Religion* into another sphere, that of performance. This time, it would be more than simple speechmaking. The vehicle was a good old-fashioned courtroom drama titled *The Case of Civilization against Hitlerism*.

In "Trial as Theater," Mark Bernstein and Laurence Milstein assert that trials take on many of the characteristics of theatrical performance, functioning as dramatic events to satisfy the needs of the audience, or in this case, the jury. They observe:

> America's public fascination with trials is strikingly similar to the popularity of classical Greek theater. Trial drama satisfies the same inherent cathartic needs as does stage drama. The juror's vicarious participation in human tragedy and suffering engenders personal pride in the victor's success or relief in the knowledge that the loser's problems were never really the juror's own . . . Once pulled in, our imaginations captured, we are ready to be educated and perhaps even enlightened.[69]

If the courtroom itself is only a short step from the footlights of the stage, the reverse is also true. Not only is it possible for a trial to imitate theater, but theater may also appropriate the trappings of a trial. The genre of courtroom trial has proven to be an enduring American standby in both theater and cinema, eliciting a heightened, collective sense of civic pride, a comforting reaffirmation of values, and the satisfaction of aligning oneself on the side of justice.

By the early 1930s, courtroom drama was well established in the American theater. The year 1934 marked the Los Angeles premier of Ayn Rand's *Woman on Trial*, which began a successful Broadway run the following year as *The Night of January 16th*. It owed its popularity in large measure to the gimmick of using the audience as a jury pool, "empaneling" twelve new jurors for each performance, who, at the end of the play, found the defendant either guilty or not, thus blurring the distinction between courtroom and theater even further.

The American Jewish Congress's choice to create a theatrical production of indictment and persecution in *The Case of Civilization against Hitlerism* afforded it possibilities that had not been available the year before. Then, the shocking developments in Germany had called for a swift response that produced a hurried program, consisting mainly of whatever politicians, Christian clergy, labor leaders, and representatives of the Jewish community had been close at hand. With more lead time, the event's organizers had greater freedom to plan and could recruit speakers from a broader field.

They chose a staged prosecution of the Nazi government not only for its dramatic impact but also for the sake of a greater variety of speakers who assumed the guise of witnesses for the prosecution, thus reinforcing one another's arguments. This device also promised to heighten the effectiveness of the climax of the condemnation of the Nazi government by drawing the audience into the proceedings as jurors who, at the end, could render a just verdict almost as though it were a real trial.

The March 7 date for the drama coincided closely with the first anniversary of the March 5, 1933, German election from which Hitler derived unbridled dictatorial power. Unlike the protest events of 1933, which had been hurriedly assembled, Wise had ample time not only to prepare a program but also to publicize his intensions. Beginning in January 1934, the Jewish Telegraphic Agency published a series of releases that supply valuable material about the background of this event, the process through which it came about, and those responsible for guiding it to fruition.

The Agency reports that the event's committee of sponsors, none of whom were speakers, was drawn from a pool of distinguished academics, including William T. Neilson, president of Smith College; John Dewey, the Columbia University philosopher and educator;

and Arthur O. Lovejoy, head of the philosophy department at Johns Hopkins University. Eight governors also served, including Herbert H. Lehman of New York, I. C. Blackwood of South Carolina, Wilbur Cross of Connecticut, Clyde L. Herring of Iowa, Hill McAlister of Tennessee, Leslie A. Miller of Wyoming, William H. Murray of Oklahoma, and Gifford Pinchot of Pennsylvania. Other committee notables include Carrie Chapman Catt, the suffragette and founder of the Woman's League of Voters, and Alvin Johnson, head of the New School for Social Research.[70] The New School also served as the site of the initial planning to coordinate the participation of forty-five anti-Nazi and Jewish organizations. Later that month, the Agency reported:

> A special session of the administrative committee of the American Jewish Congress, which met yesterday at the Hotel Commodore on the eve of the first anniversary of Adolf Hitler's appointment to the German chancellorship, announced that arrangements had been completed for the presentation of "The Case of Civilization Against Hitlerism," in Madison Square Garden on March 7.
>
> With the cooperation of all anti-Nazi organizations in this country, this review, to be based on factual evidence only, will be the most formidable indictment of Hitlerism and its threat to civilization which, according to Dr. Stephen S. Wise, honorary president of the American Jewish Congress, "has yet been made."
>
> "While the Jewish case against Hitlerism will also be presented, it will form but a single link in the chain of evidence against Hitlerism; its threat to civil liberties and democracy; to science; to the arts; the liberal professions; the churches; the status of women. Outstanding American representatives of these various fields will have part in the presentation," he said.[71]

Clearly, Wise had ample opportunity to convene a much more disparate panel of speakers than the political and religious leaders he had rallied the previous year. Yet one thing that had not changed was that the majority was non-Jewish. As he had done previously, Wise made skillful use of non-Jewish personalities to take the lead in making the case against the German government. In so doing, he once again carefully avoided the appearance of pitting Hitler and the Nazis solely against the Jews. Instead, Wise negotiated a complicated path to strike a balance between promoting the concerns of his own constituency and making his appeals to a larger group of interested parties who he hoped would add additional weight to his argument. As Klaus Fischer notes, "the sponsors of this mock trial, headed by Rabbi Stephen Wise, wished to avoid a purely partisan attack on Hitler and portrayed the sponsors as representatives of humanity who wanted to defend the civilized values of Judeo-Christian heritage."[72]

On the night of the event, as the courtroom drama unfolded, the diverse coalition of Christians and Jews indicting Hitlerism hammered home their points. The evening began with a solemn moment during which victims of the Nazi terror were remembered to the accompaniment of a rendition of "Taps." A crier declaimed, "Hear ye! Hear ye! Hear ye! All those who have business before this court of civilization give your attention and you shall be heard. May I ask you to rise while the Court takes its place?"[73]

Former Secretary of State Bainbridge Colby convened the court with these portentous words:

> The thousands who crowd this huge auditorium make up a mighty host, but they are only a fraction of the millions whose thoughts are centered here and who await with eagerness every word that shall be spoken. America is speaking tonight—not only for herself, but for civilization and brotherhood. We are piously met. We bow reverently before the Lord and Master, who has commanded of us that we love our neighbors as ourselves.[74]

Thus, the hosts of civilization and the righteous of the Lord were arrayed against Nazi barbarism. This was the tone throughout the evening. Speaker after speaker appealed mainly to values assumed to be held by civilized peoples or else to what were touted as the shared religious values of Judaism and Christianity to make their case. As first witness, Bernard S. Deutsch, who was president of both the

American Jewish Congress and New York City's Board of Aldermen, stressed further the antithetical relationship between Hitler's ideology and American democratic values, particularly freedom of worship. Indicting Hitlerism for threatening the long history of German education and culture, for endangering world peace, for enslaving the German people, and for exporting Nazism through subversive means, Deutsch declared, "Public opinion contrasts with the charges in this indictment the principles which are the concern of civilization—safeguarding democratic ideals and institutions; the freedom of the individual; the progress of society."[75]

As advertised, the panel was drawn from a broad sample of public leaders. Luminaries pressed indictments from a variety of angles, drawing from a diversity of fields, including law, medicine, labor, journalism, literature, academia, and even sports. Politicians comprised a significant component of the proceedings, as had been the case the previous year, a number of whom were called on to argue the case for American public opinion. Al Smith spoke again, his speech marking a change in attitude toward Germany from that of the year before. Reflecting on his remarks at that time, Smith said he felt compelled to revise his earlier view, echoed by so many of the speakers the previous year, that the German people as a whole could not be held responsible for the depredations of their government. Speaking of the Nazi platform, its antisemitic plank, Smith urged his audience to reconsider the cautious attitude of so many who refused to believe the first alarming reports concerning German Jewry. He declared that those who had given Germany the benefit of the doubt had erred, and "after a year, we are compelled to change that opinion and, much as we dislike to do it, we have to bring ourselves to the frame of mind that leads us to believe the German people are behind that program plank."[76]

Foremost among the newly recruited politicians who played a role in making the case for American public opinion was Mayor Fiorello LaGuardia. LaGuardia, whose mother was partly Jewish, was a colorful figure who relished the ethnic mixture of the largely immigrant population that had given him political life and who could please his various constituencies with a few simple phrases in a number of languages, including Yiddish. Even before he took office as mayor in 1934, he had been an outspoken opponent of the Hitler regime, and one of his first public acts as mayor was to declare support for the boycott of German goods initiated by the American Jewish Congress.[77] In years to come, he would continue to be a staunch ally of the Jewish community.[78] Although his address was short, he was startlingly prescient: "Our concern for conditions in Germany is not local . . . We, as Americans, have a grave concern because we see the same philosophy, the same arrogance, the same conceit, the same ruthlessness that precipitated a peaceful world into a World War."[79]

Another influential political figure who weighed in on this issue was US Senator Millard Tydings of Maryland. In January 1934, he introduced a resolution instructing President Roosevelt to lodge a protest with the German government over the treatment of its Jewish citizens.[80] His case contains some of the bluntest language regarding Germany's departure from civilized values and its persecution of the Jews:

> Now, in the back-wash of the great international holocaust which began in 1914, in this period of world-wide economic, financial, and political disaster, these enduring principles in some parts are threatened with extinction; for we have learned with pain and displeasure that in a great nation there have been singled out 600,000 of its citizens who have been commanded not to bear the common burden of their fellows, but, to suffer, as a group, the loss of personal liberties for no other reason, forsooth, than they are the sons of their fathers.[81]

These foreboding words would prove to be truer than either speakers or audience knew. Soon enough, it would be more than enduring principles that would be threatened with extinction. In the next decade, the word "holocaust" would take on a yet-unimagined dimension not only in Germany but throughout Europe.

Other speakers came forward one by one to speak from the perspectives of the disciplines out of which they had been recruited. Making the case for civil liberties, Roger Baldwin, director of the American Civil Liberties Union, berated the Nazis for their suppression of a free press, freedom of speech, and freedom of assembly, characterizing them as a "handful of adventurers, backed by big industry, ruling by decrees enforced by the violence of an irresponsible army of Storm Troopers."[82] Articulating the case of the liberals, Raymond Moley, former undersecretary of state and editor of *Today*, said that Jewish persecution was an affront to the liberal values of social justice embodied in American political ideology: "It is not merely a battle in behalf of Jews. It is a fight for the integrity of American principle."[83] Seth Wakeman, a professor of education at Smith College, stepped up for the case of academic freedom to protest the draconian Nazi takeover of the German educational system, declaring, "The whole educational system in Germany has become a means of furthering and stamping into the young, the political creed of the National Socialist Party."[84] The journalist Stanley High cautioned his audience to guard against the proliferation of groups in America that were sympathetic to Nazi ideology, such as the Silver Shirts, warning, "That is why tonight's meeting is not exclusively to provide a protest against Germany's return to Medievalism, but, also, to develop a solidified opinion against those who would drag us in the same direction."[85]

The suffragette and historian Mary Ritter Beard was the lone woman to take the stage. Long active in feminist causes and a prolific author, she became the founding director of the World Center for Women's Archives the following year. Co-author of *The Rise of American Civilization* (1927) with her husband and fellow historian Charles A. Beard, her presence on the platform was likely due to her connection with Alvin Johnson and the New School, which her husband had helped found.

Arguing the case for woman, Beard lit into Hitler and his cohorts on behalf of her "client, Woman," characterizing the Nazis as "a grim collection indeed of embattled bachelors" and as "errant soldiers who never found their way back from the Front to civilization."[86] Warming to her subject, Beard castigated the Nazis for putting women out of public life and attempting to subjugate them all, rich and poor, Aryan and Jewish, feminist and nonfeminist alike. If anything, she characterized Aryan women as being in even more desperate straits than the Jews: "Thus the Aryans suffer; the most purely Germanic of the Germans—the peasant girls—are dispossessed as ruthlessly as Jewish intellectuals. And there is no Palestine for them."[87] She ended her speech with a tribute to the German Social Democrat Toni Pfulf, who committed suicide rather than submit to the new regime: "She would not bend her neck. But she was not Jewish; there was no Palestine for her, no refuge but death. She took poison rather than submit to Hitler, enslaver of woman, the Accused of Tonight."[88]

Beard's equating of the plight of all German women with that of the persecuted Jews of Germany could not have gone down well with her Jewish listeners. Neither, too, would the reference to Palestine, not once but twice, as a refuge for only Jews. For one thing, the assumption that the Jews should flee Germany for Palestine, even if they could, was at this stage a hotly contested issue within the Jewish community both in America and in Germany. For another, such a path was simply not a viable choice for any but a small number. Real as the reduced circumstances of Aryan women were under Hitler's rule, their problems were not the priority of the evening's organizers or audience.

If there was one area where the Nazis were truly vulnerable to a rising tide of negative American public opinion and were deeply concerned about bad publicity, it was the immense propaganda value they hoped to derive as hosts to the 1936 Berlin Summer Olympics. For some months beginning in June 1933, Wise strove behind the scenes for Germany's assurance of the participation of German Jewish athletes, under the threat that Germany would pay dearly if it did not cooperate. A US boycott of the Olympics would reduce the prestige of the games immeasurably, and in March 1934 American participation was not yet fully assured. For this reason, the Reich was particularly vulnerable to criticism regarding its treatment of

German Jews. Vocal protest of Germany's exclusion of German Jewish athletes from membership in the sports associations from which their Olympic athletes were drawn was therefore a potential public-relations disaster for them.[89]

In this connection, Gustavus Kirby, treasurer of the American Olympic Committee, made the case for sports. In his speech, he forthrightly condemned Germany's flagrant disregard of the Olympic spirit, patiently dismembering Germany's deceptive and specious arguments that its government was not at fault if German sports clubs chose to exclude Jews or if a Jew chose not to try out for the German team. He forcefully declared:

> We know that he cannot, and until he can, and until we have assurance that they are not only being officially permitted to do so, but also that no harm will come to them, or their families, or their associates, if they do so, will we, the sportsmen of America be in a position to look with favor upon the invitation of Germany for us to come and play with them in Berlin in 1936.[90]

Given the broader range of speakers, it is understandable that representatives of Christian churches played a greatly reduced role in the proceedings compared with the previous year. Although references to God and country were commonly invoked, in only two instances did Christian speakers specifically address the objections of the Christian faith to Nazi ideology.

Arthur Judson Brown, secretary emeritus for the Presbyterian Board of Foreign Missions, argued the case for the Protestant churches. In a lifetime of activism until his death in 1963 at age 106, Brown sought to balance his firm commitment to Christian missions with his role as a pioneer in the ecumenical movement. Active in the FCC from its inception, Brown was also, among his many other commitments, a member of the American Palestine Committee.[91]

Praising Germany's illustrious history, as so many had done, and laying much of the blame for Hitler's rise at the feet of the crafters of the Treaty of Versailles, Brown lamented, "It was this ill treatment that gave opportunity to a fanatic like Hitler to ride into power on a mighty wave of popular indignation."[92] However, he went on to sternly chastise the Hitler regime for its ill treatment of its Jewish population, claiming that, if anything, it was underreported and that, despite voices that counseled silence, loud protest was the moral imperative of right-thinking people.

Brown's indictment of Hitlerism only indirectly employed the language of religion. Instead, his address enlisted the concept of "natural rights." Conceding Germany's right to organize its own affairs, he nonetheless affirmed:

> We are concerned solely with the question of justice and humanity, the common and inalienable rights of men everywhere, irrespective of race or religion; rights imbedded in the legislation of all civilized nations. But laws and treaties do not create, they simply express a basic right of humanity binding upon all nations, whether incorporated in a formal treaty or not.[93]

By contrast, Michael Williams, who argued the case for the Catholic churches, relied heavily on his religious affiliation and theological convictions to condemn Hitler's policies. Careful to clarify that he was speaking only for himself as a Catholic layman and journalist, Williams declared in no uncertain terms:

> My deliberate opinion, then, is that the Catholic religion in Germany is threatened with a most serious danger of being crushed out of existence by the power of a State Religion of paganism, which is the most potent power of the Hitler movement, and which is opposed to the spirit and the practice of Catholic Christianity.[94]

Building his argument on the pronouncements of various German Catholic ecclesiastical leaders, Williams summarized:

> The National Socialist movement is not merely a political party, but also a Weltanschauung, or world view. It contains in its cultural-political [system] heresies, as it rejects or misrepresents essential

doctrines of the Catholic faith, and because, according to the declaration of its leaders, it intends to substitute a new world view for the Christian faith.[95]

Given the warm relations Williams enjoyed with the Jewish community and his forthright condemnation of the Nazi treatment of the Jews in *The Jews in Nazi Germany* and *The Voice of Religion*, his speech contained surprisingly little regarding German antisemitism, and that mainly in passing reference to Jewish converts to Christianity who had been forced out of their professions. He dwelt primarily on the rapidly vanishing freedoms of the Catholic Church and press, despite the July 1933 concordat between the Reich and the Vatican. Yet by depicting the rise of Hitler as a spiritual battle between Christianity and paganism, he gave elements of the Protestant public a reason to oppose Hitler that was comprehensible to them, even if the case were being made by a Catholic spokesman.

Out of the almost two-dozen speakers who testified at Hitler's "trial," only five were Jewish. In addition to Bernard Deutsch, they were Arthur Garfield Hays, Abraham Cahan, Samuel Margoshes, and finally, as the last witness called, Stephen Wise. They all brought different perspectives, born of differing experiences and convictions from which they had formed their core commitments and their reputations. Arthur Garfield Hays, general counsel for the American Civil Liberties Union, supplied one of the evening's most jolting moments with the case of an eye-witness I. There, at the mock trial at Madison Square Garden, he offered a compelling eye-witness report of the real trial held in Germany for five Communists accused of setting the fire that destroyed the Reichstag in February 1933.[96] One notable aspect of Hays's speech is that it offered the only reference to Hitler's vigorous persecution of Communists. Careful to distance themselves from Communism, as was the case the year before, the event's organizers ensured that Communists were barred from the microphone that night.

Speaking for the case of an eye-witness II, Samuel Margoshes, who was instrumental in organizing the Garden event the previous year, provided a sobering account of the conditions in Germany that he had observed in November 1933:

> Nine months after the imposition of the Nazi yoke, I found Jews as well as the rest of the population still living in fear of their lives. The constant complaint that assailed my ears was that people are disappearing from the streets and are never found again. Others are dragged away to concentration camps to reappear God knows when . . . I left Germany with the feeling that the entire country has been converted into a huge prison.[97]

Margoshes concluded his testimony with an appeal for economic sanctions against Germany, expressing hope that "a Germany isolated may yet turn out to be a Germany brought to her senses."[98]

Judging from the words he uttered that evening as witness for the case of the Socialists, Abraham Cahan's greatest grief seemed to be reserved for the downfall of the German Social Democrats and the demise of the Weimer Republic, which he depicted as a veritable paradise "without a vestige of political inequality or racial prejudice," and which was "the bulwark of German Liberty and political and moral progress."[99] As others had done in the previous year's speeches and at this event, Cahan assigned the blame for the Nazi rise to power to the Treaty of Versailles and its crippling effect on the nascent German democracy. Speaking confidently of Hitler's demise at the conclusion of his brief address, Cahan declared, "It is not Hitler but Hitlerism. The manikin who bears that unsavory name is merely a historical accident, a human form assumed by a sad set of circumstances. And the economic disaster that brought this man to his crownless throne will sooner or later bring about his destruction."[100]

Finally, Wise took the podium as the final witness to testify before the summation and verdict that drew the evening to a close. By shrewdly positioning himself as the final witness in the program, he could confidently align the case of the Jews with every other aspect of civilization's indictment of Hitler covered by the non-Jewish witnesses. By placing himself last, he was poised to sum up and interpret the testimony of those who had spoken before him.

He began by contrasting the evening's proceedings with the program of the previous year. The latter, he asserted, had begun as a more local protest against the first harsh decrees of the Nazi regime. Now, in light of worsening conditions, the protest had grown into an indictment lodged by civilization itself against Hitlerism. Wise depicted the case of the Jews as a particularly heinous injustice not only because the Jews were the first victims of Nazi oppression but because they had already suffered the most from the policies executed under the banner of Aryan purification. Circling back to the theme of common cause, Wise hastened to add that Jews were not alone in suffering, as Catholics and Protestants also felt the increasing weight of Nazi paganism and its oppressive actions. It is somewhat ironic that Rabbi Wise spoke the most unambiguous words of the evening regarding the relationship between Hitlerism and Christianity and was, in fact, the only speaker to directly mention the central figure of the Christian faith:

> But in this hour we, the Jews, find ourselves together with all groups and factors including the great Catholic Church and Protestant churches of the land—Hitlerism being at one and the same time a denial of Jesus and the negation of every type and manner of Christianity in favor of an ancient pagan cult of hate.[101]

Wise continued to invoke the language and imagery of Christianity to depict the plight of the Jews in Germany, characterizing Jewish people as the "brothers of Jesus and Mary, Peter and Paul and John," who, deprived of liberty and legal protection, were imprisoned in a society where they were "wronged, mocked, and crucified."[102] Wise did not neglect to mention the contributions of Judaism, expressing the core of his Reform convictions regarding Judaism's role in world history, "We protest, not for our own sake, for we have always been watchmen at the gate who at the cost of life itself safeguarded the ineffably precious values of threatened civilization."[103]

This was the heart of his argument, the core of what he hoped would create a united front of Jews and non-Jews to oppose Nazi Germany. By conflating Christianity and the democratic values of Western civilization in opposition to Hitlerism, and by placing Hitlerism in opposition to the Jews, Wise skillfully aligned Christianity and civilization in sympathy with the special case of Jewish persecution. In doing so, he provided the dominant Christian culture in America with a reason to stand up for Jews while at the same time preserving Jewish difference.

The pretext of the courtroom drama was maintained until the conclusion of the program. In the lengthiest speech of the evening, Samuel Seabury, a distinguished New York jurist, summarized the arguments set forth in the course of the long night. After defining civilization as "an advanced stage of social development and of the forces in society which make for human progress," Seabury enumerated the most salient points of the indictment.

In a nutshell, Seabury indicted Hitlerism for promoting concepts that stood diametrically opposed to the values of civilization. These included religious persecution and race hatred; the "deification of force" in the form of "multiple tyrannies, oppressions, brutalities, cruelties and injustices"; censorship by state control; the suppression of organized labor; the co-optation of "religious, cultural, charitable, scientific and political" entities; the suppression of academic freedom; and, most particularly, the outrages to which the German Jews had been subjected, whom he characterized as "galley slaves in the Nazi ship of state."[104] At the conclusion of Seabury's soaring rhetoric, he exhorted his audience: "The emergency is great; the need for immediate action is vital. It must be crystallized at once and it must find expression in a boycott against Hitlerism—a boycott as wide as civilization and as powerful and as strong as humanity."[105]

The role of judge fell to Wise's close friend John Haynes Holmes, who pronounced and rendered judgment in the form of a resolution that followed another lengthy enumeration of the Reich's transgressions. The resolution reads:

> We, the citizens of the United States of America, assembled together in Madison Square Garden in the City of New York, on Wednesday, March 7, 1934, upon the first anniversary of the Hitlerite coup d'état, solemnly declare that the National Socialist Government of Germany has turned its face against historic progress and the positive blessings and achievements of modern civilization. It has shown itself by doctrine and practice to be the avowed enemy of those methods of peace and freedom by which the march of civilization has been enabled and the progress of mankind accomplished.[106]

As *The New York Times* reported the following day, when the roughly fifteen thousand audience members who remained in the hall until shortly after midnight were asked if they agreed with the verdict, a mighty shout of agreement issued forth, with only one dissenting voice, a woman who said she "believed in Hitler" and had to leave the Garden under police escort.

It stands to reason that the longer lead time and the more thoughtfully conceived program would have worked to the advantage of the American Jewish Congress in terms of garnering greater publicity in the mainstream English-language press, particularly as the date of the event approached. However, such was not the case. As in the previous year, the *Times* provided the most extensive coverage, although there are striking differences in the amount and the kind it provided. As was true the year before, the Yiddish press weighed in with differing perspectives grounded in ideology and alternative viewpoints about how best to serve and to represent its leadership.

On March 6, the day before the event, in "Fears Nazi Disturbance," the *Times* reported a request from the American Jewish Congress for special police protection against members of Nazi cells whose presence was anticipated at the event. The brief piece also listed a number of the speakers who would be appearing and noted that the event would be broadcast, although it failed to inform readers when and where they could tune in. Apart from that, unlike the previous year, there was hardly any reportage in the mainstream press about how the event had been conceived and organized. By contrast, the Jewish Telegraphic Agency, which disseminated stories to the Jewish and the general press, generated at least a half-dozen stories, beginning on January 1, 1934, about the program, its participants, and the radio stations that would broadcast the speeches.

Part of the significant drop in publicity leading up to the event can be attributed to the fact that Hitler's policies were no longer the dramatic news they had been the previous year. In 1933, the sensational events surrounding the abrupt change in the status of German Jews that followed so quickly on the heels of Hitler's ascent to power had driven the program. The stories the *Times* was already running about the plight of the German Jews generated a context of urgency that amplified the coverage of the Garden rallies and their counterparts across the country. In 1934, this context was absent. The overall reduced coverage in the *Times* conveyed the impression that Jewish persecution in Germany was no longer news.

Without the charged news climate of the previous year, *The Case of Civilization against Hitlerism* lacked the same sense of immediacy. In addition, Jewish leadership also failed to organize rallies in other cities, as it had done in 1933. This reduced the scope of the event's importance and deprived it of the afterlife in the press from which it had benefitted the previous year.

Another reason that *The Case of Civilization against Hitlerism* did not attract the same degree of publicity was that the ritualized form of the mock trial was harder to treat as a realistic expression of outrage. What had helped the organizers to dramatize their case had also hurt it. The indictment formula was too closely akin to theater, and this perception detracted from the seriousness of its content. The few publicity notices for the event that the *Times* did run appeared in early March in the Amusements section, where it was treated as a show in styled playbills alongside other theatrical events on offer in the city that week. On March 7, the day of the event, a single item on the *Times* front page listed the speakers and noted that it had been organized "under the auspices of the American Jewish Congress, the

American Federation of Labor and other liberal, anti-Nazi and Jewish groups" with the participation of members of "more than 1,000 organizations."[107]

Yet, in stark contrast to the tepid publicity during the days that preceded it, the reporting that followed the performance of *The Case of Civilization against Hitlerism* could not have been more fulsome. The event garnered generous front-page coverage due to the packed house and heightened police security, which supplied an atmosphere of tension and signaled potential trouble. As in the previous year, inside pages carried lengthy excerpts of the many speeches plus a number of dramatic photos. The front-page headline, "Nazis 'Convicted' of World 'Crime' by 20,000 in Rally," was followed by descriptive lines such as "Hitlerism Is Held Threat to Civilization and Peace in 'Trial' at Garden," "German People Absolved," and "Police Every 20 Feet around Hall and Inside to Prevent Threatened Disorder."[108]

The front-page story, which summarized the proceedings, spilled over to page 14 and went on to describe the heightened security measures, which included 325 uniformed police, detectives, bomb squads, and an honor guard for the speakers composed of 200 members of the Jewish War Veterans and 200 members of the Youth Division of the American Jewish Congress. In addition, a group of detectives accompanied and stuck close to a contingency of fifty members of the pro-Nazi Silver Shirts who had obtained tickets. The story also reported that petitions to President Roosevelt were distributed to the audience, urging him to use his influence to gather support to pressure Germany to restore the Jews' civil rights. Audience members were encouraged to gather additional signatures and to return them to the office of the American Jewish Congress by March 17.

The lead story was written with dramatic flair, stressing the theatricality of the event: "The floodlights in the balcony were directed toward the speakers' platform and the 'court' filed in."[109] According to the story, "The greatest ovation of the night came a little after 10 o'clock, when former Governor Smith arrived and seated himself between Mayor LaGuardia and Arthur Garfield Hays."[110] The reporter spoke warmly of Smith's stage presence, as well as that of

Mayor LaGuardia. When, at the conclusion of more than three hours of speeches, the final "verdict" was read by Rev. Holmes and the audience was called on to participate, "Mr. Colby asked for a vote. When he asked all those in favor of the resolution to say 'Aye' there was a great swelling roar of approval from all over the hall."[111]

In the almost three full pages of inside coverage, the greatest amount of space was given to Judge Seabury's speech, which was printed in its entirety and prominently placed. The resolution read by Rev. Holmes was also recorded in full. Other speakers, such as Matthew Woll, vice president of the American Federation of Labor, and Al Smith, received columns devoted entirely to their remarks, as did Mayor LaGuardia, Gustavus Kirby, and Dr. Lewellys Barker. Others, such as Bainbridge Colby, Bernard Deutsch, Rev. Brown, Michael Williams, Senator Tydings, and even Abraham Cahan, who had been slighted the year before, were quoted at some length.

The demotion of Stephen Wise was the most noticeable change. Although his address, "The Case for the Jews," had been positioned for maximum effect, for reasons that are unclear his presence was noted only in passing. Far from being one of the centers of attention, as he had been the year before, his remarks were viewed almost as an afterthought. A brief excerpt from his speech was given at the end of an article in which other speakers had received far greater attention.[112]

The one dark cloud of negative publicity that night came in a short piece placed alongside the speeches, in the midst of the multiple accusations leveled at Hitler's government. A group called the American Citizens League of Ohio lodged a strenuous protest against the proceedings, "in the interest of continued friendly relations between the United States and Germany and against the 'farce' of placing Hitler on trial before public opinion." They asked, "What right has the American Jewish Congress to embarrass our government?"[113]

Other New York City dailies also took note of the proceedings, although not to the same extent as the *Times*. *The New York Evening Journal*, a Hearst publication, ran a story on page 3 that contained a list of the "witnesses" and stressed that extra police would be on hand to deal with Nazi sympathizers. The following day, under the front-banner headline "Hitler Perils World Peace, Cry 21,000," its colorful copy proclaimed, "In an atmosphere surcharged with emotion, the assemblage, jamming every nook and cranny of the immense arena, roared approval of the vigorous denunciations of the Nazi chieftain as voiced by many speakers."[114] The *Evening Journal* also took up Seabury's call for a boycott, which the *Times* avoided mentioning, as did *The New York Herald Tribune* in its front-page story on March 8.[115]

Of course, the influential Yiddish press weighed in, beginning, in contrast to the English press, with headline coverage the day before. On March 6, *Forverts* ran a front-page article that began with an account of reported threats by local Nazi sympathizers to the American Jewish Congress to break up the meeting, and the preventative measure of increased police protection. The story went on to describe the great demand for tickets and how, after less expensive tickets had sold out, the event organizers had decided to reduce the price of the more expensive seats so as to ensure that as many people as possible would be able to participate.[116]

The day of the event, March 7, *Forverts* again ran a story on page 1, "Hitler Trial Today in Madison Square Garden." Not surprisingly, the brief description of the program beneath the headline spotlighted the *Forverts* editor: "Ab Cahan to Make the Case for Socialism." The article stressed the prominence of the speakers and what it claimed to be the international importance of the event to a world waiting to hear the judgment of the court. The mock trial was reported with all seriousness: participants were seen in their roles of judge, prosecuting attorney, and witnesses, and the audience of twenty thousand onlookers were taken as the jury. The story supplied a comprehensive list of the speakers and urged ticket holders to arrive a half hour early to find their seats. *Forverts* also listed radio stations that would carry the speeches for "tens and hundreds of thousands that would not be able to personally attend."[117]

The day following the event, *Forverts* went all out. Bold headlines proclaimed "Hitler Barbarism Guilty," "Huge Meeting Renders

Judgment," and "Important Leaders Condemn Nazis, Demand Boycott." Although *Forverts* supplied copious extracts from the previous evening's program, as did the English-language press, there were predictably sharp differences in its emphasis. The first, given the editorial policy of the paper and the importance of its editor, was no surprise. Ab Cahan was given pride of place on the front page under the headline "'Socialists Fight for Human Freedom,' Declares Ab Cahan."[118]

As the *Evening Journal* had done, *Forverts* emphasized Seabury's call for a boycott under the bold headline "'Boycott and World Protest Will Vanquish Hitler,' Says Seabury." Turning to page 6, the point was repeated in bold letters, "'The Public Opinion of the World Together with Boycott Will Smash Hitlerism,' Thunders Judge Samuel Seabury in His Concluding Speech," which appeared under the headline "Famous American Jews and Christians Indict Hitler before the Conscience of the World." Through its emphasis on political action, which mirrored Cahan's own perspective, *Forverts* took its coverage a step further than simply reporting the evening as a staged event.[119]

Der Tog, whose editor Samuel Margoshes spoke so eloquently at the meeting, provided ample publicity beginning on March 7 with a front-page story that proclaimed, "Important representatives of American social opinion will indict the Hitler regime," and promised that "representatives of a thousand organizations" would be present in the audience.[120] The following day, it too gave extensive coverage to the mass meeting in front-page articles under the banner headline, "The Civilized World Renders Guilty Verdict against Hitler: Twenty Thousand in the 'Jury.'" As *Forverts* had done, *Der Tog* stressed Seabury's closing demand for the implementation of a boycott against Germany and stressed that "Jews, Catholics, Protestants, Socialists, and Liberals unite in the trial against Hitler."[121]

Morgn Frayhayt's ideological differences with the American Jewish Congress had kept the Madison Square Garden rally of 1933 largely beneath its notice, except for ridicule. Its 1934 coverage continued in the same vein. On March 6, *Frayhayt's* front page took the

American Jewish Congress sorely to task for an open letter it published on the first anniversary of Hitler's ascent to power, penned by Bernard Deutsch. Reproducing the letter's quote from Matthew 7:1–5, beginning, "Judge not, that you be not judged," *Frayhayt* derided this admonishment to Hitler as ridiculously irrelevant: "Suddenly, Hitler will read these verses and become good and *frum* [pious] as all the good and *frum* Jews of the American Jewish Congress and Jesus and the apostles call him to do."[122] This jeering note is a noticeable departure from the uniformly respectful tone that mainstream Jewish leaders used with the general public when referring to Christian religion. In Yiddish, they could afford to be less guarded.

Frayhayt gave no advance notice of the event. On March 8, the front page carried a brief notice at the bottom describing the speakers as representatives from "the Catholic church, Protestants, and Presbyterians," and printed an abbreviated list of the speakers, including Abraham Cahan and Stephen Wise.[123] There were no quotes from any of the speeches, and the article misidentified Rev. John Haynes Holmes, the reader of the resolution of judgment, confusing him with Senator Millard Tydings, who had spoken earlier.

Although the courtroom drama was successfully employed in the theater, sometimes with spellbinding effect, its effectiveness in the political arena was questionable. One discordant note was struck by Dorothy Jones, who characterized the evening as "[an] elaborate piece of make believe that threatened no one, despite rumblings of diplomatic displeasure . . . the speakers . . . could judge as well as anyone the very slight effect—if any—that their words and actions would have in the real world of international politics."[124]

More recently, the legal historian Louis Anthes has been more respectful, taking the "diplomatic rumblings" that Jones dismisses so casually far more seriously. Noting the connection between the courtroom and the theater, Anthes maintains that the law is not merely a political instrument fashioned for the sake of orderly society but is also shaped by "received cultural understandings of law's dramatic effect," which can lend the mock trial a power that transcends the merely make believe to actually shape public understanding of the law itself. As he observes, "Therefore, the story of the mock trial shows how the cultural meanings of law have been instrumentally mobilized to reconstitute legal culture itself."[125]

Anthes's point is borne out by the Nazi government's vociferous protests against *The Case of Civilization against Hitlerism*, which show that it took the proceedings seriously enough. Germany knew it could be hurt by a boycott. It did not like being cast in the role of barbarian. Above all, at this point, it wanted to host a spectacular theatrical event of its own—the Olympic Games of 1936. But in the end, despite the publicity, the loud calls for a boycott, and other forms of pressure, the Roosevelt administration was simply unwilling to extend itself to promote Jewish interests.

Despite the sensational flurry of press attention and the program's turn in the spotlight, there was little aftereffect. Although it had succeeded in commanding enormous attention in New York City for a brief moment, *The Case of Civilization against Hitlerism* was essentially a one-night wonder, even if it did have a brief run later that month when it was adapted at Temple Emanu-El in Providence, Rhode Island. There, as in New York City, Hitlerism was found guilty as charged.[126]

Nonetheless, the courtroom drama it fantasized would one day become reality. The case it tried in an atmosphere of suspended disbelief on the stage of Madison Square Garden would be conducted in a future courtroom with real lawyers, convictions, and sentences. It is remarkable that the indictment brought against accused Nazi war criminals after the war so closely resembled the brief by earlier, make-believe prosecutors. A little more than a decade later, the Nuremburg trials legally defined and prosecuted crimes against humanity; to all intents and purposes, this was how Nazi crimes were presented to the American public in 1934.

Meanwhile, brief though its impact may have been, the behind-the-scenes organization and the positive notices for *The Case of Civilization against Hitlerism* strengthened the bonds that Jewish and Christian activists had begun to forge. The year that followed the first public rallies in 1933 against Hitler's treatment of German Jews was a time of mutual discovery for Jews and Christians who were united by a common concern for the rapidly unfolding catastrophe overtaking Germany's Jewish citizens. Both the American Jewish Congress and the American Jewish Committee reached out to Christians in an attempt to find allies; the methods they used reflected the internal culture of their respective organizations. Each, in its own way, succeeded in challenging Christians to more fully articulate and express support for Jews. The American Jewish Committee, which valued education and the power of the pen so highly, turned primarily to publications and produced *The Jews in Nazi Germany* and *The Voice of Religion*. The more vocal American Jewish Congress leaned more to public demonstration and concerted action, resulting in *The Case of Civilization against Hitlerism*. In order to secure the keys that would unlock Christian cooperation, both groups were forced to probe the theological spectrum and religious understanding of Christianity more seriously than they had done previously, and they had to find a language more closely attuned to the Christian ear.

Christians, on the other hand, were faced with a set of different challenges. Foremost among them was the need to discover a way to encounter Jews in an affirming manner, without abandoning the distinctive claims of their own Christian doctrine. As the digest of editorial commentary assembled by *The Voice of Religion* demonstrates, Christian perspectives regarding Jews differed widely. In order to express support for the Jewish cause, the representatives of various American Protestant groups had to search within their own traditions and understandings to find reasons to do so that were congruent with the worldviews they upheld.

During the years leading up to the war, Jews and Christians continued to gingerly enter the largely uninhabited region of mutually respectful interreligious relationship. In so doing, they would discover things that altered their understanding of each other and of themselves. Stimulated by the early stages of the Nazi persecution in Germany, their encounter would greatly intensify as the shock waves generated by the war reverberated throughout American secular and religious culture.

3

Differing Jewish Responses to the Final Solution in 1943 and Their Effects

Prior to the outbreak of World War II, the American Jewish Congress and the American Jewish Committee each in its own way sought to mobilize efforts among influential non-Jewish politicians and Christian clergy to persuade the American public that the plight of the Jews caught in the net of Nazi power was worthy of attention and meaningful intervention. Although these agencies, often rivals for recognition as American Judaism's most authoritative voice, held widely disparate ideological positions, advocated differing tactics based on their respective priorities, and sometimes worked at cross-purposes, they were united in their concern for the immediate relief of Jewish suffering. Their shared concern would turn to desperation during the war as persecution spread and intensified from the dreaded to the unimaginable. Regardless of their differences, each of these prestigious organizations understood that Christian cooperation was indispensable to their cause and worked to obtain it, mainly through political and religious channels. In so doing, they and their Christian counterparts sought to reconfigure the image of Jewry in Christian understanding in such a way as to align it with the Protestant establishment's version of American patriotic values.

As well connected as the American Jewish Congress and the American Jewish Committee may have been with their own considerable constituencies, they did not speak for all sectors of the Jewish community. A far broader range of Jewish cultural and political organizations also sought representation. Their leaders sometimes vocally balked at conforming to mainstream Jewish institutions, objecting to a relationship that they were convinced was too subservient to the elite brokers of political power, especially as the war unfolded and the situation of European Jewry grew more desperate. These conflicting views would bring about more-widening fissures in the Jewish community as minority voices sought ways to broaden their influence.

The continuing degradation of German Jewry in the 1930s and the beginning of World War II changed the face of the map, broadening and deepening the European Jewish nightmare beyond measure. The sharp ideological differences and contrasting Jewish responses to the war and the increasingly horrific facts that emanated from Europe burst into public view in the form of two more extraordinarily well-attended mass meetings at Madison Square Garden that occurred within a week's time, both of which generated significant aftereffects. The first, held on March 1, 1943, was called "Stop Hitler Now." It represented a throwback to 1933, an evening consisting mainly of dignified speechmaking emphasizing Jewish-Christian solidarity in service to American civil unity. The second, the pageant *We Will Never Die*, on March 8, followed another track, that of the defiant courtroom drama *The Case of Civilization against Hitlerism*.

Although both events represented a response to catastrophic developments abroad, they took place in the context of an internecine battle at home over the mantle of Jewish leadership triggered by the dreadful news surrounding the implementation of the Final Solution. This rivalry at a time when Jewish unity was most urgently needed was sparked in large measure by the ideological and personal differences between the seemingly omnipresent Stephen Wise and Hillel Kook, aka Peter Bergson (1915–2001), who, along with the celebrated American screenwriter and playwright Ben Hecht (1894–1964), represented the vociferous and militant Zionist revisionist faction. The sharp disparities between these two camps and their constituencies not only enlarged the conversation among Jews but also brought non-Jews into the discussion as they chose sides.

Wise at that time functioned in a dual leadership role with the American Jewish Congress and with the Zionist Organization of America. As such, he was aligned closely with the position of the so-called general Zionists who had held the reins of leadership in the World Zionist Organization since Theodor Herzl's death in 1904, and whose president at the time was Chaim Weizmann. Although politically diverse, general Zionists represented themselves as the centrist, mainstream segment of Zionist ideology, committed to the establishment of a Jewish State primarily through the development of settlements in Palestine and diplomatic alliances in the wider world.[1]

Zionism was, however, far from univocal. In 1925, the Odessa-born Vladimir Jabotinsky (1880–1940), whose more militant outlook was shaped by fighting in World War I under British auspices in the Jewish Legion, formed the World Union of Zionist Revisionists. Impatient with what he perceived as too soft an approach on the part of the general Zionists, he advocated less conciliatory, more forceful methods of provoking the British to live up to the promises of the Balfour Declaration.[2] In keeping with this goal, he helped establish the Irgun Tzvai Le'umi (The National Military Organization), a paramilitary force, which conducted armed reprisals against Arab attacks and eventually declared war on the British in 1944.[3] Jabotinsky was also instrumental in the formation and the leadership of Betar, a Jewish Palestinian youth movement that adopted a military culture along with the accoutrements of martial discipline.[4]

Jabotinsky's aggressive approach and unwillingness to submit to control set him at odds with the Jewish Agency, the Zionist leadership in Palestine. Frustrated with what he considered to be the World Zionist Organization's puny program to attain statehood, Jabotinsky broke with the World Zionist Organization in 1935.[5] Jabotinsky also ran afoul of the British authorities who viewed him as dangerous, and they refused to readmit him to Mandatory Palestine in 1930.[6] From that point, Jabotinsky traveled extensively, seeking to build support for his movement abroad and influencing the course of events in Palestine from afar.

In 1937, at a meeting in Warsaw, Jabotinsky met a young representative from Irgun who was sent to consult with him. His name was Hillel Kook, a twenty-two-year-old rising star in that organization who was also a member of one of the most prestigious rabbinical families in Europe. Kook, who would shortly join forces with Ben Hecht, had a storied history of his own. He was born in 1915 in Kruk, Lithuania, the son of Dov Kook, an influential regional rabbi, whose brother, Avraham Yitzhak Hacohen Kook, became Palestine's first Ashkenazi chief rabbi in 1921.[7] Greatly impressed with Jabotinsky's demeanor and program, the younger man had found a mentor who returned his devotion by treating him as a trusted colleague who could be counted on as an able deputy.

Like many members of the Irgun underground network, Kook had already used a number of false identities in his travels. In his case, the use of an alias also enabled him to shield his renowned family name. In 1939 he settled on the name Peter H. Bergson.[8] It was under that name that Kook, as Irgun's appointed representative to America, sailed to New York City with Jabotinsky. At their last meeting on August 1, 1940, Jabotinsky charged Bergson with the task of doing all he could to promote his cherished dream of "a fully mechanized Jewish Army, to fight by the side of the Allied forces."[9]

On August 4, while visiting a Betar camp in Hunter, New York, Jabotinsky died suddenly of a heart attack, leaving his young colleague to take up the cause as best he could.[10] After some months of struggling to find his footing, Bergson, who had read Hecht's writing and knew his reputation, arranged a fateful meeting with Hecht at the 21 Club, a renowned watering hole in Manhattan, that would instigate a political war between Zionist factions represented by Stephen Wise in one corner and Bergson and Hecht in the other. The outcome of their antagonism would draw the attention of tens of thousands of Jews and Gentiles across the country.

Madison Square Garden was the arena of the battle between the differing visions of these determined individuals. The frictions that arose between Wise and those who came to be known as the "Bergson boys" in this brief space of time demonstrate how the internal conflicts within Jewish life created repercussions that had far-reaching effects. In this instance, the infighting between differing Zionist movements played an integral part in the complex cortège of the evolving Jewish-Christian encounter and the articulation of its developing values.

The trigger that eventually led to the confrontation was the accelerated pace of the destruction of European Jewry. As early as August 1942, word of the Final Solution reached Stephen Wise via telegram from Gerhard Riegner, then representing the World Jewish Congress in Switzerland.[11] At that time, uncertain of the reliability of the facts, at the behest of Undersecretary of State Sumner Welles, Wise chose not to publicize what information he had received.[12] In the ensuing months, upon confirmation that hundreds of thousands, and finally millions, of Jews had perished, the realization dawned that this was a catastrophe that so far outstripped previous calamities in the lengthy narrative of Jewish suffering that it defied description. Even as American Jews clung to the hope that something could be done to rescue their remnant, they began to realize that a way of life that they or their parents or grandparents had known had already been irretrievably altered and was in danger of complete annihilation.

The increasing urgency of the situation placed Wise in a difficult position. Ever mindful of conserving what political capital he had, or thought he had, with the Roosevelt administration, Wise was reluctant to risk embarrassing the president by making what could be interpreted as untoward demands. But at the same time, his constituents were impatient for concrete measures and growing resentful at what some perceived to be the timid posture of the establishment Jewish organizations. Their dissatisfaction threatened to weaken the hold Wise sought to maintain as the primary spokesman for Jewish interests and increased the pressure on him to take more meaningful steps.

One example of the pressure Wise faced came from Bergson and the revisionists in response to a *New York Times* report in February 1943 about the possibility of ransoming Romanian Jewish inmates in concentration camps in Transnistria at the cost of fifty dollars per person. On February 16, Bergson's Committee for a Jewish Army of Stateless and Palestinian Jews placed an ad in the *Times* that read, "For sale to humanity 70,000 Jews. Guaranteed human beings at $50 apiece. Attention America! The Great Rumanian bargain for this month only," and urged readers to send contributions to "the Committee for a Jewish Army."[13]

Alarmed at this audacious proposal emanating from a group over which he had no control, Wise urged American Jews to ignore this plea for support with the assurance that "authorized Jewish organizations" were looking into the matter.[14] *New Palestine*, a Zionist Organization of America publication, hinted darkly that contributions might be used for nothing more than to purchase more such ads.[15] This bit of public sparring was only the opening salvo in what would soon escalate into a bitter feud between Wise and Bergson, whom Wise regarded as irresponsible and a dangerous influence. Bergson's committee would prove to be a sharp thorn in his side. Even so, its highly vocal, skillfully deployed propaganda doubtlessly goaded Wise to act decisively to recapture public attention in order to retain his mantle of leadership.

According to the Holocaust historian Haskel Lookstein, the proximate cause of the March 1 "Stop Hitler Now" rally was a January 21, 1943, cable from Riegner, which was immediately brought to Wise's attention.[16] Far less ambiguous than his telegram the previous August, it reported that the Germans "were killing Jews in Poland at a rate of 6,000 a day."[17] Acting swiftly, Wise attempted to organize a rally on February 2, which failed to materialize. This proved to be fortuitous, for additional time for planning and publicity produced an unprecedented turnout at the Garden on March 1 for a mass meeting cosponsored by the American Jewish Congress, the American Federation of Labor (AFL), the Congress of Industrial Organizations (CIO), and the Peace Church Union. Although not officially listed as sponsoring organizations, B'nai B'rith and the Jewish Labor Federation lent their support. True to its deeply rooted instincts, the American Jewish Committee remained aloof from such highly public proceedings.[18]

The major New York daily newspapers, including the *Herald Tribune*, the *Journal-American*, and the *Times*, diligently covered the March 1 meeting. The latter offered the fullest coverage, although not nearly as much as it had given the events of the previous decade, beginning with a brief lead on page 1 that continued with a single page of inside copy. Excerpts from the speeches were relatively short. The lead, however, was straightforward, a stark description of what was at stake:

Save Doomed Jews, Huge Rally Pleads

Immediate action by the United Nations to save as many as possible of the five million Jews threatened by extermination by Adolf Hitler and to halt the liquidation of European Jewry by the Nazis was demanded at a mass demonstration of Christians and Jews in Madison Square Garden last night.

As he had done in the past, Wise assembled a platform of speakers drawn from Jewish leaders, politicians, the Christian community, and other dignitaries. In addition, there were a number of messages of support from overseas clergy, including William Temple, the archbishop of Canterbury, and the ailing Cardinal Arthur Hinsley, the archbishop of Westminster, who passed away less than three weeks later. Joseph Herman Hertz, the chief rabbi of Great Britain, sent along stern words to the assembled group and the listening public:

It is appalling to think that whole [sic] of Mid-European Jewry stands at the brink of annihilation and that the millions of Jewish men, women, and children have already been slaughtered with fiendish cruelties that baffle belief but equally appalling in fact that those who proclaim the Four Freedoms have so far done so very little to secure even the freedom to live for 6,000,000 of their fellow Jewish men by readiness to rescue those who might still escape Nazi torture and butchery.[19]

Speaking in person, as the *Times* reported, Chaim Weizmann challenged the United Nations to translate its expressions of concern into actual deeds. He passionately proclaimed, "Two million Jews have already been exterminated. The world can no longer plead that the ghastly facts are unknown and unconfirmed. At this moment expressions of sympathy, without accompanying attempts to launch acts of rescue, become a hollow mockery in the ears of the dying."[20]

Weizmann urged the democracies to negotiate, through neutral parties, the release of Jews in German-occupied territories to safety in Allied-controlled lands. He also made a bold, impassioned plea for unrestricted Jewish immigration to Palestine. "Let the gates of Palestine be opened to all who can reach the shores of the Jewish homeland. The Jewish community of Palestine will welcome with joy and thanksgiving all delivered from Nazi hands."[21]

The former presidential candidate Wendell Wilkie, Supreme Court Justice William O. Douglas, Senator Robert Wagner (New York's long-time advocate for Jewish causes), and Governor Thomas Dewey were among the politicians and other government officials whom Wise solicited for personal appearances or statements. Wilkie sent a message that called on Americans, "Christian and Jew alike," to not only protest but to demand action as well. Justice Douglas and Senator Wagner addressed the gathering from Washington by radio. Douglas characterized the essential purpose of the war as the preservation of the principle of minority and individual rights, which he called the foundation of American society. Speaking eloquently on behalf of Jewish rescue, Wagner said:

> In this work, a loaf of bread or an immigration visa speaks louder than the most heartfelt expression of sympathy. This is no problem for the Jews alone; it is a United Nations problem, and it must be dealt with through the most vigorous action of a united conscience, working through an international rescue agency. No doubt we cannot do all we wish; but happily we can still do enough to satisfy the still small voice within us which will not let us rest.[22]

Governor Dewey, speaking from Albany, sought obliquely to debunk the policy of rescue through victory that the State Department had made into a mantra to justify its inaction. He declared,

"It is our duty to frustrate to the limit of our capacity the savage purposes of the murderers. Every victim of Nazi hate is an American ally. Every life we save will speed the victory, will aid the task of creating a free world after the war."[23]

Demonstrating once again his ability to rally liberal Christian leaders to his side, Wise was able to persuade representatives of two important Christian organizations to join him on the platform. The first was Henry Atkinson, founder of the Christian Council on Palestine. Atkinson was also a leader and early member of the Church Peace Union, an international, interdenominational, Carnegie-endowed pro-democracy organization founded in 1914. In 1941, acting in response to the worsening war situation, it formulated a charter whose first point declared:

> We recognize that the present conflict arises in large part out of mistaken ideologies, such as the state as the supreme object of man's worship, and the subordination of the individual to the demands of the state and the degradation of that worth of the individual that is essential to any form of prophetic religion.[24]

Although the Church Peace Union was overwhelmingly Protestant in its makeup, its original guiding light, Andrew Carnegie, had insisted from the Union's inception that its board of trustees include influential Catholic and Jewish members as well. In addition to well-known Protestant peace activists such as John Mott and Charles S. MacFarland, the Union's original board of trustees also included James Cardinal Gibbons, chancellor of the Catholic University of America; and Reform Rabbi Emil G. Hirsch of Chicago's Sinai Congregation, who in addition to being a well-respected religious leader had a widespread reputation as a scholar and social-justice advocate. Under Atkinson's leadership, the Church Peace Union sought to foster international cooperation in the ensuing decades amid an increasingly isolationist environment in the United States.

Even as it envisioned a world at peace based on the precepts of Christian love among both individuals and nations, the Church Peace Union was not conceived as a pacifist organization. In spite of its lofty goals, it recognized that the use of force was sometimes required to maintain the conditions where such a world was possible. For that reason, it recognized the importance of winning the war.[25] During World War II, it organized a series of over thirty "Win the War—Win the Peace" institutes, which not only fostered morale for the grim work of defeating the Axis powers but also articulated its vision for a post-war peace that would be monitored by an international body to peacefully adjudicate conflicts.[26]

In addition to the "Win the War" institutes, the Church Peace Union composed an interreligious declaration of its vision for the postwar world. Titled *Pattern for Peace*, its authors included Father Edward A. Conway, S. J.; G. Ashton Oldham, the Episcopal bishop of Albany; and Rabbi Louis Mann, who succeeded Rabbi Hirsch not only at Sinai Temple but also as a trustee for the Church Peace Union. Although it proclaimed that a just peace was based on a shared vision of moral law dependent on the sovereignty of God, *Pattern for Peace* was sufficiently imprecise in its wording so that it would present no difficulties for the non-Protestant trustees. Published in October 1943, the original hundred thousand copies were soon distributed, and by June 1944 that number had grown to over five hundred thousand.[27]

After over a quarter century of vigorous service as a churchman, Atkinson was still active in his various responsibilities as an ecumenically minded Protestant. In response to the invitation to speak at the Garden, he argued that the pernicious effects of antisemitism affected more than just the Jews:

> Let us not forget that those who thrust this war upon us used antisemitism as the basis of the attack not only upon our way of life, but upon all the freedoms of men and women everywhere. Just as Hitler used antisemitism as the opening wedge in his attack, so we must turn our attention to the means and methods by which antisemitism will be forever wiped out and its emergence shall be a crime against the common good.[28]

Another influential voice Wise brought on board was that of Henry St. George Tucker, the presiding bishop of the Episcopal Church and president of the Federal Council of Churches. Although he did not offer specifics, Tucker disclosed that the FCC was already conferring with Jewish leadership in order to extend the "utmost cooperation possible in efforts to relieve the persecuted Jews of Europe." He also appealed specifically to the conscience of his co-religionists, saying that "the Christian people of America must join with their Jewish fellow citizens not only in protesting against brutal and cruel persecution, but also in using every means in our power for putting an end to it."[29]

Although the evening consisted mostly of speeches, the audience adopted by approbation a resolution directed to President Roosevelt consisting of eleven points, including the creation of safe havens for the remaining European Jews, particularly in Palestine; the organization of feeding programs for starving Jews; and the creation of tribunals for the prosecution of war crimes.[30] The proceedings were also not devoid of emotional content. As the *Times* reported, the climactic moment of the meeting occurred with the blast of the shofar and prayers for the dead, as "the huge audience waited and wept, while thousands outside, who heard the proceedings through amplifiers, joined."[31]

The Yiddish press gave the March 1 rally even more attention than its English-language counterparts. The day before the event, *Morgn Zhurnal* ran a full-page advertisement whose headline conveyed the desperation of the circumstances: "HELP SAVE THE REMNANT OF JEWS IN EUROPE! COME TOMORROW TO MADISON SQUARE GARDEN TO DEMAND JUSTICE FROM THE WORLD."[32] The notice also demanded an answer to the question of how the free world could stand idly by and allow such suffering to continue, and it exhorted its readers, "Save the survivors! Do not let the Murderer exterminate the remnant of Israel."[33] The following day, *Morgn Zhurnal* issued a call to Jewish storekeepers to close their doors by 6 pm and join the rally.[34]

On the day of the meeting, *Forverts* likewise urged its readership to action: "Today the Jews of America need to demonstrate to the world and to themselves how great their grief is for the millions of their brothers who have been killed by the Nazi murderers."[35] In an about-face, *Morgn Frayhayt*, which had snubbed and denigrated the American Jewish Congress and Wise's leadership during the previous decade, also gave "Stop Hitler Now" enthusiastic front-page publicity, including photos of the main speaker, Governor Dewey; the labor leader Phillip Green; and even Rabbi Wise.[36]

The following day, each of these papers carried articles that described the proceedings and quoted the speakers. *Forverts* began with a front-page story that continued with extensive inside coverage, including quotes from both Jewish and Christian speakers, the full text of the resolution, and gripping details about the tenor of the evening.

Though its reporting was less extensive, *Morgn Frayhayt* essentially covered the same territory. In contrast to the more factual articles of *Forverts* and *Frayhayt*, *Morgn Zhurnal* was far less restrained, offering insight into the deeply wounded collective Jewish sensibility, the expression of which was understandably greatly accentuated in the Yiddish press. In addition to thorough coverage of the speeches and photographs, its front page carried several emotionally charged articles. The first, penned by the veteran journalist Moshe Duchovny, begins: "On Forty-Ninth Street, on Eighth Avenue and on the streets of New York, Jews wept. Thousands of Jewish men, women and children lifted up their eyes to the starry sky, and the cry tore from of their aching hearts, 'Dear God, see our suffering. Have mercy on your people, great God in heaven.'"[37] In another front-page piece, Meyer Nurenburger wrote: "The tens of thousands of New York Jews who were gathered in and around Madison Square Garden not only protested, not only cried out to God and to the conscience of the world against the mass extermination of European Jewish life. They mourned together. They poured out their tears together. They prayed together."[38]

In addition to garnering enormous numbers who either listened to the speeches in person, heard them on the radio, or read about them in the papers, the March 1 rally at Madison Square Garden allowed the various Jewish organizations that had been so painfully at odds with one another to once again attempt to coordinate their efforts. Dubbed the Joint Emergency Committee on European Affairs (JEC), this latest stab at unity was composed of a spectrum of groups, including the American Jewish Congress, B'nai B'rith, the Jewish Labor Committee, and the American Emergency Committee for Zionist Affairs. The American Jewish Committee entered in as well, shedding at last, in light of the escalating calamity, its well-entrenched position against public visibility. Notably, the JEC failed to invite the Bergson faction to participate.[39]

The Joint Emergency Committee quickly formed a subcommittee, one of whose purposes was to give the Garden rally an afterlife in other cities. In this instance, they succeeded. "Stop Hitler Now" spawned similar events elsewhere. Working with local Jewish and Christian groups, the JEC was able to sponsor forty rallies in twenty states. Acting on Bishop Tucker's pledge in New York, the Federal Council of Churches joined the JEC in promoting these efforts most vigorously.[40] As the archives of the American Jewish Committee reveal, the JEC stressed the desire to recruit both Protestant and Catholic speakers and to "associate [sic] the non-Jewish community both in expressions of grief and in a demand for action."[41]

At least partly as a result of the connections that were reinforced through its participation in the Madison Square Garden rally, the Federal Council of Churches acted on its own to express sympathy for Europe's Jews and urge action on their behalf. On March 16, the FCC executive committee proclaimed May 2, 1943 as a "day of compassion" and urged Christians to give moral support to measures calling for the rescue of Europe's Jews. It appealed to the government to facilitate the removal of the endangered Jews to neutral countries or other temporary asylums.[42] It also urged American Christians to pray "for the deliverance of the Jewish people; that the hearts of all Christian people may be stirred to active compassion for the suffering of the Jews; that Christians in America may steadfastly oppose all tendencies to antisemitism in our own country."[43]

On May 2, in a brief article buried deep in *The New York Times*, Bishop Tucker warned against assuming that the reports of the atrocities against the Jews were exaggerated. Rather, he went so far as to suggest that they were actually underreported, and that a policy of Jewish extermination was well under way. He declared, "The Christian people of America vigorously protest against this brutal and cruel persecution. But protest is not enough."[44]

The FCC also worked closely with the Joint Emergency Committee, furnishing Christian clergy with sermon material and making available several pieces of pertinent literature: "Christians Protest Persecution," issued by the National Conference of Christians and Jews; "Hitler's War against the Catholic Church," from the Anti-Defamation League; and other material from the FCC.[45] It also produced a special bulletin titled "The Mass Murder of Jews in Europe" that contained a collection of verified reports about the treatment of the Jews in the German-occupied countries of Europe and the Nazi's goal of extermination. The bulletin also offered two specific proposals for rescue. One was "to offer financial assistance for the support of refugees that neutral governments may receive persons fleeing Nazi controlled territory, either by infiltration across their borders or by negotiations with the Axis powers." The second proposal put the American and the British governments directly on the spot, forthrightly demanding that they "provide places of temporary asylum to which refugees whom it may be possible to evacuate may be removed, with the understanding that they will be repatriated after the war or be provided with permanent homes in other ways."[46]

The Jewish Telegraphic Agency reported the statements of Dr. Samuel McCrea Cavert, general secretary of the FCC, who had maintained close ties to Wise and other members of Jewish leadership.[47] Cavert went out of his way to emphasize the gravity of the situation:

> The reports about the treatment of the Jews in Europe are so full of horror that many people assume they are merely "atrocity stories." The Federal Council's study of the evidence was undertaken for the purpose of finding out whether the reports are authentic and

trustworthy ... It is impossible to dismiss the reports as "atrocity stories." When the full story is known, the actual facts may turn out to be worse than the fragmentary reports have indicated.[48]

The efforts of the FCC were gratefully acknowledged by the Jewish community. Noting that the "day of compassion" coincided with the start of a six-week period of mourning and intercession called for by the Synagogue Council of America, Rabbi Israel Goldstein assured the congregants of Temple B'nai Jeshurun that "Jewish survivors in Nazi Europe who have survived only to await their turn to be exterminated" would find "new strength and new hope" from the message of Christian concern.[49] Rabbi David de Sola Pool of the Spanish-Portuguese Synagogue declared, "The bloody uprooting from continental Europe of the learning, the culture and the piety that are rooted in the Old Testament has made American Jews into a new generation of Pilgrim Fathers called to tend and strengthen this ancient spiritual culture in the sunshine of free American democracy."[50] These last somewhat bizarre comments demonstrate the extent to which some sectors of Jewish leadership were willing to go to identify with what they perceived to be the dominant religious and cultural powers of America. The notion that an American Christian "day of compassion" would matter much to European Jews caught in a deathtrap is difficult to fathom, and a Jewish appropriation of the role of Pilgrim Father seems, to put it mildly, a bit overbold even for the Jewish imagination.

"Stop Hitler Now" gives further clarity to the substance of the arguments that Jews and the growing coalition of concerned Christians sought to make in response to the grim realities unambiguously confirmed in the early months of 1943. The Jewish leaders, the politicians, and the Christian clergy who joined forces at Madison Square Garden displayed a solidarity united around a number of generally agreed-on points that concretized the rationale for Jewish rescue. While the speakers harshly condemned the Nazis, using terms such as "bestiality," "savage," "butchery," and "fiendish cruelties," they also built a case for Jewish rescue that drew its strength largely from a broader context, as though the murder of the Jews in and of itself, shocking though it might be, was not a sufficient case for forceful intervention.

One of the prevailing arguments that Jewish and Christian speakers alike employed was that while the Jewish murders were horrible, they were more so in light of the wider threat they posed to the common good, to the American way of life, and to individual freedom. In making the case for Jewish rescue, the speakers insistently sought to build a bridge that somehow linked Jewish concerns to those of the wider audience whose sympathetic response they sought to elicit. Dewey's remarks that characterize the Nazi victims as American allies are a good example of the underlying argument for Jewish rescue that had begun to evolve in 1933—that is, the Jews are an acceptable component of the larger group on the basis of a discoverable commonality, and therefore support for them is an approved course, for it exemplifies an instance of what separates Western civilized values from the barbarity of the enemy.

In attendance and publicity, "Stop Hitler Now" was a resounding success along the lines of the first protest rally ten years earlier. But now Christian participation had become far more than the collection of contacts with which Wise had started. Now, Jewish organizations had the cooperation of powerful Christian institutions such as the Federal Council of Churches and the Church Peace Union. This reinforced the perception that the event sponsors had captured public attention to the desperate condition of European Jewry in a way that could lead to meaningful results. This hope motivated both Jews and Christians to intensify their efforts to raise awareness and rally support for Jewish rescue, as demonstrated by the activities of the admittedly short-lived Joint Emergency Committee, and by the steps the FCC and the Peach Church Union took that spring to keep the issue alive among their respective constituencies.

"Stop Hitler Now" was also a validation of Stephen Wise's authoritative presence in Jewish affairs, both as a public figure and a behind-the-scenes mover and shaker. Yet as he gained stature, he became an increasingly visible target for his critics. Other voices were clamoring to be heard. In service to his cause, Madison Square Garden had once again showed its utility as a venue for public performance. It would do so again even more forcefully in only a week's time as the stage for the florid dramatics of Ben Hecht's *We Will Never Die.*

By March 1943, even the imperfect knowledge of the magnitude of Jewish suffering in Europe had an understandably galvanizing effect on various sectors of Jewish communal life that wanted to act but recognized that they needed allies. Drawing on previous experience, and shaped by their own internal culture and priorities, Jewish organizations reached out mainly to those with whom they had an affinity or with whom they could create a sense of sympathetic involvement, particularly among Christians. Yet they could not operate with a completely free hand.

Mindful of the political pitfalls that attended their activism, groups such as the American Jewish Committee and, to a lesser extent, the World Jewish Congress exercised a degree of caution in bringing their concerns forward for fear of making things worse for European Jews and alienating those in power to whom they naturally turned for assistance at home. Wise was particularly wary of embarrassing the Roosevelt administration, which he knew he needed, and the president himself, whose access he craved. Furthermore, having packaged their concerns as part of the larger context of Protestant American patriotism, Wise and the rest had little choice but to remain patriotic, not make waves, and hope that their lot had been wisely cast.

As the war of ideology between Western civilization and Nazi barbarism that began in the 1930s became true armed conflict, and as America went to war after Pearl Harbor, the realities of the draft, the fighting, and the dreaded telegrams that had begun to arrive with startling swiftness wove themselves deeply and dramatically into the fabric of American life. Rationing and other wartime necessities created an impact that, while more quotidian, nonetheless brought the realities of war home through a myriad of shortages and restrictions. As the government soon realized, efforts to boost morale were crucial. America had to be reminded, early and often, why it was fighting.

In response to this challenge, the government set about to create the necessary propaganda apparatus to foster a mood of patriotism, unity, and shared sacrifice. In June 1942 the newly formed Office of War Information was tasked with the creation of such a program, and those responsible for creating it turned naturally to the Hollywood dream factory.[51] Not only were studio heads recruited to make films, but movie stars of both sexes were recruited to personally promote the war effort in a variety of ways, such as entertaining troops and selling war bonds.[52] Hollywood celebrities, however, did not always take to the scripts that the studio heads or other powerful leaders handed to them. Some of them had other ideas. As the production of Ben Hecht's *We Will Never Die* shows, their creativity could be placed in service to messages that were not always in keeping with the preferences of those who sought to control them.

So far, the Madison Square Garden rallies had ranged from straightforward speechmaking to courtroom drama. Though they were encouraged by the undeniable public interest that these events stirred, Jewish and Christian activists knew that their efforts had had little overall effect in shaping the policies of world governments, including that of the United States. As the war progressed and the scope of the destruction became more fully known, it became evident that the welfare of Europe's Jews was not a priority for anyone other than the Jews themselves and what allies they had managed to recruit. To deflect Jewish criticism, political powers developed the message of rescue through victory. They were abetted in no small measure by some Jewish organizations that were willing to subordinate Jewish concerns to the larger war effort and were ready to adopt the rationale that the sooner the war was won, the sooner the Jews and the rest of the Nazi victims would gain relief.

As American Jews increasingly sensed that the intercessors of old, such as the American Jewish Committee and the American Jewish Congress, were failing to effectively represent Jewish interests, a new tone of defiance began to emerge among activists who were less inhibited about chastising the powerful for failing to act on their behalf. They demanded concrete action while there was still time, calling for a new manner of Jewish public expression. In response, some of the cogs in the same Hollywood machine serving the general war effort answered the call to address the specific concerns of the Jews.

In 1943, the Hollywood A-list screenwriter and playwright Ben Hecht, whose screen credits include *The Front Page*, *Scarface*, *Gunga Din*, and a host of other films, wrote and became the moving force behind the production of *We Will Never Die*, a tribute to fallen European Jews and the defiant, undying spirit of those Jews who yet lived. According to his autobiography, Hitler and the war had strengthened Hecht's lackadaisical connection to Jewishness and stimulated his sense of American patriotism.

Hecht's meeting with Jabotinsky's protégé Peter Bergson proved to be a turning point. Though only twenty-five years old, Bergson's passion for the Committee for a Jewish Army of Stateless and Palestinian Jews roused the older, more cynical Hecht's sympathy for, and eventual stalwart commitment to, revisionist Zionism and Irgun. Through Bergson, Hecht joined Irgun members Yitzhak Ben-Ami and Samuel Merlin in an informal steering committee to plot a course that would culminate, in large measure due to Hecht's determined efforts, contacts, and creative gifts, in the production of *We Will Never Die*.

By 1943, Hecht, like many others in Hollywood, had lent his well-honed gifts to war propaganda efforts, writing speeches and staging shows for the Red Cross and the war bond drive.[53] Hecht's activism began even prior to Pearl Harbor. One of his earlier projects had been *Fun to Be Free*, a pageant sponsored by the Fight for Freedom Committee, a group formed early in 1941 to press for US military intervention in the war.[54]

Staged at Madison Square Garden by the producer Billy Rose on October 5, 1941, *Fun to Be Free* was an all-star production featuring

Tallulah Bankhead, Burgess Meredith, and Claude Rains as narrators, with music by Kurt Weill. In answer to the question, "What is America? What is the USA?" an array of patriotic figures from America's hallowed past stepped forth with speeches containing thinly veiled warnings against isolationism. The audience heard a replay of a recent speech by Roosevelt, who was portrayed as a latter-day Abraham Lincoln, calling for decisive defensive action against German depredations in the Atlantic.

Special effects abounded in the sudden, simulated Japanese and German air attack on America, including New York City and Madison Square Garden itself, that featured sirens, blasts, and five-inch cardboard parachutes descending from the ceiling. The show's finale, which included Ethel Merman, Eddie Cantor, and Jack Benny, featured a number by Bill "Bojangles" Robinson tap dancing on Hitler's coffin while singing Irving Berlin's "When That Man Is Dead and Gone." The show was a smash hit and went on to play in a number of other cities.[55]

According to his own account, the silence of Jewish newspaper publishers and other influential Jewish elites about multiplying German atrocities against the Jews roused Hecht to action. Reflecting on what he perceived to be their self-serving indifference, he marveled, "Yet there was no voice of importance anywhere, Jewish or non-Jewish, protesting this foulest of history's crimes."[56] He reserved his greatest contempt for the fifty Jewish "Hollywood chieftains" who, at a meeting with Ambassador Joseph Kennedy, had, according to Hecht, acquiesced to Kennedy's stern admonition to keep their "Jewish rage" to themselves, lest their spoken advocacy "make the world feel that a 'Jewish War' was going on."[57] Rather, to Hecht's way of thinking, "The sound of moral outrage over the extinction of the Jews would restore human stature to the name Jew. In the silence this stature was vanishing. We Jews in America were fast becoming the relatives of the garbage pile of Jewish dead. There would be no respect for the living Jew when there is no regret for a dead one."[58]

In addition to the plaudits he had earned as a brilliant Hollywood screenwriter, the versatile Hecht was also a widely read newspaper and magazine columnist. Working with the damning documentation of German atrocities against Jews obtained from Dr. Chaim Greenberg, the editor of the English-language weekly *Jewish Frontier*, Hecht wrote the article "Remember Us," which appeared in the February 1943 issue of *Reader's Digest*. Upon reflection, he was inspired to take the idea further. At a gathering of about thirty Jewish creative artists at the home of Beatrice and George S. Kaufman, Hecht floated the idea for a project that might make a bigger statement and perhaps apply enough pressure to the British to open the ports of Palestine to Jews desperate to escape from Europe. To his disappointment, only Moss Hart and Kurt Weill lent him any encouragement. The rest, in his account, were too frightened to stand up and be counted as Jews.[59] Nonetheless, joined by Billy Rose as producer and buoyed with the promise that Bergson's group would supply funding, the project took shape.

From a creative and technical standpoint, Hecht did not have to reinvent the wheel for *We Will Never Die*. As an experienced professional with a collection of close, proficient colleagues, he employed several of the features and personnel from *Fun to Be Free*, including the use of well-known narrators to move the story along and a colorful, costumed, historical tableaux. His difficulties in getting the production on its feet arose mainly from political rather than artistic sources.

From the moment of its inception, the project ran into opposition from a number of quarters. Billy Rose approached the White House, hoping to obtain a message from President Roosevelt to be read aloud at the event, but was turned down for fear that *We Will Never Die* would create political pressure to admit Jewish refugees to the United States. The British Embassy in Washington also complained that the pageant was "implicitly anti-British," because, although it was never stated, the most natural haven for Jewish refugees was indeed Palestine, controlled by the British, who were fearful of displeasing the Arabs.[60]

Hecht's troubles had only begun. He also failed to build the broader coalition of endorsements he had sought among the almost three-dozen influential Jewish organizations he solicited. Some were unwilling to work with Bergson's group, afraid that such publicity would lead to a spike in antisemitism, or else were unwilling to yield turf to a rival organization.[61] Stephen Wise, no friend of revisionist ideology, proved to be a particularly adamant foe. In Hecht's recollection, Wise had somehow gotten hold of a script and called to inform Hecht that it was unacceptable, that Hecht should cancel the pageant, and that he should cease working for the Jewish cause independent of Wise's supervision.[62]

According to Hecht, Bergson had foreseen such difficulties all along.[63] Financially independent with Bergson's backing and beholding to no one, Hecht proceeded as he had originally planned. Auditions were held in February 1943 and a large cast was chosen, including one hundred students from Yeshiva University, fifty cantors, and another fifty rabbis, some of whom had been rescued from Europe and, after some prodding, agreed to pray on stage as part of a theatrical production. Some of Hollywood's and Broadway's best-known actors agreed to appear, including Stella and Luther Adler, John Garfield, Paul Henreid, Paul Muni, Edward G. Robinson, and Sylvia Sidney.[64] Muni and Robinson were recruited as narrators, assisted by Luther Adler and Herbert Rudley, a lesser-known character actor. Jacob Ben-Ami, known for his acting prowess in both Yiddish and English, would portray a rabbi. Fifty members of the NBC Symphony Orchestra provided the musical accompaniment.

We Will Never Die, which owes its title to Habakkuk 1:12, opened at Madison Square Garden on March 9, 1943. Since the twenty thousand tickets available had been sold out the week before, Hecht scheduled an encore performance for 11:15 pm that also played to a full house. It was the first time in the history of Madison Square Garden that the same event was performed twice in one evening due to an overwhelming demand for tickets.[65] The presentation was coordinated with a day of mourning and prayer throughout New York that Governor Dewey had proclaimed.[66]

The illustrated cover of the evening's program depicts Jewish misery. A soldier whose helmet bears the Star of David brandishes a machine gun in one hand and cradles a dead rabbi in the other, who in turn is clutching a Torah scroll to his lifeless breast. The inside pages include an introduction from Hecht under the bold heading "Action—Not Pity" and a prominently displayed notice of the pageant's sponsorship by the Committee for a Jewish Army of Stateless and Palestinian Jews. The program also featured a full-page call for support headlined "Ten Reasons Why a Jewish Army!" These included a mixture of appeals to national interests, such as advancing the war effort and bolstering the front in the Middle East, and specifically Jewish concerns that an army was a matter of honor and an expression of their desire to demonstrate worthiness. Hecht also wrote a plea for action to save the two-thirds of European Jewry thought to be still alive:

> When you leave Madison Square Garden tonight, there will be 4,000,000 pair of eyes watching your fading form as it merges with the night. There will be 4,000,000 hearts praying that with you will bring means of escape. They are not defeated—for with your help THEY WILL NEVER DIE! "WE WILL NEVER DIE"[67]

The spectacle consisted of three acts: "Roll Call," "Jews in the War," and "Remember Us." These three episodes reinforced one another in service to a single message, a dramatic articulation of the developing central theme, which is the indispensability of the Jewish contribution to Western civilization and especially American democracy. Thus indebted, America and its allies must take up the cause of the Jews not merely as generic victims but precisely because of their Jewishness and the contributions of Jewish religion, creativity, and culture.

Although Hecht cheerfully eschewed Jewish faith and practice for himself, he did not hesitate to use the symbols of Judaism and the faith of others to make his point. As the lights came up on the renowned Broadway designer Lemuel Ayers's impressive set, the audience first saw two large depictions of the tablets of the Decalogue, which towered over the proceedings throughout. The resounding blast of the shofar was then followed by a lengthy prayer on behalf of "the two million who have been killed in Europe, because they bear the name of your first children—the Jews." The prayer is one of sadness for the dead, but also contains a ringing affirmation of the Jewish spirit and concludes with an assembly of rabbis from many lands praying the "Shema Yisrael" with a choir of cantors singing in response. Thus dignified by the presence of the Almighty, the play begins.

As the first act unfolds, the narrators remind the audience of the debt the world owes to the ancient composers of the Hebrew scriptures, which led humanity to a heightened awareness of the qualities of goodness, righteousness, and justice. Germany, in turn, is portrayed as the archenemy of the children of Abraham, "seeking to destroy the creed written by Abraham that now belongs to the whole world." The Germans strike first against the powerless Jews who have no weapons and, as the Zionist Hecht reminds his audience, no flag.

Then, as in *Fun to Be Free*, historical figures step forward to hold the stage for a moment. This time, it is a roll call of illustrious Jewish figures, beginning with those who have the closest links to pre- and post-exilic Jewish religious history: Moses, David, Solomon, and a mighty host of other heroes, poets, and prophets—"Thunderers all, whose dreams and phrases molded the soul of man and illumined forever his tomorrow." To these, the narrator adds a lengthy list of Jewish accomplishments in the arts and letters and other fields of endeavor, which reaches a crescendo with a recitation of the names of Jewish Nobel Prize winners.

The scene shifts abruptly for the second act as soldiers enter. This section lauds the bravery of the Jewish fighting man, serving under many flags, most of all for America. But there is one flag missing: his own. Hecht pleads, "Our two million brothers in Europe have died as Jews. Let us fight as Jews to avenge them. We will fight well. This is the cry of the missing flag." This act concludes with an honor guard of Jewish soldiers with a flag bearing an emblem of the Star of David, which takes its place among other flags of the Allies that are on display. A chorus of thirty Palestinian Jews sings "The War Song of Modern Judea," followed by "The Battle Hymn of the Republic."

The setting of the final act is a courtroom at the future "table of judgment," where Germans will hear the charges brought against them by a panel representing the nations who have opposed them. But there is no Jew present on the panel for two reasons. The first is that Jews are disqualified from representation because they have no national status. The second reason is more chilling. By the time the war is won, there are no Jews left in Europe: "They have been reduced from a minority to a phantom."

The tablets of the Decalogue swing open. Two Jewish men, two women, and a child emerge. They are the dead. Standing just beyond the table, they recite a litany of German atrocities. Each one ends with the plaintive words, "Remember us." The narrator concludes, "Let them who have no voice hear our voices speaking for them. . . ." A tenor leads the choir in the Kaddish, the prayer recited to remember the deceased and to affirm the faithfulness of God, as the dead recede slowly and silently through the lighted space between the tablets. The program concluded with Muni reading Governor Dewey's proclamation.

We Will Never Die received extravagant coverage from the New York English-language papers, far more than "Stop Hitler Now." The New York dailies included the *Times*, the *Journal-American*, the *Daily Mirror*, and the *Brooklyn Daily Eagle*. While all of them described the presentation, the set, the actors, and included quotes from the script, and some included photographs, there are subtle differences in how the controversial content and a message made ambiguous by its medium was reported. For example, the *Times* featured a straightforward description of the presentation as a "tribute," a "spectacle," and "a dramatic mass memorial to the 2,000,000 Jews killed in Europe," whose purpose was to "stir the Allied nations to stop the slaughter of a people by the Germans." However, it did not mention the Committee for a Jewish Army, which had sponsored the program, or Dewey's proclamation. By sticking to an unadorned, matter-of-fact description of the pageant, the *Times* noncommittally distanced itself from its message.

By contrast, the characteristically less restrained tone of the *Journal-American* was more emotional, portraying the pageant's message as "a call to the conscience of the world, to civilization itself," issued to "open a second front against the anti-human massacre program of the Nazis."[68] It made special mention of "the poignant parade of the dead, the murdered Jewish men, women and children of Europe, who appeared in a slow, ghostly procession. . . ."[69] It also carried photographs and extended excerpts of the script in that day's pictorial review section.

The *Daily Mirror* alone framed the event in the context of Governor Dewey's proclamation and specifically mentioned the sponsorship of Bergson's group by name.[70] In addition, in contrast to the *Times'* more general description of the message, the *Mirror* described it as not only a plea to speed relief to the remaining European Jewish population but also "a plea for the formation of a Jewish army to fight under its own flag alongside the forces of the United Nations."[71] The reliable Michael Williams, writing for the *Brooklyn Daily Eagle*, described it as "one of the most extraordinary manifestations of religious faith displayed in modern times."[72] A review in the *Eagle's* theater section was the only article that carried a quote from Hecht: "Maybe we can induce a voice to sound somewhere on behalf of human dignity, a voice powerful enough to cause the Germans to pause and blink and drop their happy extermination and torture."[73]

As for the Yiddish press, it took far less notice of *We Will Never Die* than of "Stop Hitler Now." *Forverts*, *Frayhayt*, and *Morgn Zhurnal* gave front-page coverage on the day of the event but, curiously, ran the same identically worded story, which stressed that the event would be presented on Governor Dewey's officially proclaimed "day of mourning." While *Forverts* ran a single article and photo on the front page the day after, its coverage consisted of little more than a desultory description of the proceedings without a single word of praise for the production.[74] *Morgn Frayhayt* ignored it altogether until two days after the performance. Although it noted the large turnout and overflow crowd, its page 6 description was short and uninspiring.[75]

Morgn Zhurnal was more generous. Its story ran the day after the event on page 2, but above all others, including the English-language papers, it treated the pageant as having potential real-life political ramifications. Alone among any of the press reports, *Morgn Zhurnal* reported that after the performances Ben Hecht held a press conference at the Waldorf-Astoria where he explained the purpose of the play. He said, "Public opinion in America must be roused, so as not to keep silent about the Jewish tragedy, but do something immediately."[76]

The striking differences in the Yiddish-press coverage for "Stop Hitler Now" and *We Will Never Die* is instructive, particularly when compared to the coverage these two Madison Square Garden events received in the English-language newspapers. While the English press heartily boosted both events, the noticeably low level of enthusiasm for *We Will Never Die* in the Yiddish press may be accounted for not primarily in terms of their form or content but by the ideological crosswinds that were at play. *Forverts* and *Frayhayt* were simply unsympathetic to Zionism, and the revisionist brand of Zionism represented by Bergson and Hecht would hold even less appeal for them. *Morgn Zhurnal*, on the other hand, was pro-Zionist, and therefore more apt to be receptive.

All of that notwithstanding, Hecht had retained his golden touch. As in the case of *Fun to Be Free*, sold-out performances and respectful media coverage put the show on the road for four months, with stops in Washington, DC, Philadelphia, Boston, Chicago, St. Louis, and Los Angeles. On April 12, *We Will Never Die* was performed in Constitution Hall, where it was viewed before an audience that included six justices of the Supreme Court, more than two hundred members of Congress, and Eleanor Roosevelt.

Eleanor Roosevelt's presence at the event ought not to come as a surprise, for by 1943 her vocal and behind-the-scenes advocacy for Jewish people was well-established. According to John F. Sears, largely motivated by humanitarian impulses, she rubbed elbows with Jewish immigrants as early as 1903 as a volunteer at the Rivington Street Settlement on the Lower East Side of Manhattan. Over the ensuing decades, as the Roosevelts' political and social connections expanded, her progressive concerns brought her alongside politicians and other highly placed public figures, Jewish activists, and influential Christian and Jewish clergy, including Rabbi Stephen Wise.[77]

Greatly enthused by what she had witnessed in Constitution Hall, in her next syndicated newspaper column the First Lady wrote approvingly, "The music, singing, narration, and actors all served to make it one of the most impressive and moving pageants I have ever seen. No one who heard each group come forward and give the story of what had happened to it at the hands of a ruthless German military, will ever forget those haunting words: 'Remember us.'"[78] As Rafael Medoff, director of the David S. Wyman Institute for Holocaust Studies notes, "For millions of American newspaper readers, it was the first time they heard about the Nazi mass murders."[79] Yet, according to Sears, although she continued to write about the shame of bigotry, including antisemitism, she refrained from issuing a full-throated, specific call for the rescue of Europe's Jews.[80]

On April 22, *We Will Never Die* was performed in Philadelphia's Convention Hall to a crowd of over fifteen thousand, with guest stars Claude Rains and Edward Arnold as the narrators. Afterward, the *Philadelphia Jewish Exponent* observed, "*We Will Never Die* demonstrated for all to see that in order to reach the conscience of the Christian as well as to arouse the Jew himself, popular psychology must be understood and utilized. The 'old reliable' organizations . . . would do well to emulate the example set."[81]

Although Hecht had originally worked mainly through his Jewish contacts in show business, by the time the show reached Los Angeles and the Hollywood Bowl on July 21, *We Will Never Die* had acquired the endorsements of a roster of distinguished Christians, including John Cantwell, archbishop of Los Angeles, as well as politicians, including Governor Earl Warren and Los Angeles Mayor Fletcher Bowron. Whatever the merit of Hecht's earlier appraisal of the powerful Jewish "Hollywood chieftains," a special section in the bulky playbill identified Louis B. Mayer, Harry Cohen, Samuel Goldwyn, David O. Selznick, and others as "Honorary Chairmen of the Motion Picture Industry." These names were joined by several dozen less exalted "general sponsors," including rabbis, Christian clergy, educators, attorneys, and other professionals. The play now had an additional piece, "The Battle of Warsaw," inserted before the final act.

We Will Never Die succeeded in publicizing a disaster that in 1943 had still not impressed itself on the American public consciousness. Taken on these terms, and considering the enormous popularity it enjoyed throughout its brief life, *We Will Never Die* was a great theatrical success. Robert Skloot, who has written extensively on the the theater and the Holocaust, gives *We Will Never Die* high marks for its effect on the audience it sought to reach. Conceding that its script did not resemble "great dramatic literature," Skloot maintains that this deficiency does not detract from its success, because "the theatrical objectives of pageants lie elsewhere." Rather, "What is wanted is color, size, and mass together with a stridency and sentiment which allows easy access to emotional experience."[82]

In a sense, *We Will Never Die* is the culminating expression of the genre of the courtroom drama. Its concluding act, "Remember Us," is certainly reminiscent of *The Case of Civilization against Hitlerism*, in which Nazi barbarism is brought to the bar of justice. There is, however, a great difference between them. *The Case of Civilization*, presented almost a decade earlier, took place at a time when Jewish leadership might find reason to hope that disaster for Europe's Jewish culture could be averted. Now, it had become a question of what, if anything, could be salvaged.

We Will Never Die left a mixed legacy. Skloot, citing the Hecht biographer Doug Feathering, argues that although Hecht succeeded in gaining an audience for his message, he also widened the already counterproductive divisions in the Jewish community.[83] On the other hand, Medoff credits *We Will Never Die* for increasing the pressure that the Bergson group brought to bear on the government, which led Roosevelt to form the War Refugee Board in 1944 to rescue two hundred thousand Jews in the final eighteen months of the war.

At the time, the pageant's creators were uncertain about the value of their accomplishment. Hecht believed the show had at least made America aware of the extent of the disaster, as far as it was known. Kurt Weill was less sanguine, saying, "The pageant has accomplished nothing . . . all we have done is make a lot of Jews cry, which is not a unique accomplishment."[84] Although the political dividends may not have been as great as they had hoped at the time, Hecht and Bergson's group found enough reason to continue their collaboration. In September 1946 they produced *A Flag Is Born*, yet another pageant, to promote the Zionist push toward statehood. It opened on Broadway and enjoyed similar success, playing to large houses both in New York and on an extended tour.[85]

Whatever the strengths and weaknesses may have been in its theatrical and political value, *We Will Never Die* had an overlooked and perhaps unintended effect. What started in New York as a thinly veiled piece of revisionist propaganda fueled by Hecht's genuine outrage took on multiple meanings in the four months that elapsed between its first and final performance in Hollywood. At that point, it had become more than a Zionist cause célèbre. It had become yet another vehicle for Jewish-Christian solidarity.

The playbill accompanying the July 21 performance at the Hollywood Bowl is more than just the usual explanatory notes to a theatrical performance. The document serves as a multivocal commentary on the proceedings and its context in world events. The various viewpoints propounded in the articles are evidence of the further development of Jewish-Christian discourse in America aroused by the increasingly fraught circumstances of European Jewry. Among them was a reprint of New York Congressman Emanuel Celler's recently published "Diplomatic Mockery," which harshly condemned the allied nations' failure to render rescue and relief at the

Evian Conference of 1938 and the recently concluded and equally ineffectual Bermuda Conference. Celler writes bitterly:

> We explored in 1938; we explore again in 1943. Finally comes the pronouncement that the only solution is victory. Was victory the only solution likewise in 1938, or is it simply another delaying pretense? Victory *is* the complete solution; after victory disembodied spirits will not present so difficult a problem. The dead no longer need food, drink, asylum.[86]

In addition to political commentary, the playbill contained messages appealing specifically to precepts of the Christian faith, including an editorial titled "Mercy—Which We May Need One Day for Ourselves" from the Jesuit periodical *America* that challenged "the Christian conscience" to not turn away from Jewish suffering and attributed Hitler's "fiendishly cruel destruction" to a "hatred of God and Christ Himself." The noted Catholic theologian Jacques Maritain agreed and went further in his article "A Challenge to Christian Conscience," which had previously appeared in *Commonweal*: "The challenge has been hurled at Christian conscience. It . . . is Christian conscience which has the primary responsibility in the fight for the defenses of the people whence issued Christ." Moreover, he continued to identify the suffering of the Jews with that of Christ and asserted that "this anti-Semitic rage . . . by persecuting and exterminating the Jews, seeks to inflict upon Christ a new kind of passion. . . ."[87]

Maritain had already elucidated this concept in 1939, in *A Christian Looks at the Jewish Question*. There he writes, "It is no little matter, however, for a Christian to hate or to despise or to wish to treat degradingly the race from which sprung his God and the Immaculate Mother of God. That is why the bitter zeal of antisemitism always turns in the end into a bitter zeal against Christianity itself."[88]

Maritain's close identification of the crucified Christ with the Jewish people was an effort to bind the interests of Christians and

Jews to each other in a deeper and more emotional fashion. Where liberal Jews and Christians favored an approach to religious unity against the antisemitic scourge of Hitlerism based on common, humanitarian values, Maritain viewed the relationship of Jews and Christians through a more mystical lens. For him, the shared fate of dying Jews and the persecuted Christ became the unifying factor in the Jewish-Christian nexus. Whereas in *We Will Never Die* Hecht pointed to themes derived from the Hebrew Bible and Jewish history as the basis for a just redress of Jewish grievance and the rejection of antisemitism, the lesson that Maritain derives from these sources is that the shame of Christian antisemitism and its attendant evils are an ultimate rejection of Christ and, therefore, a self-contradictory distortion of authentic Christian faith. Cast in these terms, the argument for Christian compassion toward Jewish suffering is stamped with the ultimate Christian spiritual imprimatur, identification with the suffering of Jesus himself.

"Stop Hitler Now" and *We Will Never Die* have much in common, starting with their proximity to the particularly painful moment in 1943 when reports of the obliteration of European Jewish life became more widely known. Both had the same goal of motivating the public to pressure the Roosevelt administration and its allies to take concrete steps to avert the full measure of the destruction. Despite these similarities, the contrast in their respective approaches, in their style and substance, reveals widely different understandings of the nature of Jewish identity in itself and in its connection to others. Both bear the stamp of their originators' priorities, strengths, and limitations.

"Stop Hitler Now" portrays Jews as helpless victims and as supplicants to those more powerful. Its plea for intervention is based primarily on an appeal to "civilized" values, which Jews played an integral role in creating, and which ought to motivate the world to come to their rescue. By once again deploying politicians and Christian clergy to make their case, Wise and his Jewish colleagues created a protective cover under which Jewish speakers could operate, confident that their message would not sound too strident or otherwise strike a discordant note.

By contrast, *We Will Never Die* adopts a far more defiant tone. Unlike "Stop Hitler Now" and the other meetings that Wise had a hand in organizing, *We Will Never Die* does not look to others to validate its message. Instead, the Jewish presence is front and center, with Christians offstage in a minor and supplementary role. *We Will Never Die* is less an appeal to the conscience of the world and far more an unambiguous demand. Although it portrays the Jews as victim-martyrs, it strongly suggests that they are capable of being something more. The basis of its case is that Jews are entitled to exercise the same fighting instincts for survival as any other national group. Its message to the wider world is not merely a request for aid based on the finer elements of enlightened values. Its message is that the Jews, in no uncertain terms, are owed justice, which includes the right to fight for themselves.

If anything, Hecht, with the backing of Bergson, became increasingly belligerent in the latter months of 1943, particularly in light of the failure of the Bermuda Conference to provide any meaningful aid to the dying European Jews. On September 14 Hecht published "Ballad of the Doomed Jews of Europe" in *The New York Times*, a scathing indictment of the world and particularly of Christian indifference. Its final lines are:

> O world be patient—it will take
> some time before the murder crews
> are done. By Christmas you can make
> your peace on earth without the Jews.[89]

As though to illustrate Hecht's point that the Jews did not matter in the eyes of the world, on November 1, 1943, Washington, London, and Moscow issued a joint statement, the Moscow Declaration, which warned that German officers, Nazi Party members, and others would be held personally accountable for atrocities against

Polish, Dutch, Norwegian, and other nationalities, without any mention whatsoever of the Jews.[90] In response, Bergson's "Emergency Committee to Save the Jewish People of Europe" published an almost full-page notice in *The New York Times* on November 5, 1943, written by Hecht, titled "Uncle Abraham Reports." The gist of the piece was that by omitting any mention of the Jewish victims, the Moscow Declaration had reduced them to ghosts and to nonentities. The concluding paragraph depicts Uncle Abraham at the White House sitting close to but unnoticed by President Roosevelt, implying his lack of concern.[91]

These and other accusatory pronouncements that originated from Bergson and Hecht further illustrate the sharp contrast between their confrontational tactics and the more deferential approach favored by Wise. It is unimaginable to think Wise would risk alienating the Christians he had cultivated for so long, or endanger whatever real or imagined influence he may have wielded with the Roosevelt administration, especially with the president himself. Even so, their differing approaches and ideologies freed them to organize their own events and appeal to a different set of followers, thus widening the range of concerned participants.[92]

In summary, in 1943 the increasingly horrifying reports about the obliteration of the Jewish communities in Europe and the apparent indifference of the allied governments, including America, to their plight created a climate of increasing anger among American Jews and a breakdown in confidence in the established organizations and leaders who claimed to represent their interests. As a result, other less-mainstream groups seized the initiative. Capitalizing on the name recognition of Jewish celebrities who had become well known beyond the borders of Jewish life, the Bergson group successfully captured some of the spotlight. Although neither the forces represented by Wise nor those of Bergson could definitively point to tangible success in saving Jewish lives, both groups were able, each in its own way, to reinforce Jewish identity, articulate Jewish concerns, and elicit a response from the wider Christian world.

In either case, to induce Christians to respond to their concerns, Jewish leaders had to create a rapport with them on both an intellectual and emotional level. Jews were faced with the task of successfully appealing to Christians both ethically and spiritually. This meant discovering what those spiritual sensibilities were, as they searched for clues to the puzzle of how to impart to Christians the urgency they felt for Europe's rapidly diminishing Jewish community.

Another result of the newly gained ground in closer interfaith cooperation was that Christians concerned with the plight of Europe's Jews were forced to confront the evil fruits of the antisemitism they had tolerated and even nurtured among themselves. The FCC's "day of compassion," its public pronouncements and publications, were attempts to clearly portray antisemitism as a character trait of the enemy that had no place among right-thinking Christian Americans. Likewise, the Church Peace Union made it clear that antisemitism had no place in a progressive vision of world order. In speaking on behalf of American democracy, politicians such as Wagner and Dewey reified these sentiments as a part of Americanism itself. By portraying Jews as sympathetic victims of the forces of evil, their speeches sanctified Jews, divesting them of their otherness and folding them into the righteous fight America was waging on behalf of Western civilization.

As the Jews fought to project a more accessible image of themselves to the larger American public, they were sometimes able to elicit, as in the case of Maritain, a more complex response to Jewish suffering. He and others like him viewed Jewish suffering not merely as a humanitarian tragedy but in terms that resonated with their own spirituality, as the suffering of Jesus of Nazareth, the central figure of their own religious faith. Jewish figures in the arts and letters, such as Marc Chagall and Sholem Asch, had also stressed the Jewishness of Jesus in order to strike a sympathetic chord that would cultivate a more emotional level of Christian engagement, thereby reinforcing the validity of Jewish identity in Christian eyes. This strategy carried its own set of pitfalls. By encouraging an engagement with

Christianity on the ground of its own values and beliefs, Jews risked reminding Christians that in the end, the differences really mattered. For Christians, the image of real Jews was still easier to bear when bathed in the sanctity of biblical promise. Proximity was therefore perilous. Yet however long a distance there remained to travel toward each other, it is irrefutable that both sides of the Jewish-Christian equation had taken meaningful steps.

11. New York Mayor Fiorello LaGuardia, vociferous advocate for the Jewish cause. *Los Angeles Daily News*, circa 1947. Wikimedia Commons.

12. William T. Manning, Episcopal Bishop of New York. Arthur W. Page, ed., *The World's Work: A History of Our Time*, Vol. XLI (Garden City, NY: Doubleday, Page & Company, 1920–21), 423, via Wikimedia Commons.

13. John Haynes Holmes, Unitarian minister. Bain News Service, Library of Congress, Prints and Photographs Division, LC-DIG-ggbain-06550.

14. Michael Williams, the founding editor of the Catholic weekly *Commonweal*. Used by permission of *Commonweal*.

15. Ben Hecht, the A-list Hollywood screenwriter and committed Zionist. Wikimedia Commons.

16. The creative artists Kurt Weill and Lotte Lenya. Wide World Photos, 1942. Wikimedia Commons.

17. "We Will Never Die" program cover, *Tears of Rage*, by Arthur Syzk. Courtesy of the Estate of Dr. Samuel Halperin.

18. The Oscar-winning composer and conductor Franz Waxman at the Hollywood Bowl, July 21, 1943. Photograph by Floyd McCarthy. Photo courtesy of the John W. Waxman Family Photo Collection.

19. The French Catholic theologian Jacques Maritain. Unknown photographer, circa 1930. Wikimedia Commons.

THE NEW YORK TIMES, TUESDAY, FEBRUARY 16, 1943. L+ 11

ADVERTISEMENT   ADVERTISEMENT   ADVERTISEMENT

FOR SALE to Humanity
70,000 Jews

Guaranteed Human Beings at $50 a Piece

Roumania is tired of killing Jews. It has killed one hundred thousand of them in two years. Roumania will now give Jews away practically for nothing.

SEVENTY THOUSAND JEWS ARE WAITING DEATH IN ROUMANIAN CONCENTRATION CAMPS:

Roumania Will Give These 70,000 Jews to the Four Freedoms for 20,000 Lei ($50) a Piece. This Sum Covers All Transportation expenses.

COMMITTEE FOR A JEWISH ARMY
OF STATELESS AND PALESTINIAN JEWS

535 FIFTH AVENUE
NEW YORK, N.Y.
MUrray Hill 2-7237

February 16, 1943

To The FOUR FREEDOMS
Care United Nations' Leaders.

My Dear Noble State of Mind:

I know you are very busy, too busy perhaps to read the story on the left hand side of this page.

For that reason I am writing an ad. Ads are easier and quicker to read than stories.

Your admirer,

Ben Hecht

RUMANIA WILLING TO TRANSFER 70,000 JEWS TO PALESTINE

Loss of Faith in Germany's Victory Seen in Rumanian Proposal

Newspaper reports from London reveal that the Rumanian Government has proposed to the United Nations to transfer 70,000 Rumanian Jews from Trans-Dniestria to any refuge that will be assigned by the Allies.

This proposal was made through the medium of neutral diplomats. According to the reports, the Rumanian proposal implies that the Rumanian Government is ready to release the Jews which would be permitted to display the insignia of the Vatican to insure safe passage.

The Jews would be first transferred under the supervision of ex-

ROUMANIA OFFERS TO DELIVER THESE 70,000 ALIVE TO PALESTINE

Attention Four Freedoms !!!
NO SPIES WERE FOUND AMONG THE 300,000 JEWS WHO CAME TO PALESTINE SINCE HITLER ASSUMED POWER IN GERMANY
THERE WILL BE NO SPIES SMUGGLED IN AMONG THESE JEWS.
(IF THERE ARE YOU CAN SHOOT THEM)

Attention Humanity !!!
PALESTINE'S ARABS WILL NOT BE ANNOYED BY THE ARRIVAL OF 70,000 JEWS
THE ONLY ARABS WHO WILL BE ANNOYED ARE THE ARAB LEADERS WHO ARE IN BERLIN AND THEIR SPIES IN PALESTINE.

Attention America !!!
THE GREAT ROUMANIAN BARGAIN IS FOR THIS MONTH ONLY!

20. "Jews for Sale," Hecht's bitter plea in *The New York Times*, February 16, 1943. © 1943 The New York Times Company. All rights reserved. Used under license.

4

Jewish and Christian Zionists

Uncommon Allies in a Common Cause

Sympathetic Christian interest in America regarding the worsening situation for Jews in Europe during the Nazi regime sprang from distinctly different sources. The liberal factions of American Protestantism framed their concerns according to the modern, enlightened values of universal human rights and social justice. Within this framework, the ill treatment of Jews or any other group was deemed an offense because of its disregard of acceptable standards of behavior in civilized societies.

Their characterization of Nazi villainy included offenses against notions of civilized behavior generally and American patriotism particularly. This expanded ethical framework provided additional permission for members of the predominantly Christian American public to consider the Jews more favorably because their persecution represented an affront to the patriotic sensibilities of all right-thinking Americans. Though it was a realistic strategy to create public indignation, it revealed an underlying lack of confidence among American Jewish leaders and their sympathetic Christian friends that Jewish suffering was in and of itself sufficient cause for widespread concern and action. This diffidence was quite understandable, given the recent history of entrenched isolationism and rising antisemitism at home.

The non-Jewish spokespersons at the Madison Square Garden protests, drawn largely from the Protestant establishment, were recruited from a pool of public figures whose viewpoints complemented those of the American Jewish Congress and the less visible American Jewish Committee activists. These two organizations, regardless of their differences, were united in their efforts to find non-Jewish allies in order to rouse public interest and create the political pressure necessary to effect measurable relief for Europe's Jews. In seeking Christian support, both organizations quite naturally turned to the influential members of Protestant churches and organizations that by the 1930s were established as mainstream American religious oracles. Not only were some of them already known through the relationships founded in the 1920s in the goodwill movement, but they were also the ones whom progressive Jewish leaders thought could do their cause the most good.

Alongside this, a second source of Christian support sprang from another region of Protestantism that was less familiar to and in many ways far less compatible with the thinking that progressive Jewish leaders sought among like-minded liberal Christians. As the editors of *The Voice of Religion* discovered, there was also a groundswell of concern for the Jewish people among conservative Protestant denominations. Their interest was grounded not on the universality of basic human rights but on the particularity of the role of Israel and the Jews, based on an understanding of the Bible that was deeply rooted in the evangelical movement. However welcome such endorsements might be, the beliefs of this broad and diverse subculture of American Protestantism were problematic for mainstream Jewish leadership and were also, for that matter, unattractive to many mainline Christians.

The unapologetic efforts of evangelicals to achieve Jewish conversions, which was often an essential corollary to evangelical belief, had already provided ample reason for some Jewish leaders to reject out of hand participation in the goodwill movement. Evangelical Christians who held high the banner of missionary zeal were anathema to Jewish leaders and their constituencies, who deemed such approaches to be deeply offensive. Progressive Christians, aware of the fragility of their hard-won victories on behalf of goodwill, had to regularly assure their Jewish conversation partners that their efforts were not a subterfuge for missionizing, and they made certain to distance themselves from such activities. As contention among Christians arose over the role of evangelism generally, the gulf widened between progressive Christians and evangelicals whose views of Jewish people and Israel were colored by their eschatology, especially when viewed through the lens of dispensationalist theology. Jewish leaders, mindful of their own interests, stuck with their newfound progressive Christian friends, who seemed now to be in the driver's seat.

Yet there was an element of Jewish community and leadership that had not always rebuffed evangelical efforts to establish friendly relations, despite their well-known missionary agenda. This corner of Jewish life was drawn largely from the Zionist movement that arose in the late nineteenth century, which had already formed a small but growing minority among American Jews by the early decades of the twentieth century. Zionism, which experienced a surge of support among American Jews as conditions in Europe deteriorated, remembered an earlier moment in its history when it had successfully tapped the support of powerful Christian allies. Pressed by the extremity of need, Zionist leaders would attempt to revive a coalition of mutual interest that had begun even before the first World Zionist Congress in 1897.

As World War II engulfed Europe, Jewish and Christian Zionists met anew on the common ground of their determined efforts to create a Jewish homeland in Palestine, now made all the more urgent by Britain's unwillingness to open Palestine's borders to Jews attempting to flee almost certain death. The Zionist vision shared by Jews and Christians is an essential point of contact between them that helps to fill out our understanding of the interreligious relationships that developed during this period. The common cause that Jewish and Christian Zionists found in the Nazi era, despite the sometimes extraordinarily disparate reasons for their interest in each other, provides fresh insight into the pragmatic approach that Jewish Zionists were willing to take to find reinforcement, even in unlikely quarters. The willing cooperation between Christian Zionists and their

Jewish counterparts also sheds light on the faith and the mentality that prized Jewish particularity in some cases even more than Jews did themselves, and most certainly for different reasons.

Although the Christian figures that leaders of the Zionist Organization of America (ZOA) sought to enlist during the Nazi era were drawn largely from sympathetic Christian progressives, elements of American Zionist leadership also cast a wider net with an eye toward Christian counterparts from an earlier strata of support that predated the goodwill movement by over a quarter of a century. The connection that American Jews and Christians had already forged to fulfill the dream of a Jewish homeland, although limited in scope, established a precedent that Zionist Jewish leadership took steps to enlarge on as circumstances in Europe grew more desperate during the war years.

Several cooperative institutional efforts sprang up from both sides as a result. Operating under the direction of the Zionist Organization of America, the American Zionist Emergency Committee (AZEC) was tasked with the project of forming a beneficial alliance between Jewish Zionists and sympathetic Christians. The American Palestine Committee and the Christian Council on Palestine were organized to bring the plight of the Jews and the Zionist cause to the attention of the American public. The fruit of these various efforts culminated in a series of well-coordinated public protests, starting once again at Madison Square Garden, which provide another facet of developing Jewish-Christian relations in this era.

The history of Christian and Jewish Zionist ties was already well-established by the beginning of the twentieth century. These ties encompassed a period that saw dramatic conflicts within American Protestantism that realigned its balance of power not only in relation to itself but vis-à-vis society at large. These developments effected a profound shift in Jewish-Christian relationships that was already under way by the time Hitler came to power.

As William Hutchison has pointed out, at the start of the twentieth century a symbiotic relationship between the wielders of political and economic power and what came to be known as "mainline"

Protestant churches exerted a grip on American society to the point where their combined "quest for cultural authority became a matter of conscious intent."[1] As Robert Schneider points out, the coalescing mainline Protestant establishment had two broad purposes: to manifest Protestant unity and reform American society.[2]

The emergence of mainline churches as representatives of the Protestant establishment solidified with the establishment of the Federal Council of Churches in 1908. Although it included a somewhat diverse representation of American Christian traditions, in practice it was dominated by the larger denominations, including the northern Baptists, northern Presbyterians, Disciples of Christ, Congregationalists, and northern Methodists.[3] Constituted "to coordinate churches in wider service of America and Kingdom of God," the guiding lights of the FCC were determined not only to establish their influence in society in general but also to control the influence of other Christian denominations in particular.[4]

The FCC's first commissions reflected its early priorities: Christian educational resources, church and social services, temperance, family life, Sunday observance, and foreign and home missions. These seem no great departure from traditional American Christian faith and practice. But demonstrating a more liberal turn in the decades leading up to World War II, the FCC shifted from these more traditional concerns to more controversial issues of social justice that seemed to displace the priority of the "Great Commission." This shift in emphasis led some of the more conservative denominations, including the Southern Baptist Convention and most Lutherans, to steer clear of what they perceived to be a troubling new direction.[5]

By the mid-1920s, conservative efforts to turn mainline churches away from their liberalizing tendencies were largely a rearguard action. In what has been characterized as the "Great Reversal," fundamentalists who were alarmed at the direction the FCC's social activism was taking, which seemed to come at the expense of their priorities, turned away from political engagement.[6] At the same time, as fundamentalists retreated from the public square, the gaps along the Christian spectrum widened as liberal proponents of what became known as the "Social Gospel" seemed to place themselves at odds with the more traditional understanding of Christian salvation.

To the traditionalists, the goodwill movement was symptomatic of an alarming broader trend away from evangelism that had to be vigorously resisted. The progressives' rejection of the evangelization of "the chosen people" was bad enough, but it also seemed to signal a broader, troubling movement away from the church's primary mission. This difference in philosophy between Christian progressives and conservatives would only widen in the years to come.

With the progressives in ascendance by the 1930s, the widespread perception that mainline churches had come to represent not only the more reputable regions of Protestantism but also the image of American Protestantism itself was not lost on Jewish leadership in its search for allies. One result of this change in the inner dynamic of national religious power would be a recalibration in thinking among Jewish leaders regarding which Christians to cultivate in support of the Zionist cause. All but forgetting their earlier allies, Zionist Jewish leadership in the Nazi era sought Christian public support almost exclusively from among the liberal groups.

Nevertheless, the history of the unusual alliance between Christian and Jewish Zionists is vital to its continuing development in the Nazi era. That history is critical to an understanding of the strategies Jewish leaders used to reach out to this particular element of American Protestantism. The Jewish Zionist contacts with evangelical Christian sympathizers that developed in the decades prior to World War I are an essential part of the foundation on which the activities of Jewish-Christian cooperation in the Nazi era were based.

Recovering this history is important because the modern account of Jewish-Christian relations seems to suffer from a form of selective amnesia, or worse.[7] Although the term "Christian Zionism" does not appear until the twentieth century, the modern Christian movement for the return of the Jewish people to Palestine originated far earlier.[8] Beginning in Britain in the seventeenth century, it arose in connection with a heightened interest among some Christians regarding the events preceding the anticipated return of Jesus. The two most pertinent features of the Christian Zionist eschatological framework, given the central importance of the doctrine of the Second Coming, are the belief that the return of the Jewish people to the land of Israel is a precondition of Jesus's arrival and, hand in hand with this, their corporate repentance in surrender to the message of the Gospels. The unique and exalted role that Jewish people occupy in Christian Zionist interpretive understanding is the basis of a wholehearted and active commitment to their evangelization.

Beginning in the early nineteenth century, England played a prominent role in the evangelistic aspirations of early Christian Restorationists, as they were then termed, through the 1809 establishment of the London Society of Promoting Christianity among the Jews. The dual goals of restoring Jews to Palestine and of exposing them to the Gospel were given significant support in the English aristocracy by Lord Ashley Cooper, the seventh earl of Shaftsbury, who used his wealth to publicize the Restorationist message and his prestige to enlist the political support of Lord Palmerston, the minister of foreign affairs.[9] The foothold that Restorationism found in the highest echelons of British government was amply demonstrated by Lord David Balfour, an ardent Restorationist, who in his famous declaration of 1917 offered the first official endorsement of a Jewish homeland in Palestine by any Western power.

Christian Zionism had been given tremendous impetus through the dispensationalist premillennial teachings of Charles Nelson Darby (1800–1882), an Anglican cleric and leader of the Plymouth Brethren, and was well established in the United States by the latter part of the nineteenth century. The Restorationist agenda gained additional influence in America as a political force largely through the efforts of William Blackstone (1841–1935), an energetic missionary who in the 1880s helped to establish Chicago's Moody Bible Institute and was the founder and president of the Chicago Hebrew Mission.[10] Author of the widely read pamphlet "Jesus Is Coming" (1878), Blackstone subsequently visited Palestine in 1889 and found himself captivated not only by his visits to the biblical sites he had read of in the scriptures but also by the scattered communities of

Jews who had immigrated to Israel, sometimes in connection with their own messianic expectations. Blackstone returned to America more deeply convinced than ever that the restoration of the Jewish people to their ancient home held the key to the return of Christ.[11]

Blackstone's zealous attention to the program of restoring the Jews to Palestine expressed itself in practical action. As a result of his mounting concern for the increasing persecution of Russian Jewry, particularly after the assassination of Alexander II, Blackstone organized a conference in Chicago in 1890 of Christians and Jews to discuss not only the wording of a protest against the unjust treatment of Russian Jews but also Jewish restoration to their promised land. The Jewish participants, limited in number and theological scope to three Reform rabbis, were negative regarding Zionist aspirations but willing nonetheless to join Christians to voice their protest on behalf of Russian Jews.[12]

The persecution of Russian Jewry ignited Blackstone's initial spark for the Zionist cause. He embarked on a long life of political activism highlighted by the promulgation of two widely endorsed and well-publicized petitions for the creation of a Jewish homeland in Palestine, known as the "Blackstone Memorials." The first, published in 1891 and sent to President Benjamin Harrison and about a half-dozen reigning European monarchs, including Tsar Alexander III, responded directly to the difficulties of the Russian Jews. Answering its own question, "What shall be done with the Russian Jews?," it proposed the solution: "Why not give Palestine back to them again? Let us now restore to them the land of which they were so cruelly despoiled by our Roman ancestors."[13]

As a result of his perseverance, Blackstone amassed a list of 413 signatories, including the chief justice of the Supreme Court; the Speaker of the House of Representatives; a significant number of other politicians, including various congressmen and the mayors of New York City and Philadelphia; and prominent men of affairs like J. P. Morgan and John D. Rockefeller.[14] But this enthusiasm did not translate automatically into Jewish support. Widespread resistance to Zionism in the American Jewish community at that time resulted in significant opposition to the sentiments attached to Blackstone's petition, especially among Reform Jewish leadership.[15]

Although it created some sensational publicity, the first Blackstone Memorial had little if any impact on the situation of Russian Jews or in creating noticeable momentum toward prying Palestine away from the Ottoman Empire.[16] It did, however, alter the Jewish-Christian encounter, and it had a direct bearing on their relationship during the Nazi regime, for it brought Blackstone to the friendly attention of pre-Herzl Jewish American Zionist sympathizers, such as the New York City attorney Adam Rosenberg, president of Hovevei Zion (Lovers of Zion).[17] The tie between Blackstone and his Jewish counterparts was further strengthened by the formation of the Zionist Organization in 1897 at the First Zionist Congress in Basel, followed closely by the creation of the Federation of American Zionists (renamed the Zionist Organization of America in 1917) that same year. Through these organizations, Blackstone could now relate to official Jewish Zionist leaders in the United States, some of whom would remain active in the movement for years to come.

Among the earliest American Zionist advocates were Louis Brandeis and Stephen Wise. Their influence would be felt deeply over the following three decades. Both seem to have welcomed Blackstone's interest and friendship, as their correspondence demonstrates, particularly in Brandeis's case. During World War I, Brandeis took the reins of the Provisional Executive Committee for General Zionist Affairs. He and Blackstone then joined forces in 1916 to present Blackstone's second Memorial pamphlet to President Woodrow Wilson. At seventy-five years of age, Blackstone once again, petition in hand, went about gathering signatures, concentrating mainly on influential Protestant Christians, to support the creation of a Jewish homeland in Palestine. Much had changed in the twenty-five years since his first effort. By World War I, the Zionist movement had taken root in the United States and had become a force to be reckoned with within Judaism. Jewish nationalist aspirations now stood at the brink of the recognition that it would be accorded on the world stage through the 1917 Balfour Declaration announcing the British government's support for a national home for the Jewish people in Palestine.

The 1916 Blackstone Memorial drew significant support from American Protestant clergy and academics from major denominations, including some of the most respected churchmen in America, such as F. M. North, president of the FCC, and Robert Speer, general secretary of the Presbyterian Board of Foreign Missions. Blackstone also garnered support from evangelicals with whom he shared close theological affinity and from a number of rabbis, the most prominent of whom was Judah Magnes, chairman of the Kehillah of New York City.[18]

The 1916 Memorial adhered closely to the spirit of his earlier pamphlet. Beginning "WHEREAS, the civilized world seeks some feasible method of relieving the persecuted Jews," it went on to propose an international conference "to consider the condition of the Jews and their right to a home in Palestine" and petitioned for "such measures as may be deemed wise and best for the permanent relief of the Jews."[19] Signed and sealed by May 1916, the Blackstone Memorial was, however, never officially delivered to the White House. Once in the hands of Jewish leadership, the proper timing for a publicized official presentation never seemed to arrive. Even so, Stephen Wise did have the opportunity to show it to President Wilson in private, as his letter to Blackstone on June 30, 1917, indicates:

> Dear and Reverend Sir,
> I had the honor of presenting in informal fashion to the President at the White House yesterday a copy of your petition. The President accepted it, but he felt in agreement with Justice Brandeis that this was not the best time for public or private presentation thereof . . . We must therefore wait upon events and you will agree with me in permitting our friend and leader Justice Brandeis, to decide what is the most favorable hour in which to offer to the President the notable petition which you have made possible.
> With cordial greetings, believe me, faithfully yours,
> Stephen Wise[20]

The proposal for the international conference was the sticking point. It created a tangle of diplomatic difficulties that complicated the process by which decisions could be made by the United States and Britain. Wise and Brandeis had decided to exercise caution, and Wise, by referring to the Memorial as "your petition," perhaps unconsciously communicated his desire to distance himself from its contents.[21]

Although no record exists of any effect the petition had on official policy at the time, it seems evident that Wilson's own beliefs were aroused, for he confidingly spoke of himself at his meeting with Wise as "the son of a manse" who "should be able to restore the Holy Land to its people."[22] In light of Wilson's religious sensibilities, it is reasonable to assume that the Blackstone Memorial had played at least a part in wooing the Presbyterian president, who took his religion so seriously into the Zionist camp.[23]

Regardless of their efficacy, Blackstone's labors were acknowledged and greatly appreciated by Jewish Zionist leadership. In a letter dated May 8, 1916, the widely respected philanthropist Nathan Straus, founder of the R. H. Macy department store, expressed his fulsome thanks to Blackstone: "Mr. Brandeis is perfectly infatuated with the work you have done along the lines of Zionism. It would have done your heart good to have heard him assert what a valuable contribution to the cause your document is. In fact he agrees with me that you are the Father of Zionism, as your work antedates Herzl."[24]

There is no reason to doubt the sincerity of these words. Blackstone was an ardent backer and highly capable organizer who had worked with enormous energy over the course of many years to marshal support for the Zionist cause. It was no secret to his Jewish colleagues that his commitment to political Zionism existed primarily in service to his openly professed religious beliefs, which men such as Wise and Brandeis certainly did not share. Yet those with whom Blackstone developed such positive working relationships seem to have tolerated his often-expressed evangelistic fervor. A familiar figure at Zionist gatherings, to which he was warmly invited, Blackstone referred demurely to himself as "a stranger and a Gentile." Addressing a Zionist meeting on January 27, 1918, he declared:

> I wish all of you Gentiles were true Israelites in your religious life, and I wish all of you Jews were true Christians. I am and for over thirty years have been an ardent advocate for Zionism. This is because I believe that true Zionism is founded on the plan, purpose, and fiat of the everlasting and omnipotent God, as prophetically recorded in His Holy Word, the Bible.[25]

Blackstone was also forthright in his evangelistic hopes for his Jewish contacts in personal correspondence. In a letter dated March 19, 1917, Blackstone combined an effort to evangelize Brandeis with a request for his legal advice. Convinced that the sudden removal of Christians from the earth, known as "the Rapture," could now be mere months away, Blackstone was concerned to ensure that his sizable estate would be used to promote the Christian message to those left behind. If, as Blackstone inquired, Brandeis were still among the earthbound at that time, would he be willing to see to it? Blackstone also posed the question, "May I not ask you, dear Mr. Brandeis, that if such an event shall occur, will it not be convincing to you that I am holding a right understanding of Scripture prophecy?"[26] Blackstone's efforts at personal evangelism seem not to have alienated him from the Jews he so fervently wished to reach. His personal correspondence with them continued even after his Memorials had come and gone.[27]

The fact that Blackstone seems to have moved effortlessly between the Protestant establishment, as evidenced in the numerous influential names he gathered for the Memorials, and the fundamentalist movement, which more fully reflected his own beliefs, is a testimony to the force of his personality and the fact that at this earlier date the theological distance between liberal and conservative Christians was not as great as it would become during the following decades of the twentieth century and into the twenty-first. As well, the social influence of Protestant conservatives and liberals would change during the same period. As Yaakov Ariel notes, "the borderline between liberal and evangelical Protestantism was not yet fully defined.... After the modernist-conservative debate had reached its dramatic climax, evangelical Protestantism was no longer at the center of American civilization."[28]

The widening gulf that developed over the next two decades between conservative and liberal Christians would have a profound effect on the nature of Christian activism in the Zionist cause. Even so, the earlier efforts at cooperation among Jewish and Christian Zionists created a template that surely registered with Stephen Wise, since he would revisit it two decades later. The primary applicable lesson was that Jewish interests may be advanced under the cover of influential Christians, provided they are properly motivated.

The seeming demise of the fundamentalist movement as a public force and the mutual reinforcement between the Protestant establishment and the rich and powerful created a new force to define normative American identity and shape public morals. American Jewish Zionists turned to this hegemony in the early 1930s as they sought allies to help them fulfill their goal of establishing a Jewish homeland. The new alliances that Jewish leaders discovered among sympathetic Christian progressives would also affect the language in which they couched their aims, as circumstances dictated. If earlier Jewish conversation with Christian Zionists had needed to take into consideration their conservative Protestant biblical hermeneutics and their eschatological hopes, by the 1930s this was no longer the case. While this relieved Jewish conversation partners of one burden, it imposed yet another. New terms of engagement with progressive Christian Zionists were called for, but the question of what they might be remained to be answered.

Another complicating factor for Jewish and Christian Zionists alike was that by the time the war broke out, the British had turned a deaf ear to their demands. The decade that followed the Balfour Declaration was a time of disappointment and diminished expectation for the Zionist cause as England's initial hearty promotion of a Jewish homeland in Palestine faltered. British policy vacillated between

Jewish and Arab demands for a time, but unwilling to alienate itself from its Arab interests, England gradually shaped its policy to fit its own priorities.

The growing British and Arab antagonism to Jewish immigration to Palestine culminated in the Passfield White Paper of 1930. Emerging in the wake of an outbreak of Jewish-Arab violence the previous year, the White Paper was based on the findings of a committee headed by Walter Shaw and the investigations of John Hope-Simpson. These separate reports seemed to place the onus of blame for growing tensions in the region on increased Jewish colonization and influenced the writers of the White Paper to recommend restricting Jewish immigration and limiting Jewish land purchase.[29]

Although the provisions of the White Paper were softened the following year, England's attitude continued to be unfriendly and the Zionist leadership was jolted into fuller awareness that Britain was unreliable or worse. This decisive turn provided the impetus for the Zionist Organization of America to reengage with American Christians in two vital and deeply intertwined spheres: political and religious. The first renewed rapprochement by American Zionists with politically influential Christians after the Blackstone years came through the efforts of Emanuel Neumann (1893–1980), who brought about the formation of the American Palestine Committee in 1932 and later resuscitated it in 1941 after a period of dormancy. Its makeup would demonstrate the extent to which support for Zionism had penetrated the upper reaches of the American power structure and is a useful gauge of the degree to which highly placed Jewish leaders were able to enlist its sympathies.

The second avenue that Jewish Zionist leaders found to reengage with American Christians was to approach Christian clergy through the Christian Council on Palestine, which was organized in 1942 through the efforts of Rabbis Philip Bernstein and Milton Steinberg. The pains that Jewish leaders took to craft their message to these two organizations—the American Palestine Committee and the Christian Council on Palestine—reveals the Protestant powerbrokers' more general attachment to the concept of a Jewish homeland and the Christian clergy's more specific, theologically driven thinking. The activities of both groups provide insight into American Protestant perceptions of Jewish people and the challenges that assertive Jewish Zionist advocacy created for them.

Emanuel Neumann's Zionist commitment was rooted in his upbringing. Born in Latvia, his family immigrated to New York City a few weeks after his birth. His father, Sundel, was an ardent member of Hovevei Zion and the founder of a Hebrew-language religious school in the Williamsburg section of Brooklyn. From his early youth, the younger Neumann was involved in Zionist activities and organization. In 1914, at the start of World War I, Louis Brandeis brought him into the newly created Provisional Executive Committee for General Zionist Affairs and, thus, at age twenty-one, he began a long and useful career in the service of the Zionist cause.[30]

The 1930 White Paper rekindled the American Zionist leadership's motivation to cultivate support among non-Jews. In his autobiography, Neumann writes: "English pro-Zionist sentiment had eroded substantially and now seemed to be a slender reed to lean upon.... In these unhappy and critical circumstances I therefore returned [to] the idea of forming a pro-Palestine committee centered in Washington."[31] Although committed to travel abroad on Zionist business, Neumann tackled the task, as Blackstone had done almost two decades earlier, of garnering the endorsements of influential Protestant Americans.

He began with politicians and recruited an impressive number of congressmen, senators, and other important government officials. Thus encouraged, on December 17, 1931, he convened a meeting at the home of Judge Brandeis, who hosted a small but powerful group that included Senator William King of Utah; Senator Robert LaFollette Jr. of Wisconsin; Representative Hamilton Fish Jr. of New York; William Hopkins, the former city manager of Cleveland; and Assistant Secretary of State James Rogers. Vice President Charles Curtis was also present. The purpose of the gathering was to lay plans for an official launch of the American Palestine Committee on January 17, 1932 at the Mayflower Hotel in Washington, DC. Brandeis spoke of the importance of bringing influential non-Jews into visible solidarity with their cause.[32]

When the appointed day arrived, Vice President Charles Curtis presided over that event and a distinguished group of Jewish and non-Jewish leaders attended. One of the highlights of the evening came when Neumann read a letter from President Hoover that said, in part:

> I am interested to learn that a group of distinguished men and women is to be formed to spread knowledge and appreciation of the rehabilitation, which is going forward in Palestine under Jewish auspices, and to add my expression to the sentiment among our people in favor of the realization of the age-old aspirations of the Jewish people for the restoration of their national homeland.[33]

Hoover's expression of support succinctly summarizes the basis of general sympathy toward Zionism in establishment Protestantism at this time, with the caveat that the admiration for Jewish efforts to "rehabilitate" the land was congruent with a Western perspective of rehabilitation. But the phrase "age-old aspirations of the Jewish people for the restoration of their national homeland" originated in more than romanticism. Jewish Zionists began to rediscover how they could use the sympathetic, religiously based disposition of some Christians as a card played to advantage. For example, Neumann's recollection of a remark that William Hopkins made during that first meeting in 1931 shows the Zionists' growing awareness and appreciation of the powerful hold that the term "Zion" could exert on the religious imagination of even nominal Christians, provided the seed had been properly sown. As Neumann recalled, Hopkins opined, "[We] are most likely to gain supporters among a certain type of Christians who have been brought up on the Scriptures, and who have a sentimental and emotional attitude toward the Holy Land, which makes them predisposed to favor the Zionist cause."[34] Hopkins' astute thinking did not stop there, as he went on to warn the gathering to not depend too much on "politicians and liberals who have no such background and sentimental attachment to Palestine."[35]

His assessment of the level of staying power of both groups in support of the Zionist cause proved to be prescient.

The Mayflower Hotel event was deemed a great success, but despite this promising beginning, the American Palestine Committee almost immediately lapsed into inactivity. The most important reason for its lack of development was the absence of a guiding hand. Neumann, having launched this potentially quite useful lobby, departed the scene to pursue other matters. Senator William Borah of Idaho assumed the role of honorary chairman, but without a clear agenda and a determined hand to move things along, the group languished.[36] Stillborn as it may have been, the first incarnation of the American Palestine Committee served a purpose. Many of those who signed on to its principles would appear again when, in the following decade, under the direction of the American Zionist Emergency Committee, the American Palestine Committee was revived. At that time, it would be far more fully fledged.

The straitened circumstances of European Jewry had grown exponentially worse in the decade between the formation of the American Palestine Committee and its revitalization. If the 1930 White Paper had been an alarming hindrance to Zionists hoping to promote immigration to Palestine, by 1940 that avenue of escape had become a matter of life and death. Writing as a historian of the American Jewish Committee, Naomi Cohen assigns three phases to the intensifying persecution of Jews by the Nazi regime beginning in the 1930s. The first phase consisted of restrictions without the official sanction of violence, which lasted from 1933 to 1935. The second phase was the codification of the more draconian Nuremburg Laws in 1935. The third phase was the officially sanctioned, determined destruction of Jewish life in Germany as embodied by *Kristallnacht* on November 9, 1938, and the Jewish murders that commenced throughout Europe the following year with the German invasion of Poland and the start of World War II.[37]

The Zionist perspective recognized a fourth factor to Jewish oppression: the British recommitment to its policy of restricting Jewish immigration to Palestine at the worst possible moment. As stated in its White Paper of 1939, Jewish numbers would be limited to seventy-five thousand for the following five years, a policy that would have both immediate and far-reaching effects. This roadblock to Jewish escape from Europe was serious enough by itself. Combined with the Roosevelt administration's resistance to any meaningful relaxation in its closed-door immigration policy and the indifference to the plight of European Jewry displayed the previous year by world governments at the Evian Conference, this heavy blow further emphasized the vulnerability and complete isolation of Europe's Jews from the rest of the world.

As the violence in Palestine and the White Paper of 1930 had done at the beginning of the decade, the violence of *Kristallnacht* and the White Paper of 1939 galvanized American Zionists to seek support once again beyond familiar Jewish contacts. Neumann was particularly critical of the American Zionists' failure to cultivate allies among a wider circle, asserting, "[We] Zionists have isolated ourselves from the vital currents of American life and American thought. We have withdrawn into our shell."[38] Neumann set about to correct this. His efforts and those of his co-workers, which both drew on past tactics and significantly departed from them, succeeded in capturing the attention of the American public.

As America's importance as a Zionist stronghold became evident with the outbreak of hostilities in Europe, American Zionists experienced a renewed sense of urgency to find and to cement friendships with as many allies as they could find. This led to the formation of the Emergency Committee for Zionist Affairs (ECZA), which in 1942 was renamed the American Emergency Committee for Zionist Affairs (AECZA). Chaired by Stephen Wise, it was constituted as the "political arm of American Zionism." As such, its brief was to coordinate activities among its constituent bodies, including securing as broad a base of support as possible across the United States for a Jewish homeland in Palestine.[39] Toward this end, the able Neumann was tapped to head the Department of Public Relations, which was responsible for the formation of two significant subcommittees designed to foster Jewish-Christian relations: the American Palestine

Committee, formed in 1941, and the Christian Council on Palestine the following year. The activities and perspectives of these bodies provide insight into both the general attitudes prevailing among influential members of the Protestant establishment and the emerging changes in viewpoints among Christian theologians and clergy about Jews and Judaism that were stimulated by the crisis of the war.

With the encouragement and financial backing of AEZCA, Neumann went about reconstituting the American Palestine Committee.[40] Wise was particularly helpful in steering Neumann toward New York Senator Robert F. Wagner, who had proven to be such a valuable asset at the 1933 Madison Square Garden rally. Wagner agreed to head the committee once it was finally in a sufficient state of organization for its existence to be publicized. The inaugural dinner was held at the Shoreham Hotel in Washington, DC, on April 30, 1941. In Neumann's recollection, "The non-partisan gathering made up a good assortment, almost a galaxy of American political, civic, religious and cultural leaders."[41]

The evening's featured speakers included Senator Robert Wagner, already a forthright supporter of Jewish causes; Chaim Weizmann, president of the World Zionist Organization; and Senator Alben W. Barkley of Kentucky, who would go on to serve as vice president in the Truman administration. Barkley, whose interest in Zionism was inspired by his longtime friend and fellow Kentuckian Louis Brandeis, had visited Palestine in 1934 and was to return there on several occasions as an enthusiastic supporter of Jewish settlement.[42] Their carefully nuanced characterizations of Zionist aspiration serve as a reminder that the goal of statehood was not yet clearly articulated, and that although the Zionist cause had gained considerable traction since the war began, it was by no means a universal cause célèbre among American Jews.[43]

The speeches that evening differed widely in tone, from tentative to bold assertions of the Zionist agenda. Senator Barkley broached the Zionist aim in a most oblique way, noting that among the injustices taking place was a loss of "the right, which we thought had been firmly established, of the small nations to live their own lives," and linking this loss to America's hope for "a day when those small nations will again be restored to their rightful heritage."[44] Barkley went on to wonder out loud whether a place for the Jewish people could be found as the rights of the afflicted smaller nations were restored. This would be particularly fitting, he asserted, considering "the contribution of the Jewish genius" and "those great moral laws and principles which have come down to us from the days of the Hebrew prophets."[45] Finally, Barkley buttressed his case by directly linking the Zionist cause with distinctly American values, asserting "that the American people desire to see freedom reestablished for all the peoples on earth, and that the Jewish people shall again come into its ancient inheritance."[46]

Senator Wagner continued in the same vein, only in somewhat stronger terms: "Though they have been the target of the worst fury which the forces of evil have unleashed, the Jews have sometimes been omitted from the roster of small nations whose restoration is considered essential. There is no justification for such an omission."[47] While acknowledging that the committee by itself wielded no actual official powers, Wagner declared, "But it has access to a power which is enthroned above all these: the sovereign power of public opinion. It is our intention to speak to the conscience of America and of all Christendom."[48]

In Neumann's recollection, Weizmann made the strongest appeal of the evening. After making the case that Palestine, and Palestine alone, must be the location of what he phrased carefully as a Jewish "national home," he addressed the issue in the starkest possible terms. Appealing to the Christian sensibilities of his listeners, he declared, "The world has to choose between two things: between the Bible, or the Sermon on the Mount, and *Mein Kampf*, and there is no bridge between these two."[49]

The arguments to sway Christians to support the Zionist cause have both similarities and differences to those of the earlier Madison Square Garden rallies. These arguments, particularly those fashioned by progressives, repeatedly justify intervention on behalf of the Jews in the larger context of Western values. One striking similarity may be found in Barkley's argument, as echoed by Wagner, for Jewish statehood. If, in the larger context, the political fortunes of other small nations ought to be restored, so, too, should those of a Jewish nation. Even if it did not yet exist, the *concept* of Jewish statehood could be justified as part of a larger righting of wrongs inflicted on small nations generally. The basis of his argument is also remarkably similar to earlier appeals: Jewish contributions to civilization, Christendom's indebtedness to the prophetic tradition of the Hebrew scriptures, and the close affinity of Jewish values and aspirations to those of American patriotism. It too couched Christian appeals to support suffering Jews as a more general appeal to human rights and democratic values. To these, Weizmann added a final, telling argument, that Nazi goals are diametrically opposed to the values of the Bible and, more specifically (in a shrewd move from Weizmann), the teachings of Jesus.

Jewish Zionists began with an enormous advantage over other Jewish groups striving to enlist Christian assistance. Although they differed among themselves in their understanding of how to achieve a homeland, and even the meaning of Jewish nationality, they were focused on a goal that had already won the hearts and minds of substantial numbers of American Christians. Moreover, the ability to draw on this already existing reservoir of good will made a significant difference in the power dynamics of Jewish and Christian Zionist cooperation. The respectful and even worshipful reverence that some Christians had toward Zionist ambitions afforded Jewish leadership a more assertive relationship to their Christian partners than the American Jewish Congress and the American Jewish Committee could have. Because the American Palestine Committee and the Christian Council on Palestine operated under the auspices of the Zionist Organization of America, it was understood that they would function in a subordinate role. By contrast, the American Jewish Committee and the American Jewish Congress, even with Wise at its head, were much more in the position of supplicants.

Another advantage that the Zionist Organization of America enjoyed was that in a national atmosphere of stiff resistance to absorbing refugees, the notion of opening the doors to European Jews somewhere else was welcomed. Also, as a result of its relatively narrow agenda, Zionist efforts were less dispersed than those of the American Jewish Committee and the American Jewish Congress, which were more fully preoccupied with the immediate and widespread suffering of Europe's diverse Jewish population. Concerned as Zionists might be about the persecution of their fellow Jews, their gaze was already fixed on a future beyond the war.

Although Zionist activists might at times find common cause with other Jewish organizations regarding the rescue and relief of the Jewish people, Zionist cooperation would not come at the expense of their own raison d'être. As the suffering in Europe intensified, the groups that were prone to be unsympathetic to Zionist ideology, particularly the American Jewish Joint Distribution Committee, would see the need to bend in the direction of the Zionist goal to bring Jews to Palestine, even if they did so grudgingly and even if it was only for the practical reason that it was the least unfeasible avenue for Jewish survival.

Unlike its predecessor, the reinvigorated American Palestine Committee, now backed and funded officially by the Zionist Organization of America, became a useful tool with which to build support for the Zionist message across the country. From the first, it achieved an enormous amount of success in persuading politicians to lend their names to a variety of resolutions it formulated in favor of its program. One such effort was its widely circulated declaration, "The Common Purpose of Mankind," issued on November 2, 1942, on the twenty-fifth anniversary of the Balfour Declaration, which carried the signatures of 68 senators and 194 congressmen, including those of the majority and minority leaders of both houses.[50]

Zionist leadership was not only after politicians. The American Emergency Committee for Zionist Affairs, reorganized as the better-funded and more active American Zionist Emergency Council, formed a Community Contacts Committee, whose job it was to establish local emergency committees. These local cells worked at the grassroots level in cities and towns across the country to lobby local officeholders, organize petition drives, influence clergy, create speaking opportunities at local gatherings and fraternal organizations, such as the Rotary Club, Lions Club, and Kiwanis, and, in particular, to exhort members to go after more Christian support.[51] Local Zionist Organization of America and American Zionist Emergency Council chapters, where they could be found, backed the American Palestine Committee with funds, clerical services, and moral support.[52] The emergency committees were also instructed to send the names of likely Christian notables up the chain of command; they would then receive an invitation signed by Senator Robert Wagner to join the American Palestine Committee.[53] These well-coordinated efforts reached deeply and effectively into the American heartland.

Neumann set in motion another important outreach effort to the Christian world. The organization was dubbed the Christian Council on Palestine and operated in tandem with the American Palestine Committee, with which it would eventually merge at the end of the war. According to Neumann, the idea originated as a result of his frustration with what he felt was insufficient attention in the mainstream press to the present suffering of European Jewry and to the question of what the position of the Jews would be once the war was ended. For Neumann, this question was directly linked to the future of Palestine. He writes, "Articles appeared dealing with various postwar issues, but I found no word about the future position of the Jews and their problem—as if there was a conspiracy of silence despite Hitler and the Nazi Terror."[54] Determined to remedy the situation, Neumann brought the issue to the attention of Freda Kirchwey, editor of *The Nation*, who, seeing merit in Neumann's complaint, agreed to correct the omission. Understanding the influence that well-known Christians were capable of wielding, Neumann then approached Reinhold Niebuhr, already known for his Zionist sympathies, to see if he would make the Zionist case.

Niebuhr, whose standing at the Union Theological Seminary and whose published works on theology and ethics made him a Christian thinker of international stature, was a vociferous enemy of Nazism and, contrary to many Protestant isolationists and pacifists, a firm advocate of intervention. Writing in the first issue of *Christianity and Crisis*, the biweekly magazine he founded in February 1941, he defined the crisis as one in which the "most powerful state in Europe has sworn to destroy our North Atlantic civilization, and during 1940 has proved its ability to keep its word."[55] Niebuhr also spoke unambiguously against the persecution of the Jews along the same lines, as being part of a deadly threat both to Judaism and Christianity, which he linked directly, as many liberal Christian clergy had done, to the foundation of Western civilization. In the same issue, he asserted, "Nazi tyranny intends to annihilate the Jewish race, to subject the nations of Europe to the dominion of a 'master' race, to extirpate the Christian religion . . . and generally to destroy the very fabric of our western civilization."[56]

Yet in spite of his understanding of the Nazi threat to the religious values of civilization, which he shared with other progressive Christians, Niebuhr's thinking diverged sharply from his Christian liberal contemporaries who touted good will and tolerance as a panacea for prejudice. In contrast, he regarded such sentiments with deep suspicion. In "Jews After the War," a two-part article for *The Nation* that he penned in February 1942 in response to Neumann's request for greater publicity, he states, "American theories of tolerance in regard to race are based upon a false universalism which in practice develops into a new form of nationalism. . . . The majority group expects to devour the minority group by way of assimilation. This is a painless death, but it is death nevertheless."[57]

Niebuhr's determination to oppose what he considered to be a false utopianism, the real effect of which was to obliterate national identity, was the basis for his advocating the Zionist cause. Prejudice against the Jews, he maintained, will not be eradicated "by a little more enlightenment."[58] Therefore, noting that an Allied victory in itself would not solve the problems of the Jews, and that the bigotry of the majority toward minority groups is "a perennial aspect of man's collective life," he determined that the Jews deserved a place "where they are not 'tolerated,' where they are neither 'understood' nor misunderstood, neither appreciated nor condemned, but where they can be what they are, preserving their own identity without asking, 'by your leave' of anyone else."[59]

Niebuhr's effort, thought by Neumann to be the first of its kind published during the war years in the non-Jewish press, was well received and opened doors to other similar works that found footing in other periodicals and the press.[60] Encouraged by the positive attention that Niebuhr's article received, Neumann was further inspired to test the depth of current support among non-Jews, particularly Christian educators and clergy. He became aware of an informal group of Christians sympathetic to the Zionist cause that had already begun to mobilize. On December 16, 1942, the Jewish Telegraphic Agency carried the following story:

> A statement of principles declaring that "the destiny of the Jews is a matter of immediate concern to the Christian conscience" was issued last night by the National Committee of Christian Leaders, Clergymen and Laymen on Behalf of Jewish Immigration Into Palestine, following an all-day conference at the Hotel Pennsylvania addressed by Bishop Francis J. McConnell, Prof. Reinhold Niebuhr and others. The statement also pointed out that "of all lands available for post-war immigration of Jews, Palestine is the most practicable."[61]

Stephen Wise also spoke that evening, urging the free immigration of Jews to Palestine after the war. Seeing an opportunity to consolidate Christian support, Neumann wanted to draw it more completely into the orbit of the Zionist Organization of America, where it could be more firmly guided. Toward this end, Neumann tapped Milton Steinberg and his brother-in-law Philip Bernstein, both rabbis, to contact this group. As a result, the Christian Council on Palestine, "committed to the establishment of a Jewish commonwealth in Palestine in relation to the overall settlement in the post-war era," was established in December 1942.[62]

Friendships with Wise, whose connections stretched back to the earlier conservative Christian Zionists represented by Blackstone, seem to be a common link between members of the Council's leadership circle, such as its chairman, Dr. Henry A. Atkinson, a distinguished Congregational minister with a lengthy resume in ecumenically minded organizations; his fellow Congregational minister Carl Voss, who would later pen the highly laudatory *Stephen Wise: Servant of the People*; and Bishop Francis John McConnell, who had taken the podium alongside Wise at Madison Square Garden a decade earlier. One of the earliest issues they faced was to bring the Council more fully in line with ZOA's determination to form a Jewish state. Atkinson, who had evidently not thought much beyond opening Palestine more completely to Jewish immigration, was taken aback by the adamant support for nothing less than full Jewish statehood voiced by fellow committee members, including the biblical archaeologist William Foxwell Albright and Niebuhr.[63] In fall 1943, Rabbi Abba Hillel Silver, the newly elected co-chairman (along with Wise) of the American Zionist Emergency Council, Steinberg, and Bernstein seem to have persuaded Atkinson to their way of thinking, at least outwardly, that only statehood with "a self-governing Jewish majority could achieve justice for a harassed and homeless people."[64] Atkinson continued to work assiduously to assemble as many famous and well-regarded Christians as he could, bringing in other influential churchmen, including the Methodist Ralph Sockman of New York's Christ Church, and Daniel Poling, the editor of the *Christian Herald*.

Among this group, Poling was something of an outlier, a throwback to the religious sensibilities of the earlier coalition to whom Jewish Zionists had once turned, and who had served them so well. In addition to his work on the vigorously evangelical *Christian Herald*, Poling was the longtime president of the World Christian Endeavor Union, an international evangelistic society founded in Portland, Maine, in 1881. Despite his firm fundamentalist convictions, Poling was known to be willing to find commonality where possible with those of differing theological convictions.[65] In addition, he was a particularly valued Zionist advocate due to his influence and excellent reputation.[66] Unlike others on the committee, such as Niebuhr, who seasoned their arguments for a Jewish state with a large measure of political pragmatism, Poling's Zionist convictions were nourished first and foremost by his conservative interpretation of scripture.[67]

Like the American Palestine Committee, the Christian Council on Palestine actively lobbied for the Zionist cause at the national and local levels. On March 9, 1944, the two organizations cosponsored a "National Conference on Palestine" at the Statler Hotel in Washington, DC, while Congress was considering passage of the identically worded Wagner-Taft (SR 247) and Wright-Compton (HR 418) resolutions, which called on the United States to "use its good offices" to loosen immigration restrictions for Jews to Palestine "so that the Jewish people may ultimately reconstitute Palestine as a free and democratic Jewish commonwealth."[68]

The Christian Council on Palestine acted in a number of other ways. In 1943 it published a set of resolutions drawn up by its executive committee, one of which recommended that "America take the lead in helping to save millions of Jews from the horror created by the Nazi terror in Europe." It also pressed for the repeal of the 1939 White Paper and for the formation of an international commission to analyze Arab-Jewish problems in Palestine, and it lobbied to make "the outbreak of political antisemitism anywhere *prima facie* evidence of incitation of crime, and punishable as such under the law."[69]

As Voss recalled, Atkinson was so elated by his successful recruits that he said:

> You know, Voss, it really will be a matter of only a few months. Then you'll see: the British are going to be so impressed by that letterhead of ours with all those top-notch names on it that they will realize we really do have public opinion on our side. They'll grasp the fact that the Christian world will not allow the gates of Palestine to remain closed to the Jewish refugees left in Hitler's Europe. They'll open the gates of Palestine and refugees will pour in. We'll fold up the Committee and congratulate ourselves on a job well done.[70]

Shortly before he died some fifteen years later, Atkinson said ruefully to Voss, "How wrong I was, lad . . . how wrong I was."[71]

The growth of the American Palestine Committee and the Christian Council on Palestine, and their coordinated efforts in connection with the American Zionist Emergency Council are well attested in the literature of both organizations through the end of the war. If anything, Zionist activists increased their lobbying efforts after the war ended as the predicament of displaced Jewish persons in the devastation of postwar Europe came to light. Public events and demonstrations on behalf of Jews became more frequent, better coordinated, and better funded, especially under the leadership of Rabbi Abba Hillel Silver.[72]

Overall, Neumann's efforts on behalf of the Zionist Organization of America produced the broadest platform of Jewish-Christian cooperation during this period. That platform encompassed some of the most elite members of the US's political establishment, as represented by the American Palestine Committee, and some of the most influential Christian clergy of the day through the Christian Council on Palestine. Neumann understood how deeply the chord that Zionist aspiration struck in Protestant mentality resonated. During the war years, his organizational ability enabled him to mobilize Christian support not only among intellectuals such as Niebuhr but also within the Christian heartland in ways that others had not. Individuals such as Atkinson had reason to value the combined efforts of the Committee and the Council and the commitment of advocates such as Neumann and Niebuhr even if they did, in the end, badly miscalculate the extent of their ability to shape events.

For these individuals, one of the most painful reminders of their failure to convert the world to the Zionist point of view was that despite their efforts, Britain stubbornly persisted in maintaining its White Paper policy of 1939, restricting Jewish immigration to Mandatory Palestine. During the war, this policy resulted in thousands being turned away to die at sea and thousands more being apprehended and sent to Cyprus to languish in refugee camps. Britain's insistence on standing by this frustrating policy, and the circumstances surrounding its decision to do so even after the end of the war, further inflamed an already indignant Jewish community.

Although the war in Europe was over by mid-May 1945, the official cessation of hostilities made little difference at first to thousands of inmates in German concentration camps. Many for whom liberation came too late died from the effects of their prolonged ordeal. Others remained in the camps with nowhere to go, in desperate need. The finest example of the collective efforts of the American Zionist Emergency Council, the American Palestine Committee, and the Christian Council on Palestine to fire public imagination and generate action on behalf of displaced persons is the series of protest rallies they coordinated not long after the conclusion of the war. Beginning on September 30, 1945, these demonstrations were a direct response to an announcement that autumn by Britain's newly formed Labour Cabinet under the leadership of Clement Attlee that it would continue enforcing the 1939 White Paper provisions.[73] In effect, this signaled Labour's refusal to meaningfully address the subject of Jewish immigration to Palestine even in light of the horrendous situation faced by surviving European Jews in the aftermath of the war.

This was an especially stinging rejection, coming as it did after years of prevarication by the British government, which had pleaded that war pressures had prevented a more open immigration policy. Now the war was over and the pitiful remnant of European Jewry suffered still, unable to return to homes that had ceased to exist or had been stolen from them. They badly needed not only immediate relief but as many options as possible for resettlement. In addition, the disposition of the Attlee Cabinet was in direct contradiction to the earlier assurances of the Labour Party, which as recently as May 1945 had promised to scrap the provisions of the White Paper and open Palestine to unrestricted Jewish immigration.[74]

On September 23, 1945, when the Jewish Agency executive in London cabled news of this about-face to the American Zionist Emergency Council, it urged the organization to mobilize American public opinion to protest what it viewed as nothing less than betrayal. Spurred on by the immediacy of the problem, the Council sprang into action. Over the next month, it used every means at its disposal to rouse public indignation to pressure Britain to alter its stance, including coordinating a massive national letter-writing and cable campaign to President Truman and other notables through the American Palestine Committee's regional emergency committees that it had so patiently nurtured.[75]

Zionist leaders also turned to an old standby. They booked Madison Square Garden for the night of September 30, a scant week after the London cable arrived, for what they hoped would be a massive demonstration against British policy and for the creation of a Jewish commonwealth. Once more, it turned to the English and Yiddish press and other media to bring out the crowd and rally public opinion to its side.

Despite the haste with which it was organized, the Garden protest received plenty of advance publicity. Taking a page from Ben Hecht's aggressive playbook from two years earlier, to build attendance, the American Zionist Emergency Committee ran the provocative ad "AREN'T SIX MILLION JEWISH DEAD ENOUGH? PROTEST AGAINST THE BETRAYAL OF THE JEWISH PEOPLE." Advance publicity came especially from the *New York Journal-American*, whose publisher, William Randolph Hearst, had lauded Zionist aims on the editorial pages of his substantial newspaper empire on other occasions.[76] Ever mindful of good publicity for himself, Hearst did not hesitate to publish the letters of appreciation he received from Wise, Silver, and other Zionist leaders for the fine coverage the paper had given the event.[77]

On September 30, the *Journal-American* ran the front-page headline "GARDEN RALLY TONIGHT WILL DEMAND BRITAIN OPEN DOOR TO PALESTINE." This story briefly summarized the program and noted that pickets would be out in force at New York's British Consulate and British Empire Building, and that a mass prayer service organized by the Synagogue Council of America would take place at the Central Park mall.[78] This account of Britain's intransigence was made even more powerful by another, related scandal brewing in the press at the same moment over the mistreatment of European Jewish concentration-camp survivors by the US military forces that were charged with their care.

Directly beneath the front-page headline, the *Journal-American* ran a second story, "TRUMAN ACCUSES US FORCES OF MISTREATING REICH JEWS." This story told of a report released by President Truman, written by Earl G. Harrison, the US representative on the Intergovernmental Committee on Refugees, containing the shocking accusation that US forces in Germany and Austria "appear to be treating the Jews as the Nazis treated them." It described how Jews were still being housed in concentration camps while Germans enjoyed far better living conditions.[79] It revealed a letter from President Truman to General Eisenhower instructing him to evict Germans from their homes if necessary to remedy the situation, and reported that Truman had also appealed to Attlee to open Palestine to as many as one hundred thousand Jews who desired to emigrate.

That same day, *The New York Herald Tribune* ran a similar story on its front page. It also ran the full text of Eisenhower's letter and of Harrison's report, which described the high death rate of Jewish survivors and detailed the deplorable conditions, the lack of adequate food, and the fact that some had no clothing other than those they had been issued as inmates.[80] The *Daily Mirror* followed suit, as did the *Times*, and in numerous instances the stories linked the atrocious situation of the surviving Jews with Truman's appeal to the British to open up Palestine. Thus, the press conflated the facts of the deteriorating conditions of the remnant of Europe's Jews with what it portrayed as the practical solution of their resettlement in Palestine, which must have been enormously pleasing to the Zionist organizers of the rally.

After the sensational buildup in anticipation of the event, the *Journal-American* followed through with more on its front page on October 1, reporting the attendance of the rally at seventy thousand, almost twenty-five thousand more than that reported the same day by the *Herald Tribune*. The *Journal-American* quoted Dewey's speech most extensively under the heading "Dewey Leads Huge Rally in Appeal for Palestine." Dewey spoke forcefully, emphasizing the Jews' distress and their long-deferred hopes for succor: "There is one place they can call their own—their very own—and to which they should be entitled to go as their right to live in peace and security . . . to be free forever from all the horrors of the dreadful past. That place is Palestine, the homeland."[81]

Although quoted more briefly, Wise and Silver were given their say. Wise spoke hopefully, expressing confidence in the goodwill of the British people and the hope that Attlee would reverse course. The *Journal-American* also quoted Wise's earlier strong and evocative statement for Jewish statehood: "Justice to the Jew does not mean a Jewish ghetto in an Arab empire. The only status for a free and great people is the status of statehood."[82] Silver's words were even more direct: "You propose to continue to keep these doors shut against our survivors, after 6,000,000 of our people perished, for whose death your country is not without blame. You will not succeed, Mr. Attlee."[83]

The *Journal-American* also quoted Mayor Fiorello LaGuardia, by now a familiar face who had proven over the years to be a stalwart ally of his Jewish constituents in New York City not only in word but also in deed. In his speech, the mayor sarcastically derided the British for their eagerness to reap the benefits of US generosity during the war, only to turn their backs on the Jews. He declared, "Let Britain give just a little bit of lend-lease justice for the people of Palestine."[84]

Daniel Poling was also among the speechmakers whose comments the press reported. Reminding the Garden crowd of the Christian stake in the Zionist dream, he urged the British government to honor the Balfour Declaration. Poling proclaimed himself a Zionist, "not because Jews are Zionists, but because I am a Christian. In the present crisis, I could not remain silent without denying my conscience and without betraying my faith."[85]

As it had for earlier rallies, the *Times* gave generous front-page space to the September 30 proceedings. Its description of the overflow crowd that arrived early to fill every seat and then spilled out to the streets was almost identical to its coverage over a decade before. The *Times* quoted excerpts of speeches, with that of New York Governor Thomas Dewey receiving by far the most attention, followed by

Mayor LaGuardia, who called on Britain to facilitate the passage of one hundred thousand Jewish refugees to Palestine and on the United States to welcome another hundred thousand to its shores.[86] But Wise was not quoted directly at all, and Silver only briefly. Speaking in support of a Jewish state, Silver vilified statehood's opponents, who were booed and hissed by the audience, singling out the *Times*, as well as anti-Zionist fellow Jews, whom he characterized as "an insignificant number of our people who are afraid lest the establishment of a Jewish State will endanger their own comfortable existence here."[87]

Silver's pointed remarks about American Jews who did not agree with Zionist objectives were no doubt directed to the American Council for Judaism, which that same day had issued a statement critical of the mass meeting and the Zionists' position. It took particular umbrage at the assertion that political Zionism was the only valid position concerning the Jewish future. On October 1, the *Times* ran a story under the headline "Council for Judaism Objects to Implication That All American Jews Back Zionist Aims," which appeared on the same page as the inside coverage of the rally.[88] In a quote that appeared directly above Silver's remarks, the Council's president, Lessing J. Rosenwald, declared, "We reject all those self-appointed spokesmen who presume to make their partisan claims in the name of all Americans of the Jewish faith."[89]

Challenges to Silver's assertions from other quarters also made it into print. In addition to its piece on the opposition of the American Council for Judaism, the *Times* ran a story on the same page about a meeting between the American Jewish Committee leaders Joseph Proskauer and Jacob Blaustein and President Truman, at which the Committee leaders counseled Truman on humanitarian priorities: "Political questions relating to Palestine should be put aside and the humanitarian factor be placed foremost."[90] Clarifying their position, Proskauer and Blaustein stated that the American Jewish Committee position favored an international trusteeship of Palestine over the alternative option of statehood.[91]

To add to the controversy, the same issue of the *Times* carried a lengthy letter to the editor from Rabbi Morris Lazaron, whose credentials as a board member of the American Jewish Joint Distribution Committee and as a committee member of the National Conference of Christians and Jews lent substantial weight to his remarks. In the letter, Lazaron warned Zionist leadership against applying political pressure against Britain and the United States to realize its goals. He predicted not only violence in Palestine as a result of any ill-considered action but also a rupture in Jewish-Christian relations in the United States.[92]

Noting what he considered to be the Zionists' inappropriate tactics against Britain, he wrote disapprovingly, "It was also determined to exert similar pressure in Washington and to enter upon a vigorous and aggressive campaign among American Jews and Christians to organize public opinion behind these Zionist demands." He went on to warn, "Propaganda pressure will not better things. It will make them worse. It will involve the American Jewish community in Zionist pressure politics to the detriment of relations between Jewish and Gentile Americans."[93]

At first glance, an internal battle among Jews splashed across the pages of the press that threatened to widen the fissures among Jewish community factions and draw Christians into the fray was not the kind of publicity Jewish leaders of any stripe would have chosen. Many Jews would construe any public airing of internecine conflicts to non-Jews as unseemly and embarrassing. But there is another side to consider. The rhetoric, especially that of the Wise and Silver faction, dispensed with the self-censorship that had characterized many previous efforts by Jewish leaders to cultivate the good will of others. It is as though, after over a decade of anxiously and vainly hoping that world powers would render meaningful assistance to displaced Jews, something had snapped.

"An Open Letter to Mr. Attlee" is one example of the new freedom of mainstream Zionists to express themselves more candidly. The letter appeared in about forty newspapers nationwide, including the Yiddish press, in autumn 1945. Written by Wise and Silver and published by the American Zionist Emergency Council, it is a strongly worded condemnation of British immigration policy.

The letter blames not only Hitler for six million Jewish deaths but also the Christian world and democratic powers who gave Hitler the green light by their indifference and inaction. Polite requests for sympathy had at last given way to passionate demands for justice. There is a certain freedom that comes with a sense of irrevocable betrayal and shattered expectations. As a result, in the words of Doreen Bierbrier, at last "Jews could be openly preoccupied with themselves as Jews, without shame."[94]

The Yiddish press also took great pains to publicize the September 30 rally. In light of what had happened to European Jews by 1945, it is not surprising that the press addressed its highly invested readership with far more intensity and passion than did the English-language press. Speaking in its characteristically unfiltered way, *Morgn Frayhayt* issued an emotional summons to its readership: "Jewish hearts are grieving. Sunday let us all together cry out our anguish. We are calling not for just an ordinary meeting. We must give an answer to the war declaration of the British government."[95]

Frayhayt's coverage included details that the *Times* and other dailies had left out, such as the fact that the gathering derided not only the British government but the American State Department as well, with placards that read, "Is Attlee Another Chamberlain?" and "What Is Our State Department Doing for the Jews?" and "An End to Imperialistic Treason." Not surprisingly, it also quoted Jewish speakers far more extensively than had the English press. Dewey, to whom the English press had devoted the lion's share of the copy, was hardly mentioned, although Poling and LaGuardia's remarks were reported in an approving manner.[96]

Morgn Zhurnal also carried front-page coverage before and after the event. On September 28, it promised that the gathering would be "the greatest and most important Jewish demonstration New York has ever seen" and that "a number of prominent Americans will participate in the demonstration to express the true feelings of American society about Israel and the desire of the American government to take energetic steps."[97] In a separate editorial asserting the right of Jews to a homeland in Palestine, the paper boldly declared, "We do not come as supplicants. The world owes us a debt and we come to collect our debt."[98]

The day following the demonstration, *Morgn Zhurnal* carried by far the most complete and sensational coverage of all, including front-page headlines, stories, and lengthy quotes. A notable front-page subheading read: "Madison Square Garden Filled. Streets around the Garden Black with People. Governor Dewey and Mayor LaGuardia Rouse Meeting with Their Fiery Speeches. Famous Christian Leader, Dr. Poling, Declares America Will Be Friendly to England When It Keeps Its Word to the Jews. Proud Speeches From Silver, Wise . . . and Others."[99]

Forverts also did its part to turn out a good crowd beforehand in a piece on page 1 and a full-page ad on page 9 urging participation: "Only Many Thousands on the Streets Will Make an Impression."[100] The coverage of the meeting itself, beginning on the front page, stressed the enormous turnout that filled the arena and the surrounding streets with a crowd of fifty thousand.[101] The inside coverage included excerpts of the speeches and photographs of the chief speakers.

On October 2, *Forverts* also weighed in with an editorial. Ideologically opposed to Zionism, it stressed that although many of the thousands that attended the rally were Zionists, many thousands were not. What brought them together was the injustice of British policy and the pressing need to find a home for thousands of displaced European Jews. However, the Socialist *Forverts* also rebuked the Zionists for berating the Socialist-leaning British Labour Party so harshly, assuring its readers that many of its members were eager to ease immigration restrictions to Palestine for Jews. This great need, the editorial seemed to imply, should trump the ideological differences endemic to the Jewish community, at least for the moment.[102]

Regardless of the continuing ideological fault lines in the Jewish world regarding statehood, and Rabbi Lazaron's counsel about forcing Christians to choose sides, Christian Zionist sympathizers remained unstinting in their support. Although earlier in the year the American Palestine Committee and the Christian Council on Palestine had voted to form one organization, the American Christian Palestine Committee, and planned to operate more independently of the American Zionist Emergency Council, its membership was still firmly committed to Zionist goals and cooperative efforts with the Emergency Council.[103] In the weeks that followed the September 30 Madison Square Garden protest, these efforts took the form of a further series of conferences and demonstrations to pressure the British to abandon the White Paper policy.

On October 14–16, a meeting sponsored by the American Christian Palestine Committee of Greater New York drew about three hundred members of the Christian clergy and one thousand other non-Jews who demanded that Britain lift its immigration restrictions in Palestine against Jews and fulfill its pledge to form a Jewish state.[104] A little over a week later, on October 24, an astonishing crowd estimated at twenty-five thousand people attended an open-air rally in Madison Square Park sponsored by the American Zionist Emergency Council. Participants adopted a resolution, sent to President Truman and to Prime Minister Attlee, supporting efforts "to rebuild the national life of the Jewish people and to restore dignity and honor to the broken remnants of European Jewry."[105]

Two weeks later, the American Christian Palestine Committee sponsored a two-day International Christian Conference for Palestine in Washington, DC, which included like-minded representatives from other countries. Those present reiterated the demand for the removal of immigration restrictions against Jews who wished to enter Palestine and the repeal of anti-Jewish land laws in Palestine, and urged a quick decision by the United Nations to establish Palestine as a Jewish democratic state. Expressing opposition to the impending formation of the Anglo-American Commission of Inquiry, the conferees resolved, "The facts with regard to the tragic condition of the displaced Jews in Europe are established. . . . Further commissions of inquiry are unnecessary and obstructive. More dallying with the problem of rescue of these unfortunate people is intolerable to Christian men and women."[106]

Despite opposition from various quarters, the series of well-executed efforts by the American Zionist Emergency Council and the American Christian Palestine Committee that occurred in such rapid response to the unfriendly position of the British Labour government demonstrates the considerable measure of institutional cooperation among different sectors of American Jewish and Christian organizations that had been achieved by that time. Each group cherished its own multifaceted image of Zion. Spurred on by the gruesome destruction of European Jewish life during World War II and the indifference of those on whom they counted for relief, their combined efforts to finally bring about a Jewish state created levels of collaboration that were unknown up to that point.

In their efforts to achieve their goal, Jewish Zionists fought a battle on two fronts: Jewish and non-Jewish. First, Zionists had to reconcile the diverse definitions of nationality and the diverse motives at play among themselves. Then they had to make a case to skeptical fellow Jews who remained outside the fold that theirs was a more authentic choice than the ideology of "hereness" that urged Jews to strive to participate wherever they were. The rise of Hitler and the destruction of European Jewry made this a far easier task. Without a "here" in which to abide, the ideology of "hereness" no longer meant anything.

From the first, Zionist leaders well knew that they could not succeed without outside help. As they measured the formidable obstacles that stood between them and the realization of their ambition, leaders like Wise understood the urgent need for non-Jewish allies. By skillfully tapping into the religious imagination of Christians, they were able to find allies on this second front. In doing so, they found Christian advocates who held widely differing theological positions. Those of a more conservative, scripturally based viewpoint were drawn in by the vision of a future kingdom in which the destiny of Israel and the Jewish people played an integral part. To them, Jewish statehood, important as it might be, was only the penultimate stop along the way to a more permanent consummation.

Others, such as the "Christian realists," represented by Reinhold Niebuhr, were more deeply moved by the pressing needs of the present. Informed by considerations that seemed to be more fully grounded in ethics than in eschatological expectation, the progressive Christians who rallied to the Zionist cause did so from the commitment to a more abstract idea of justice. They were therefore able to embrace the Jewish cause in service to a higher, universal truth that owed more to natural law than to the Sermon on the Mount.

By the war's end, Christian members of organizations such as the Federal Council of Churches, the Christian Council on Palestine, and the Church Peace Union had already found some way to fold Jewish otherness into their world. American Zionist Emergency Council activists could make the same claim, having co-opted the influence of the progressive Christian Zionists they had wooed. Their success rested on the truth that much as progressives might claim to eschew the future proffered by their ever-more-distant fundamentalist cousins, they could not completely cast away the power of the past. The echoes of the Zion they had learned about as children in Sunday school still reverberated within them, more than they may have wanted to believe. The Jewish leaders who coveted their support read them well, and on this score perhaps knew them better than they knew themselves.

Conclusion

Madison Square Garden and the Staging of Judeo-Christian Values

The various interreligious alliances that American Jewish and Christian leaders formed amid the chaos of the Nazi era achieved a lasting afterlife following the war. Their efforts in the years up to and including the Nazi genocide resulted in a new form of encounter that repositioned the Jewish people in the landscape of American life. These prewar relationships became the platform on which postwar interfaith dialogue was founded. The effects that are still with us can be traced directly to the ties that were either formed or else significantly strengthened in the cauldron of those fraught times. Furthermore, the articulation of an American rationale for Jewish affirmation as opposed to Nazi negation contributed to an emerging American narrative of civic self-understanding that politicians and other oracles at times deployed practically word for word against the Communists during the ensuing Cold War.

Jewish-Christian cooperative efforts in the Nazi era certainly did not result in one overall pact or arrangement. For one thing, many Jews and Christians were not interested in or were opposed to embarking on such a project. Even among Jews and Christians who were willing to cooperate, sharp internal ideological and theological differences within each group precluded the possibility of such an inclusive venture. Rather, Jews and Christians occupying varying points along the spectrum of their respective traditions formed different coalitions depending on their common aims and their ability to enter and maintain productive working relationships. Some proved to be enduring, others not. In the end, the two most lasting partnerships among American Jews and Christians that have had the greatest lingering effect were those between politically progressive, theologically liberal Jews and Christians and those between Jewish and Christian Zionists.

In the first instance, the partnership forged between progressive elements of the Federal Council of Churches and Jewish leaders such as Rabbis Isaac Landman and Stephen Wise coalesced into what eventually became the National Conference of Christians and Jews. The initial goodwill efforts of the 1920s cohered around social issues, bringing Protestant, Catholic, and Jewish members together in what William Hutchison terms "constructive coalitions for commonweal."[1] The like-minded pool of participants in the goodwill movement provided many of the names on the roster of activists who later stood shoulder to shoulder at Madison Square Garden.

Among the highest priorities of the National Conference of Christians and Jews was opposition to antisemitism. The agreeable comfort level that Jewish and Christian activists found on this subject provided a basis for common action. Their combined efforts against antisemitism strengthened their mutual trust and laid the foundation for other arguments for a sympathetic and an inclusive attitude on the part of Christians toward the Jews. The proving ground for this newly emerging Jewish-Christian partnership arrived with the rise of Hitler.

Jewish and Christian progressives' growing mutual awareness in the Nazi era had a profound and continuing effect on the Jewish-Christian encounter. Among the most important aspects of this change was a new willingness on the part of progressive Christians to promote a more equitable footing for Jewish-Christian interreligious relations. One corollary of this shift in attitude that has had lasting consequences in interfaith dialogue moving forward was the progressive Christians' reevaluation of the goal of Jewish evangelization. Beginning with members of the Federal Council of Churches who left to join forces with willing Jewish leaders to form the

National Conference of Jews and Christians, Christians who wanted to create new pathways for Jewish-Christian dialogue had no choice other than to leave behind their earlier zeal to convert their Jewish neighbors.

The implications of this viewpoint had ramifications beyond the simple matter of Jewish-Christian relations. Choosing dialogue above proclamation signaled a growing trend in the Federal Council of Churches toward bifurcation over the issue of Christian evangelism that generally placed more theologically liberal members on one side and those who strenuously objected to what they viewed as a withdrawal from Christian duty and a denaturing of the gospel message on the other. The theological rift between liberal and conservative Christian traditions on this issue persists to this day and, if anything, has widened.

The trend toward respectful Jewish-Christian conversation, and the progressives' efforts to disown the Christian antisemitism that had intensified from the beginning of Hitler's rise to power, greatly accelerated in the war's aftermath. As the full scope of the destruction of European Jewry became more widely known, a cascade of self-accusatory statements regarding antisemitism and Christian indifference to the destruction of European Jewry came tumbling from a wide variety of denominations and ecumenical organizations. The first, commonly known as the "Stuttgart Declaration of Guilt," was adopted by the Council of Protestant Churches in Germany in October 1945. It declared, "With great anguish we state: through us has endless suffering been brought to many people. . . . We accuse ourselves for not witnessing more courageously, for not praying more faithfully, for not believing more joyously and for not loving more ardently."[2] Similarly, the Synod of the Evangelical Lutheran Church of Saxony published a "Declaration of Guilt toward the Jewish People" in April 1948. Reflecting on the role it played in the "forceful extermination of Jewry," it states, "It would be too easy to push off the responsibility to the ruling authorities of that time. . . . Insofar as racial hatred has been fostered among us or simply has been tolerated without vigorous resistance, we share in the guilt."[3]

The World Council of Churches also faced the subject of Christian antisemitism at its founding assembly in Amsterdam in 1948. Its Committee on the Christian Approach to the Jews declared, "We call upon all the churches we represent to denounce antisemitism, no matter what its origin, as absolutely irreconcilable with the profession and practice of the Christian faith. Antisemitism is a sin against God and man."[4] In the years that followed, other rejections of antisemitism and numerous expressions of amity toward Jewish people followed from the Catholic Church and various Protestant denominations, including Episcopalians, United Methodists, Baptists, and Mennonites.

These and other postwar asseverations of guilt, stimulated by the soul-searching of conscience-stricken Christians, had a considerable effect on their approach to Jews and Judaism. Sympathetic toward a people that was reeling from its losses, and ashamed of their role in contributing to that suffering, their awakened sense of moral responsibility fostered a desire for broader, more constructive interfaith relations. Such contrition created a chastened frame of mind, tamping down whatever remaining temptation this category of Christians may have had to strongly assert their religious claims.

One of the foremost theologians to argue for a hands-off evangelistic policy toward Jewish people after the war was Reinhold Niebuhr. Already a staunch and influential supporter of Zionism and a committed advocate for Jewish self-determination, Niebuhr's reservations about conversionary tactics directed toward Jewish people were conditioned by his sensitivity to the position of minorities generally and the history of the persecution of the Jewish minority by dominant Christian culture in particular. His 1957 address at a regular meeting of the faculties of the Jewish Theological Seminary and the Union Theological Seminary, "The Relations of Christians and Jews in Western Civilization," discouraged the evangelization of Jews because he thought such activity failed to recognize the right of the Jewish minority to refuse religious and ethnic assimilation and rather sought to draw Jewish people into what was to them "an oppressive majority culture."[5]

Moreover, from Niebuhr's theological viewpoint, Jews already existed as a valid covenant community and not merely as "an inferior form of religion such as must ultimately recognize the superiority of the Christian faith; and end its long resistance by capitulation and conversion."[6] For Jews who were willing to pursue closer relations, Niebuhr's pluralistic views were a welcome step away from the centuries-old triumphalist stance that negated the value of Judaism as a faith in its own right. As such thinking developed in the following decades, what has come to be known as "dual-covenant theology" allowed Christians who are so inclined to consider Jews to be included in their reading of Christian salvation history on the basis of the Jews' already existing covenant relationship with the God of Israel.

In the decades following World War II, some Jewish religious leaders responded in kind to such expressions of Christian affirmation of Judaism. Statements issued jointly with Christians, particularly through the International Conference of Christians and Jews, established in 1974, sought to foster greater interfaith understanding. Jewish groups have also published their own statements about the nature of interfaith discussion. Perhaps the most comprehensive expression of the possibilities and the limitations of Jewish-Christian discourse from the Jewish side is "*Dabru Emet* 'Speak the Truth': A Jewish Statement on Christians and Christianity," issued by the National Jewish Scholars Project in 2000. Bearing the signatures of over two hundred rabbis and prominent Jewish thinkers drawn from a broad spectrum of religious and intellectual life, it begins by acknowledging the sincerity of the church's remorse about its mistreatment of Jews and its mischaracterization of Judaism, welcoming its willingness to accept Judaism as a valid expression of God's enduring covenant with the Jewish people.

The document goes on to outline its vision of interfaith amity. While it acknowledges what it deems to be presently irreconcilable religious differences, its main thrust is to emphasize from a Jewish perspective the commonalities that both faith traditions can share and build on. These include worship of the same God, a compatible view of the authority of the Hebrew scriptures, and a shared set of moral precepts derived from them, as well as a shared responsibility to work both separately and jointly to bring about justice and peace. *Dabru Emet* also extends an olive branch to Christians regarding the Christian relationship to antisemitism and Nazism. While asserting that Nazism could not have found a foothold in a culture that had not already been steeped in antisemitism, *Dabru Emet* states unambiguously that "Nazism was not a Christian phenomenon" and expresses gratitude for the instances where Christians acted sacrificially to save Jewish lives at that time.[7]

Catholics also played a vital role in advancing interfaith relations in the decades following the war, particularly with the landmark *Nostra Aetate*, the Declaration on the Relation of the Church to Non-Christian Religions. Issued by Pope Paul VI in 1965, its purpose was to clarify the stance of the Catholic Church toward other world religions. In section 4, he addresses the church's relationship to Judaism. While maintaining that the church is "the new people of God," *Nostra Aetate* disclaims the ancient and stubbornly persistent accusation of deicide against all Jews, warns against speaking of them as "rejected and accursed," and emphasizes that the church "deplores all hatreds, persecutions, displays of antisemitism directed against the Jews at any time or from any source."[8]

In a statement issued in December 2015 in recognition of the fiftieth anniversary of the *Nostra Aetate*, a group of over two dozen Orthodox rabbis from Israel, the United States, and Europe acknowledged it as a noteworthy milestone in Jewish-Christian relations. Their statement "To Do the Will of Our Father in Heaven: Toward a Partnership between Jews and Christians" affirms Christianity as "neither an accident nor an error, but the willed divine outcome and gift to the nations."[9] The statement continues:

> We recognize that since the Second Vatican Council the official teachings of the Catholic Church about Judaism have changed fundamentally and irrevocably . . . Nostra Aetate and the later official Church documents it inspired unequivocally reject any form of antisemitism, affirm the eternal Covenant between G-d and

the Jewish people, reject deicide and stress the unique relationship between Christians and Jews . . . We appreciate the Church's affirmation of Israel's unique place in sacred history and the ultimate world redemption. Today Jews have experienced sincere love and respect from many Christians that have been expressed in many dialogue initiatives, meetings and conferences around the world.[10]

Important as they are, it must be emphasized that the constructive statements of Christians and Jews in postwar religious history did not arise in a vacuum. Their origins must be traced to the earlier changes that American Jewish and Christian leaders set in motion as a response to Hitler and his allies. They were the indispensable prelude to what came later. By ignoring the ties between Jews and Christians in the Nazi era, we acquiesce to the false premise that the interfaith movement in America was primarily a product of postwar Christian remorse. Mid-twentieth-century American Jewish-Christian relations are far richer and more complex than this one-dimensional image implies.

The other instance of closer Jewish-Christian ties that flourished during the rise and fall of Hitler is the enduring partnership that Jewish and Christian Zionists have continued to forge to this day. Over the years, that partnership has proven to be at least as durable as that of the Jewish and Christian progressives. The labors that Emanuel Neumann undertook beginning in 1932 with the formation of the American Palestine Committee, followed by the Christian Council of Palestine, bore fruit through coordinated efforts with the Zionist Organization of America and, finally, in the emergence of the fully fledged American Christian Palestine Committee.

As the war concluded and as Jewish agencies focused on the immediate needs of Jewish survivors, the American Christian Palestine Committee continued to press the British government to open the gates of Palestine to Jewish refugees. In addition, the Committee lobbied the United Nations Special Committee on Palestine on behalf of Jewish statehood, organizing meetings and petitions drives and using other means it had employed during the war years to publicize its agenda. This culminated in the crowning achievement of the Jewish political Zionists who, assisted by their American Christian partners, reached their goal of statehood at last.

When at last the UN General Assembly voted for partition on November 29, 1947, and Israel proclaimed statehood on May 14, 1948, the American Christian Palestine Committee faced the question of whether it should continue its existence, now that its goal had at last been reached. But as things developed, the newly established state of Israel encountered opposition not only from expected quarters but also from those who had so recently professed friendship for the Jews' during their darkest days. The Committee for Peace and Justice in the Holy Land, which boasted such illustrious members as Harry Emerson Fosdick of Riverside Church, deeply opposed Jewish statehood.

Fosdick, who had written the eloquent text of the petition protesting the treatment of German Jewry following the first Madison Square Garden rally in 1933, was joined on the Committee for Peace and Justice by Union Theological Seminary President William Sloan Coffin and Rabbi Morris Lazaron of the American Council for Judaism. Faced with such formidable opposition, the American Christian Palestine Committee decided its work was not yet over and continued its program of advocacy for the Jewish state until, as American opposition to Israel's statehood declined, it became increasingly irrelevant. Finally, pressed for funds, it dissolved in 1960s.

The decline of the American Christian Palestine Committee coincides to some extent with the decline of mainline Protestantism, which had once been a stronghold of influence, and the revival of the evangelical movement. As Caitlan Carenen notes:

> They were replaced by a new group of politically motivated Evangelicals who supported Israel not out of a sense of humanitarianism, Christian guilt, or political pragmatism—as had the mainstream Protestants before them—but for eschatological reasons ... Diplomatic support for Israel, built so carefully by members of the ACPC, would be replaced by a new kind of Christian Zionism.[11]

It is ironic that the evangelical Christianity that had been so active in the Jewish Zionist movement at the turn of the twentieth century was largely excluded from Jewish partnerships during the Nazi era. The ascendency of mainline Protestantism consigned evangelicalism to the periphery of American religious life; by the 1930s it was a quaint relic of America's religious past. But contrary to progressive expectations, the resurgence of political and social activism among evangelical Christians beginning in the 1970s and their concurrent commitment to Zionism provides a striking counterpoint to the liberal ideology of the interfaith movement that emerged in the postwar years. With the rise of the religious right in the 1970s, the once-discarded evangelical Christian Zionists are now an important political force in the United States whose geopolitical influence must be reckoned with.

Although they remained largely in the background in the Nazi era, religious conservatives had nonetheless played their part to shape the rhetoric deployed to sway public opinion toward the Jews at that time. They may not have been invited to share the platform with their more liberal co-religionists, but their conservative scriptural perspective tapped into dimensions of the Christian psyche left unmoved by the more general humanitarian arguments of the progressives. The conviction that the destiny of the Jewish people is the linchpin of all history remains axiomatic for many conservative American Christians, and the current beliefs of the religious right remain completely congruent with the Christian Zionism that began to emerge in the nineteenth century.

The creation of the Jewish state in 1948 provided an immeasurable degree of vindication for evangelicals, whose biblical hopes and reading of history were fulfilled. This was especially true for the dispensationalists, who drew a direct connection between the establishment of Israel and biblical prophecy. A restored Israel was an essential element of their eschatology. Although on some level they may have realized that the modern state of Israel was not the same thing as the long-awaited messianic kingdom, they responded like some Orthodox Jews who struggled at first to accept the existence of a secular Jewish state, but reasoned that the Lord's hand was in it somehow and that it would do until the real thing came along. Meanwhile, it could not be denied that Jews were returning to the Promised Land, as the Bible foretold.

In contrast to the postwar movement away from the evangelization of Jewish people among more liberal Christian traditions, the evangelical longing for Jewish conversion that had gone hand in hand with Christian Restorationism from its inception has increased in past decades. The current of dispensationalist thinking that undergirds Christian Zionist theology and its impetus is still a major element in Jewish evangelistic missions, such as the Chosen People Ministries, which after some initial hesitation has for some time incorporated full-throated support for the State of Israel into its commitment to bring Jewish people into its fold.

As this brief set of observations highlights, beginning with the goodwill movement, ideological fault lines appeared among Christian organizations in the United States over the question of how to approach interfaith relations. As progressive American Protestants responded to the challenges posed by Nazi Germany, they formed partnerships with like-minded Jewish leaders. This approach, in reaction to Nazi antisemitism, formed the foundation of the more fully formed postwar religious pluralism movement. Conservative Christians, alarmed by this trend, formed their own coalitions and continued to encounter Jews on the basis of their theological convictions.

The partnership between Jewish and Christian Zionists established before the turn of the twentieth century was the first close working political relationship between Jews and Christians in the United States. Beginning with the Blackstone Memorials, the dream of a Jewish homeland that energized both Jewish and Christian adherents provided a common ground that endures to this day. While Zionist leadership in the Nazi era could be confident in the powerful presence of mainline, progressive Christian leadership for support, this is no longer the case. It may be something of an understatement to say that in light of recent events in the Middle East, progressives' attitude in this fraught moment toward the State of Israel has soured considerably. As a result, Jewish Zionists have rediscovered the loyalty of conservative evangelicals. They now court them accordingly, like a disillusioned middle-aged lover returning to a long-lost sweetheart of his youth.

The anti-Nazi rhetoric honed at the Madison Square Garden protest meetings has likewise worn well for political purposes. In December 1952, President-elect Dwight D. Eisenhower expounded his understanding of the relationship between religious faith and the democratic system of the US government in a speech delivered to the Four Freedoms Foundation in New York. He said, "Our form of government has no sense unless it is founded in a deeply felt religious faith, and I don't care what it is. With us, of course, it is the Judeo-Christian concept, but it must be a religion that all men are created equal."[12] This statement has been parsed by many scholars who are intrigued by Eisenhower's not fully articulated understanding of the relationship between religion and American democracy. For my purpose, it is a logical last stop in the continuing saga of Jewish-Christian relations staged at Madison Square Garden at the junctures I have chosen.

Although the term "Judeo-Christian" had existed previously in biblical studies, at the time of Eisenhower's speech it had only been recently added to the lexicon of American political discourse as a descriptor for a set of modern societal values. Mark Silk posits that its appearance and increased usage came about in the 1940s as liberal Christians sought to counter the appropriation of the term "Christian" by various American antisemitic organizations, such as Father Coughlin's Christian Front.[13] K. Healan Gaston, in *Imagining Judeo-Christian America*, places its genesis even earlier, in the developing thought of theologians such as Paul Tillich, Reinhold Niebuhr, and Jacques Maritain in response to the emerging worldview posited by the term "totalitarianism," which soon came to stand for secularism or paganism. As Gaston notes, "Judeo Christianity gained far greater currency with the public after syndicated columnist Dorothy Thompson's audience of ten million read her words in late 1937 that Hitler's Germany had 'officially repudiated Judeo Christianity.'"[14]

Will Herberg, in his book on 1950s American religious life, *Protestant-Catholic-Jew*, offers an early reflection on Eisenhower's characterization of the Judeo-Christian American religious formulation. He identifies it as the settled, pluralistic expression of "spiritual ideals" and "moral values" that are congruent with "the American way of life."[15] Herberg does not specify what these loosely defined ideals and values are in the context of Eisenhower's remarks, other than to say that they refer to "the indispensability of religion as the foundation of society."[16]

Eisenhower's "Judeo-Christian concept" is more than merely a wooly notion of Americanism. Its origins involved too much passion for that to be the case. From the first of the Madison Square Garden events in 1933, America was treated to a ringside seat to witness the struggle through which the shapers of their times elevated the status of Jewish Americans as an indirect result of the persecution and destruction of European Jewry. From that time, Protestant and Catholic Christians found the rationale and the language to condemn the persecution of Jews not only as a religious failing but also, increasingly, as antithetical to the values of the civilized world, and in particular, to the values of American democracy.

Portraying Nazi antisemitism as antithetical to authentic American values posed another challenge to sympathetic politicians and Christian clergy. They were also forced, as never before, to condemn antisemitism at home and to embrace Jews as fellow Americans. In so doing, and acting as America's oracles, they prodded American Christian culture to accept Jewish religious difference on the condition that it could exist under the shared umbrella of a larger mutual understanding of American identity.

That identity incorporates the elements that emerged in the Nazi era as American political leaders and Christian clergy sought to articulate why Jewish persecution overseas mattered to them at home. The amalgam of religious reasons, such as Christianity's dependency on its Jewish roots and its faith-based ethical values, as well as an offended sense of civilized democratic values, proved to be a useful rhetorical weapon against Nazi ideology. As the United

States and the Soviet Union faced each other across the ruins of wartorn Europe, the same ideology, repackaged as the "Judeo-Christian tradition," likewise proved serviceable during the Cold War.

On the face of it, the term "Judeo-Christian tradition" is the epitome of post-Enlightenment Jewish aspiration in America. At last, the tiny Jewish minority achieved twin-billing with the dominant Christian culture that it has struggled to cope with for all these centuries. This apparent elevation is, however, not without its hazards. As Anita Norich points out, "The hyphen of hyphenated adjectives cannot be considered an equal sign. More often than not, the first part of 'Judeo-Christian' has implicitly or deliberately been subsumed by the second part. The hyphen is a gesture toward universalism, but is held together by an awkward balance of power."[17]

This dilemma brings me full circle, back to Sholem Asch. As I discovered in *One Destiny*, Asch was a great proponent of the "Judeo-Christian idea," which he placed in the shadow of a generalized messianic longing. That longing, he claimed, is the unique hallmark of authentic Jewish and Christian faith and the founding and uniting principle of Western civilization. On that basis, Jews hold a valid claim on an equal share in its construction. Yet the animosity that his ideas roused in both Christian and Jewish quarters makes for a cautionary tale. Harmony is not so easy to achieve. As long as the borders of religious difference are so vigilantly patrolled and the substance of faith so highly contested a matter, détente may be the most we can hope to attain.

NOTES

BIBLIOGRAPHY

INDEX

Notes

Introduction

1. Michael Wyschogrod, "Orthodox Judaism and Jewish-Christian Dialogue," unpublished essay, January 28, 1986. https://www.bc.edu/content/dam/files/research_sites/cjl/texts/center/conferences/soloveitchik/sol_wyscho.htm.

2. Abraham J. Peck, Mazal Holocaust Collection, and Jewish Institute of Religion, Hebrew Union College, eds., *Jews and Christians after the Holocaust* (Philadelphia: Fortress Press, 1982).

3. Carol Rittner and John K. Roth, eds., *From the Unthinkable to the Unavoidable: American Christian and Jewish Scholars Encounter the Holocaust* (Westport, CT: Praeger, 1997).

4. Jack R. Fischel and Susan M. Ortmann, *The Holocaust and Its Religious Impact: A Critical Assessment and Annotated Bibliography* (Westport, CT: Praeger, 2004).

5. William R. Hutchison, ed., *Between the Times: The Travail of the Protestant Establishment in America, 1900–1960* (New York: Cambridge Univ. Press, 1989), xii.

6. Bruce Lincoln, *Discourse and the Construction of Society: Comparative Studies of Myth, Ritual, and Classification* (New York: Oxford Univ. Press, 1989), 7.

7. Lincoln, *Discourse and the Construction of Society*, 8.

8. For the sake of clarification, I do not use the terms "Christian" and "non-Jewish" interchangeably. I identify Christians as clergy or others who are acting in their capacity as religious representatives. Non-Jews, though possibly Christians, are those people, such as politicians, who are speaking in other than a specifically religious capacity.

1. Setting the Stage

1. A lively account of the Bund's celebration of George Washington's birthday at the Garden on February 20, 1939, may be found in Arnie Bernstein, *Swastika*

Nation: Fritz Kuhn and the Rise and Fall of the German-American Bund (New York: St. Martin's Press, 2013), 172–98.

2. Leonard Dinnerstein notes that while prior to 1933 there were no official antisemitic organizations in America, by 1939 there were over one hundred, including the German American Bund, the Silver Shirts, the National Union for Social Justice, the White Knights of the Camellia, and the Christian Front. Dinnerstein, "Antisemitism in Crisis Times in the United States: The 1920s and 1930s," in *Antisemitism in Times of Crisis*, ed. Sander L. Gilman and Steven T. Katz (New York: New York Univ. Press, 1991), 219.

3. First organized in Philadelphia under the leadership of Louis Brandeis, Julian Mack, and Stephen Wise, the American Jewish Congress emerged to some degree in response to what was perceived to be the elitist ways of the American Jewish Committee. Philosophically divided over the question of Jewish national identity and contrary to the American Jewish Committee's anti-Zionist stance, the Congress affirmed a Jewish national identity that transcended national residence and could therefore embrace Zionism. See World Jewish Congress, *Unity in Dispersion: A History of the World Jewish Congress* (New York: Institute of Jewish Affairs of the World Jewish Congress, 1948).

4. Formed in 1906 in response to the Kishinev pogroms, the American Jewish Committee saw itself as the authoritative voice of American Jewish advocacy. Its stated mission was "to prevent infringement of the civil and religious rights of Jews and to alleviate the consequences of persecution." The Committee was staunchly anti-Zionist, discouraged the idea of Jewish national identity, and, particularly in America, eschewed the concept of a "Jewish vote." Naomi Wiener Cohen, *Not Free to Desist: The American Jewish Committee, 1906–1966* (Philadelphia: Jewish Publication Society of America, 1972).

5. Shlomo Shafir sums up the mood of the period succinctly: "Much of the support America had extended to defending human dignity in earlier times had been weakened due to post-Versailles disillusionment, and the interpretation of U.S. interests had become narrower. Indeed, the deepening depression, affecting millions of Americans, only added more hurdles to immigration under the quota system, and news from abroad made little impact on American consciousness." Shafir, "American Jewish Leaders and the Emerging Nazi Threat (1928–January 1933)," American Jewish Archives, 1979, https://sites.americanjewisharchives.org/publications/journal/PDF/1979_31_02_00_shafir.pdf, 182–83.

6. American policy toward European Jews in the period leading up to and including World War II has been the topic of extensive research. Among the most important works are Richard Breitman and Alan M. Kraut, *American Refugee Policy and European Jewry, 1933–1945* (Bloomington: Indiana Univ. Press, 1987); Henry L. Feingold, *Bearing Witness: How America and Its Jews Responded to the*

Holocaust (Syracuse, NY: Syracuse Univ. Press, 1995); Yehuda Bauer, *Jews for Sale?: Nazi-Jewish Negotiations, 1933–1945* (New Haven, CT: Yale Univ. Press, 1994); Yehuda Bauer, *My Brother's Keeper: A History of the American Jewish Joint Distribution Committee, 1929–1939* (Philadelphia: Jewish Publication Society of America, 1974); Saul S. Friedman, *No Haven for the Oppressed: United States Policy toward Jewish Refugees, 1938–1945* (Detroit, MI: Wayne State Univ. Press, 1973); David S. Wyman, *Paper Walls: America and the Refugee Crisis, 1938–1941* (Amherst: Univ. of Massachusetts Press, 1968); David S. Wyman, *The Abandonment of the Jews: America and the Holocaust, 1941–1945* (New York: Pantheon Books, 1984); Michael Beizer and Mikhail Mitsell, *The American Brother: The "Joint" in Russia, the USSR and the CIS* (New York: American Jewish Joint Distribution Committee, 2004); and Henry L. Feingold, *The Politics of Rescue: The Roosevelt Administration and the Holocaust, 1938–1945* (New Brunswick, NJ: Rutgers Univ. Press, 1970).

7. "For ninety-one straight issues beginning on May 22, 1920, Ford's weekly newspaper, the *Dearborn Independent*, purported to describe an international Jewish conspiracy based on the notorious antisemitic forgery known as *The Protocols of the Elders of Zion*." Jonathan D. Sarna, *American Judaism: A History* (New Haven, CT: Yale Univ. Press, 2004), 217.

8. "35,000 in Streets Outside Garden," *New York Times*, March 28, 1933.

9. Robert G. Waite, "'Raise My Voice against Intolerance.' The Anti-Nazi Rally in Madison Square Garden, March 27, 1933, and the American Public's Outrage over the Nazi Persecution of Jews," *New York History Review*, October 20, 2013, https://newyorkhistoryreviewarticles.blogspot.com/2013/.

10. Writing in 1924, Louis Marshall expressed his contempt for Hitler and his followers: "From all that I have been able to learn, the utterances of that unspeakable group are nothing more than sound and fury. . . . There is not the slightest likelihood that their plan will ever be carried out to the slightest extent." Cohen, *Not Free to Desist*, 147.

11. Shafir, "American Jewish Leaders," 180.

12. "German Fugitives Tell of Atrocities at Hands of Nazis," *New York Times*, March 23, 1933.

13. "German Jewish Mistreatment Confirmed, but Considered Virtually Ended, Says Hull," Jewish Telegraphic Agency, March 28, 1933.

14. "German Fugitives Tell of Atrocities."

15. "German Fugitives Tell of Atrocities."

16. "Churches Aid Fight against Hitlerism," *New York Herald Tribune*, March 23, 1933.

17. "Nazi Foes Here Calmed by Police," *New York Times*, March 20, 1933.

18. "Nazi Foes Here Calmed by Police."

19. Gurock, *America, American Jews, and the Holocaust*, 139.
20. "Protest on Hitler Growing in Nation," *New York Times*, March 23, 1933.
21. "O'Brien Reviews 4,000 Hitler Foes," *New York Times*, March 24, 1933.
22. "O'Brien Reviews 4,000 Hitler Foes."
23. "O'Brien Reviews 4,000 Hitler Foes."
24. The *Times* reported that individual merchants were severing commercial ties with Germany: "Protest on Hitler Growing in Nation."
25. "Reich Is Worried over Our Reaction," *New York Times*, March 23, 1933.
26. Robert Waite notes, "While the US Secretary of State moved cautiously and did not issue a formal protest to the Nazi regime, the German diplomatic mission in Washington kept track of the mounting opposition. The information it sent to the Foreign Office in Berlin was extensive and included a 17-page chronology of protests from labor organizations against Nazi measures as well as numerous letters of protest from across the nation. Already on March 17, a telegram from the New York City consular office to Berlin described a recent speech by Albert Einstein calling for protests against Hitler as filled with 'anti-German sentiment' which "dominated New York with Jews heavily dominating the press.' The slogan 'persecution of Jews' is similar to the Belgium atrocity propaganda [of the First World War] and is used as part of a broader, anti-German campaign." In Waite, "'Raise My Voice against Intolerance.'" Tragically, propaganda stories about German cruelty during World War I that were later proven to be false contributed to a reluctance, particularly among some church leaders, to give credence to the later reports of Jewish annihilation that proved to be all too true. See Gerald Lawson Sittser, *A Cautious Patriotism: The American Churches & the Second World War* (Chapel Hill: Univ. of North Carolina Press, 1997).
27. "Reich Is Worried," *New York Times*, March 23, 1933.
28. "Rabbis Stress Loyalty," *New York Times*, March 23, 1933.
29. "250,000 Jews Here to Protest Today," *New York Times*, March 27, 1933.
30. "250,000 Jews Here to Protest Today."
31. "250,000 Jews Here to Protest Today."
32. "'We Ask Only for the Right,' Says Wise," *New York Times*, March 28, 1933.
33. In contrast to Wise's intensifying concern about Hitler's rise to power, the Wise biographer Melvin Urofsky characterizes the opposition of the American Jewish Committee and B'nai B'rith to the public meetings as symptomatic of their unwillingness to face the looming disaster, which Urofsky claims had already manifested itself through their denial as late as January 1933 of the possibility that Hitler could ever come to power. Melvin I. Urofsky, *A Voice That Spoke for Justice: The Life and Times of Stephen S. Wise* (Albany: State Univ. of New York Press, 1982), 265.

34. Stephen S. Wise, *Challenging Years: The Autobiography of Stephen Wise* (New York: Putnam's Sons, 1949).

35. This represented a change of position for the American Jewish Committee, which, under the leadership of Louis Marshall in the 1920s, evidenced no interest in cultivating ties with Christians. As the founding member Cyrus Adler put it, "What possible advantage can come from making the Christian clergymen and Christian religious press acquainted with the organization of our Committee?" Cohen, *Not Free to Desist*, 21.

36. The biographer Melvin Urofsky portrays Wise's rising concern about German antisemitism as dating from the early 1920s and notes his alarm at the growing power of the Nazi Party, which had become the second strongest presence in the Reichstag by 1931 and the largest party by 1932, although Hitler failed to win the election that year. Urofsky, *A Voice That Spoke for Justice*, 260–62.

37. Stephen S. Wise, "Germany at the Crossroads," in *As I See It* (New York: Jewish Opinion Publishing Corporation, 1944), 84–85.

38. "Sorrows for Germany—Rabbi Wise Asks Christians to Bring Change of Heart," *New York Times*, March 20, 1933.

39. "Protest on Hitler Growing in Nation," *New York Times*, March 23, 1933.

40. "Protest on Hitler Growing in Nation." Curran's comments are surprising, given his steadfast support of the virulently antisemitic Catholic priest Charles Coughlin. Curran would grow increasingly antagonistic toward the Jews later in the 1930s and became vocally critical of America's war efforts in the following decade.

41. "Churches Aid Fight against Hitlerism," *New York Herald Tribune*, March 23, 1933.

42. "Jews of New York! Go to Madison Square Garden!" *Der Tog*, March 27, 1933.

43. "Attacks on Jews Scored in Pulpits," *New York Times*, March 23, 1933. The subject of widespread anti-immigrant sentiment among the general public, the unwillingness of the Roosevelt administration to risk the displeasure of the electorate, and the antisemitism of highly placed members in the State Department contributed to the enormous numbers of Jewish deaths in Europe has been well researched by scholars such as Breitman and Kraut, *American Refugee Policy and European Jewry*; Deborah E. Lipstadt, *Beyond Belief: The American Press and the Coming of the Holocaust, 1933–1945* (New York: Free Press, 1986); Friedman, *No Haven for the Oppressed*; and Wyman, *The Abandonment of the Jews*.

44. "Thanks Christians for Reich Protests," *New York Times*, March 27, 1933.

45. Tony Michels, *A Fire in Their Hearts: Yiddish Socialists in New York* (Cambridge, MA: Harvard Univ. Press, 2005), 217.

46. Waite, "'Raise My Voice against Intolerance.'"

47. The press's role in portraying the Nazi threat before and during the war is a matter of some debate. Deborah Lipstadt is particularly critical of the press in America for downplaying antisemitism as a fundamental principle of Nazism, and she especially criticizes *The New York Times* for burying stories of importance to Jewish interests in an attempt to not be seen as "too Jewish." However, the *Times'* front-page and inside coverage of the Madison Square Garden events I focus on were anything but buried. In these instances, the content of a number of the speeches the *Times* reported drew an early and unmistakable connection between antisemitism and the Nazi program. See Lipstadt, *Beyond Belief*, 15.

48. "35,000 in Streets Outside Garden."

49. "Ban on Jews Spreads," *New York Times*, March 28, 1933.

50. "55,000 Here Stage Protest on Hitler Attacks on Jews; Nazis Order a New Boycott," *New York Times*, March 28, 1933.

51. "Smith Calls for a World-Wide Fight on Religious Bigotry," *New York Times*, March 28, 1933.

52. "Smith Calls for a World-Wide Fight."

53. "Human Tolerance, Not Judaism, Is the Issue, Wagner Declares," *New York Times*, March 28, 1933.

54. "Human Tolerance."

55. "O'Brien Pays Tribute to Jewish Contribution to German Culture," *New York Times*, March 28, 1933.

56. "O'Brien Pays Tribute."

57. Urofsky asserts that Lehman told Wise that he had been warned from appearing at the Garden by Jewish representatives who feared negative results from such a public action. Urofsky, *A Voice That Spoke for Justice*, 265.

58. "Lehman Appeals to German People," *New York Times*, March 28, 1933.

59. "Lehman Appeals to German People."

60. "55,000 Here Stage Protest."

61. "55,000 Here Stage Protest."

62. "'We Ask Only for the Right.'"

63. "'We Ask Only for the Right.'"

64. "'We Ask Only for the Right.'"

65. "'We Ask Only for the Right.'"

66. "'We Ask Only for the Right.'"

67. "'We Ask Only for the Right.'"

68. "55,000 Here Stage Protest."

69. "Hitlerism to Be Condemned by Federation of Churches and Interfaith Committee," Jewish Telegraphic Agency, March 22, 1933.

70. Urofsky, *A Voice That Spoke for Justice*, 238–40.

71. Urofsky, *A Voice That Spoke for Justice*, 239.

72. Bishop Manning's criticism of Nazi Germany would earn him the disapprobation of the antisemitic *Der Sturmer*, which in December 1937 called him "a child of hell, a pseudo-priest and a wolf in sheep's clothing." William E. Nawyn, *American Protestantism's Response to Germany's Jews and Refugees, 1933–1941* (Ann Arbor, MI: UMI Research Press, 1981), 75.

73. "Bishop Manning Denounces Acts of Racial or Religious Persecution Anywhere in the World," *New York Times*, March 21, 1933.

74. "Bishop Manning Denounces."

75. "Bishop Manning Denounces."

76. "Bishop Manning Denounces."

77. "55,000 Here Stage Protest."

78. "55,000 Here Stage Protest."

79. "55,000 Here Stage Protest."

80. Susan Curtis, *A Consuming Faith: The Social Gospel and Modern American Culture* (Baltimore, MD: Johns Hopkins Univ. Press, 1991), 173.

81. "55,000 Here Stage Protest."

82. "55,000 Here Stage Protest."

83. Sittser, *A Cautious Patriotism*, 54–55.

84. "55,000 Here Stage Protest."

85. "Bishop Dunn Takes No Part in Meeting," *New York Times*, March 28, 1933.

86. "Boycott of Jews," Keesing's Contemporary Archives (1933),737.

87. Michels, *A Fire in Their Hearts*, 98–99.

88. Michels, *A Fire in Their Hearts*, 103.

89. Dovid Katz, *Words on Fire: The Unfinished Story of Yiddish* (New York: Basic Books, 2004), 328.

90. Michels, *A Fire in Their Hearts*, 79–80.

91. "Ab Cahan's Speech," *Forverts*, March 28, 1933.

92. "Appeals to German Women and the Whole World," *Forverts*, March 28, 1933.

93. "Dr. Margoshes Brings the Word," *Forverts*, March 28, 1933.

94. "'Day,' Yiddish Daily, Marks 15th Anniversary," Jewish Telegraphic Agency, November 12, 1929.

95. Circulation figures are difficult to ascertain. Yosef Gorny estimates the circulation of *Der Tog* during the war years as 55,000–57,000. Yosef Gorny, *The Jewish Press and the Holocaust, 1939–1945: Palestine, Britain, the United States, and the Soviet Union* (New York: Cambridge Univ. Press, 2012), 3.

96. David Passow, *The Prime of Yiddish* (Hewlett, NY: Gefen, 1996), 26–27.

97. "The Father of the Idea," *Der Tog*, March 28, 1933.

98. "Dr. Margoshes' Passionate Speech," *Der Tog*, March 28, 1933.

99. "The American Christian Religious World Lets Its Voice of Protest Be Heard," *Der Tog*, March 28, 1933.

100. "Jewish Women Protest," *Der Tog*, March 28, 1933.

101. Margoshes resigned after becoming embroiled in a controversy that developed as a result of his pre-election attack on Mayor LaGuardia for refusing to revoke a parade permit for the German-American Bund. "Dr. Margoshes Resigns as Editor of the Day in Election Controversy," Jewish Telegraphic Agency, November 14, 1937.

102. "Perspectives," *Der Tog*, March 28, 1933.

103. "Perspectives."

104. "Perspectives."

105. As Gennady Estraikh puts it, "Journalists of the *Morgn-Frayhayt* and the Forverts were involved in perennial ideological warfare with one another. The former accused its larger rival of promoting assimilation, accepting capitalism as an economic model, and preferring low intellectual pabulum." Gennady Estraikh, "Professing Leninist Yiddishkayt: The Decline of American Yiddish Communism," *American Jewish History* 96, no. 1 (2010), 34.

106. Estraikh, "Professing Leninist Yiddishkayt," 44.

107. Estraikh, "Professing Leninist Yiddishkayt," 47.

108. "Speakers at Garden Meeting from 'Jewish Congress' Speak Vague Phrases," *Morgn Frayhayt*, March 28, 1933.

109. *Morgn Frayhayt* would change its policy a decade later when Soviet Communists briefly reversed their position, stressing the wartime heroism of Russian Jews by creating the Jewish Anti-Fascist Committee, which sent the noted actor and director Solomon Mikhoels and the poet Itzik Feffer as ambassadors to raise funds for Russia and drum up support for a second front to fight the Germans. *Frayhayt* lent full support to their tour and to the Jewish Anti-Fascist Committee's American counterpart, the American Committee of Jewish Artists, Writers, and Scientists.

110. "Resolution Petitioning the Government of the United States to Make Vigorous and Proper Representations to the German Government to Put an Immediate Stop to These Barbaric Persecutions and to Restore to German Jewry Its Civil and Religious Rights and the Protection of the Laws of the Reich," March 28, 1933, in Proceedings of the Board of Aldermen and Municipal Assembly, The City of New York, quoted in Waite, "'Raise My Voice against Intolerance.'"

111. "1200 Clergymen Sign Nazi Protest," *New York Times*, May 26, 1933.

2. Broadening the Jewish-Christian Alliance against Nazi Germany

1. Jonathan J. Golden, "From Cooperation to Confrontation: The Rise and Fall of the Synagogue Council of America," PhD diss., Brandeis Univ., 2008, 39.

2. Lance J. Sussman, "'Toward Better Understanding': The Rise of the Interfaith Movement in America and the Role of Rabbi Isaac Landman," *The American Jewish Archives Journal* 34, no. 1 (1982), 45.

3. Isaac Landman, quoted in Sussman, "'Toward Better Understanding,'" 47.

4. Sussman, "'Toward Better Understanding,'" 46.

5. Matthew S. Hedstrom, *The Rise of Liberal Religion: Book Culture and American Spirituality in the Twentieth Century* (New York: Oxford Univ. Press, 2012), 147.

6. Urofsky, *A Voice That Spoke for Justice*, 194.

7. Urofsky, *A Voice That Spoke for Justice*, 197.

8. Urofsky, *A Voice That Spoke for Justice*, 195.

9. Yaakov S. Ariel, *Evangelizing the Chosen People: Missions to the Jews in America, 1880–2000* (Chapel Hill: Univ. of North Carolina Press, 2000), 22–23.

10. In an editorial published in March 1931, B'nai B'rith criticized John Mott's public commitment to Jewish evangelism, asserting that it was incompatible with the objectives of the goodwill movement. See Benny Kraut, "A Wary Collaboration: Jews, Catholics, and the Goodwill Movement," in Hutchison, *Between the Times*, 228, note 31.

11. Kraut, "A Wary Collaboration," 210.

12. Hoffman's commitment to Jewish evangelism did not preclude friendly relations with prominent Jewish figures. During the war, he began and maintained a friendship with Sholem Asch that would come to include John Mott. Asch's controversial views on Jewish-Christian relations and his bestselling New Testament historical fiction doubtlessly contributed to the spark of attraction.

13. Ariel, *Evangelizing the Chosen People*, 128–29.

14. Conrad Hoffman, *The Jews Today: A Call to Christian Action* (New York: Friendship Press, 1900), 2.

15. Hoffman, *The Jews Today*, 29.

16. Hoffman, *The Jews Today*, 50. Jacques Maritain would express the same view in *A Christian Looks at the Jewish Question*, published in 1939.

17. Hoffman, *The Jews Today*, 54.

18. Perhaps Hoffman was somewhat reassured by a letter he received on June 3, 1936, from Reform Rabbi Morris Lazaron, a member of the National Conference of Jews and Christians. Reflecting on the subject of evangelization, Lazaron wrote, "I can see no reason, however, why if conversionist activities are conducted

in the proper ways—that is without the temptation of candy and play and enticements of all sorts calculated to lure the immature—I say I can see not [sic] reason why anyone should demand that you cease such activities. I personally feel that I should like to spread my Judaism to the four corners of the earth . . . I do not see why either of us should not offer what we have for healing, inspiration and peace." "Letter from Morris Lazaron to Conrad Hoffman," June 3, 1936, Lazaron-Hoffman Correspondence, Manuscript Collection no. 71, Box 4, Folder 11, Morris S. Lazaron Papers, American Jewish Archives.

19. Hoffman, *The Jews Today*, 60.

20. The American Jewish Committee, minutes of the Executive Committee, March 19, contain a lengthy discussion about the inadvisability of joining the American Jewish Congress in cosponsoring the Madison Square Garden rally, characterizing similar demonstrations as "intemperate expressions of the masses." American Jewish Committee Archives.

21. Cohen, *Not Free to Desist*, 195–96.

22. American Jewish Committee, minutes of the Executive Committee, April 9, 1933. American Jewish Committee Archives.

23. The emergence of Butler's name at all, let alone as first choice, is curious given his inconsistent record of support for Jewish faculty and students during his lengthy tenure at Columbia. Regardless, the suggestion generated much interest among the American Jewish Committee leadership. The minutes of the Executive Committee meeting on April 19 record that Butler was "deeply interested in the situation," and although he declined a role on any committee, Proskauer and Strook assured the others that Butler was eager to promote their cause to the board of the Carnegie Endowment for International Peace, of which he was president. However, the Butler biographer Michael Rosenthal notes that he did not press very hard and failed even to obtain from them the gesture of an official statement of sympathy for German Jewry. Rosenthal, *Nicholas Miraculous: The Amazing Career of the Redoubtable Dr. Nicholas Murray Butler* (New York: Farrar, Straus and Giroux, 2006), 363.

24. American Jewish Committee, minutes of the Executive Committee, April 9, 1933.

25. American Jewish Committee, minutes of the Executive Committee, April 9, 1933.

26. American Jewish Committee, minutes of the Executive Committee, April 9, 1933.

27. American Jewish Committee, minutes of the Executive Committee, June 5, 1933. American Jewish Committee Archives.

28. Rendering aid to people who fell within the Nazi classifications of *Mischlinge*, "of mixed religious or ethnic heritage"; *Halbjuden*, "with two Jewish grandparents"; or "*Geltungsjuden*, a *Mischlinge* who embraced Judaism," would prove

to be an especially vexing problem. Often perceived as being neither fully Jewish nor fully Christian, and protected to some extent from the full brunt of Nazi persecution, they were the priority of no one. For a comprehensive treatment of their circumstances, see James F. Tent, *In the Shadow of the Holocaust: Nazi Persecution of Jewish-Christian Germans* (Lawrence: Univ. Press of Kansas, 2003).

29. American Jewish Committee, minutes of the Executive Committee, June 5, 1933.

30. American Jewish Committee, *The Jews in Nazi Germany: The Factual Record of Their Persecution by the National Socialists* (New York: American Jewish Committee, 1933), i.

31. "American Jewish Committee Issues 'White Book' Refuting Allegations of Hitlerites," Jewish Telegraphic Agency, June 19, 1933.

32. American Jewish Committee, *The Jews in Nazi Germany*, 92–99.

33. American Jewish Committee, *The Jews in Nazi Germany*, 14.

34. American Jewish Committee, *The Jews in Nazi Germany*, 15.

35. American Jewish Committee, *The Jews in Nazi Germany*, 16.

36. American Jewish Committee, *The Jews in Nazi Germany*, 16.

37. "Morris D. Waldman to Executive Committee," June 12, 1933, General Correspondence files June–July 1933, Box 2, Folder 5, American Jewish Committee Archives.

38. "Confidential Bulletin," June 29, 1933, General Correspondence files June–July 1933, Box 2, Folder 5, American Jewish Committee Archives.

39. "Confidential Bulletin," June 29, 1933.

40. "The Record of Nazi Ruthlessness against the Jews," *The Literary Digest* 116, no. 2 (July 8, 1933). The following five articles were also taken from this issue of *The Literary Digest*.

41. "The Jewish 'White Book,'" *New York Herald Tribune*, June 19, 1933.

42. "Not Quite Siegfried," *New York Times*, June 30, 1933.

43. "Hitlerism Indicted," *Evening Journal*, June 21, 1933. The *Evening Journal* notes, "This editorial appeared in all the other evening papers of the Hearst chain."

44. "Aryan Germany," *Lowell Courier-Citizen*, June 30, 1933.

45. "Jewish White Book," *The Nashville Tennessean*, July 8, 1933.

46. American Jewish Committee, minutes of the Executive Committee, November 1, 1933. American Jewish Committee Archives.

47. American Jewish Committee, minutes of the Executive Committee, November 1, 1933.

48. Cohen, *Not Free to Desist*, 26.

49. Elesha J. Coffman, *"The Christian Century" and the Rise of the Protestant Mainline* (New York: Oxford Univ. Press, 2013).

50. American Jewish Committee, *The Voice of Religion: The Views of Christian Religious Leaders on the Persecution of the Jews in Germany by the National Socialists* (New York: American Jewish Committee, 1933), 13.

51. Deborah Lipstadt characterized *The Century's* skepticism about reported atrocities against Jews as "an almost reflexive action." Lipstadt, *Beyond Belief*, 249.

52. J. William T. Youngs, *The Congregationalists* (Westport, CT: Greenwood Publishing Group, 1998), 189.

53. American Jewish Committee, *The Voice of Religion*, 13.

54. American Jewish Committee, *The Voice of Religion*, 17.

55. American Jewish Committee, *The Voice of Religion*, 12.

56. American Jewish Committee, *The Voice of Religion*, 11.

57. American Jewish Committee, *The Voice of Religion*, 12–13. The quote from the Tanakh is from the Jewish Publication Society edition.

58. John Bunyan Robinson, *The Epworth League: Its Place in Methodism: A Manual* (Cincinnati, OH: Cranston and Stowe, 1890), 3.

59. American Jewish Committee, *The Voice of Religion*, 18.

60. American Jewish Committee, *The Voice of Religion*, 18.

61. American Jewish Committee, *The Voice of Religion*, 18.

62. Ariel, *Evangelizing the Chosen People*, 123.

63. Ariel, *Evangelizing the Chosen People*, 126.

64. American Jewish Committee, *The Voice of Religion*, 28.

65. The Jewish Telegraphic Agency notes the antisemite accusations leveled at Belloc. Belloc's great friend G. K. Chesterton is quoted as saying, "In our early days Hilaire Belloc and myself were accused of being uncompromising anti-Semites. . . . I am quite ready to believe now that Belloc and myself will die defending the last Jew in Europe. Thus does history play its ironical jokes upon us." "Hitler Turns G. K. C., Once Anti-Semitic, into Friend of Jew," Jewish Telegraphic Agency, October 8, 1933.

66. Hilaire Belloc, *The Jews* (Boston: Houghton Mifflin, 1922), 3, 4.

67. American Jewish Committee, *The Voice of Religion*, 8.

68. American Jewish Committee, *The Voice of Religion*, i.

69. Mark I. Bernstein and Laurence R. Milstein, "Trial as Theater," *Trial* 33, no. 10 (1997), 64.

70. Johnson was among the first to respond to the 1933 crisis of ostracized German academics and artists, moving swiftly to obtain funds to gather a faculty of fifteen émigré social scientists to form the core of a "university in exile." See Gerald Steinacher and Brian Barmettler, "The University in Exile and the Garden of Eden," in *Reassessing History from Two Continents: Festschrift Günter Bischof*, ed. Martin Eichtinger et al. (Innsbruck: Innsbruck Univ. Press, 2013), 49–68.

71. "To Present Case against Hitler at Madison Square," *Jewish Telegraphic Agency*, January 30, 1934.

72. Fischer also notes that in keeping with the dramatic device of the mock trial, the sponsors went so far as to invite representatives of the German government to act as defendants. Not surprisingly, they refused and complained to the State Department that the trial was slanderous and should be stopped. Klaus P. Fischer, *Hitler & America* (Philadelphia: Univ. of Pennsylvania Press, 2011), 51.

73. "Nazis 'Convicted' of World 'Crime' by 20,000 in Rally," *New York Times*, March 8, 1934.

74. American Jewish Congress and Bainbridge Colby, *The Case of Civilization against Hitlerism, Presented under the Auspices of the American Jewish Congress at Madison Square Garden, New York, March 7, 1934: The Pleaders, Bainbridge Colby, Bernard S. Deutsch, Arthur R. Brown . . . [et al.]* (New York: R. O. Ballou, 1934), 3. Hereafter cited as *The Case of Civilization against Hitlerism*.

75. *The Case of Civilization against Hitlerism*, 10.

76. *The Case of Civilization against Hitlerism*, 106.

77. Robert Rosenbaum also notes that in the years that followed, LaGuardia's outspokenness would prove to be an embarrassment to the State Department and would incense the Third Reich, whose newspapers referred to him as a "dirty Talmud Jew," "Jewish lout," and "pimp," among other things. Robert A. Rosenbaum, *Waking to Danger: Americans and Nazi Germany, 1933–1941* (Santa Barbara, CA: Praeger, 2010), 165–66.

78. As antisemitic rhetoric in America intensified in the years approaching the US entry into the war, New York City saw a spike in acts of vandalism, such as attacks on Jewish businesses and synagogues. In response, the mayor established a special squad of detectives tasked with tracking down the perpetuators. LaGuardia also used the power of his office to annoy his political enemies. In one memorable incident, when the New York German Consulate applied for police protection against New Yorkers who were angry about Nazi injustices, LaGuardia thoroughly incensed them by assigning a forty-member contingent of the Jewish policemen's fraternal order to protect them. Diane Cypkin, "Mayor Fiorello H. LaGuardia and His Rhetoric vis-à-vis the Jews, 1934–1945," Proceedings of the New York State Communication Association 2010, article 5 (April 16, 2012), 81, https://docs.rwu.edu/cgi/viewcontent.cgi?article=1013&context=nyscaproceedings.

79. *The Case of Civilization against Hitlerism*, 111.

80. This resolution, opposed by members of the Roosevelt administration as potentially embarrassing to the president, never made it to the floor of the Senate. See Sheldon Spear, "The United States and the Persecution of the Jews in Germany, 1933–39," in Gurock, *America, American Jews, and the Holocaust*.

81. *The Case of Civilization against Hitlerism*, 55.

82. *The Case of Civilization against Hitlerism*, 42.
83. *The Case of Civilization against Hitlerism*, 103.
84. *The Case of Civilization against Hitlerism*, 52.
85. *The Case of Civilization against Hitlerism*, 84.
86. *The Case of Civilization against Hitlerism*, 86, 90.
87. *The Case of Civilization against Hitlerism*, 88.
88. *The Case of Civilization against Hitlerism*, 92.

89. In the end, Wise's boycott threats came to naught. At the American Olympic Committee convention in November 1933, Kirby moved that Americans boycott the games unless the Germans lived up to the spirit of their pledge to not exclude their Jewish athletes. Avery Brundage, who opposed the boycott, lent his considerable prestige as the head of the Committee to the cause of American participation, and in the end he carried the day. See Allen Guttman, "Berlin 1936: The Most Controversial Olympics," in *National Identity and Global Sports Events: Culture, Politics, and Spectacle in the Olympics and the Football World Cup*, ed. Alan Tomlinson and Christopher Young (Albany: State Univ. of New York Press, 2006), 65–82.

90. *The Case of Civilization against Hitlerism*, 65.

91. Conceived by the prominent Zionist Emanuel Neumann and formed in 1932, the American Palestine Committee was another example of Jewish outreach to Christian allies, this time to the potentially potent political force of Christian Zionism, which shall be examined more closely in the final chapter. See Paul Charles Merkley, *The Politics of Christian Zionism, 1891–1948* (Portland, OR: Frank Cass, 1998), 99–106.

92. *The Case of Civilization against Hitlerism*, 12.
93. *The Case of Civilization against Hitlerism*, 14.
94. *The Case of Civilization against Hitlerism*, 20.
95. *The Case of Civilization against Hitlerism*, 23.

96. Drawn into the affair by his friend and fellow attorney Edward Levenson, an American Communist living in Moscow, Hays was present at the trial, which took place over a three-month period beginning that September, and was permitted to collaborate with the defense. He did more than collaborate in the courtroom. Hays also gained public notice by helping to organize the London Commission prior to the trial. It was referred to as a "counter trial" and functioned, in effect, as a mock trial that succeeded in intimidating the Germans to the point that prosecutors devoted a significant amount of time attempting to rebut the exculpatory findings of the "counter court." In the end, only one of the accused was convicted, an unlikely outcome given the tenor of the times. See Louis Anthes, "Publicly Deliberative Drama: The 1934 Mock Trial of Adolf Hitler for 'Crimes against Civilization,'" *The American Journal of Legal History* 42, no. 4 (1998): 391–410.

97. *The Case of Civilization against Hitlerism*, 67, 69.

98. *The Case of Civilization against Hitlerism*, 70.
99. *The Case of Civilization against Hitlerism*, 32.
100. *The Case of Civilization against Hitlerism*, 35.
101. *The Case of Civilization against Hitlerism*, 114.
102. *The Case of Civilization against Hitlerism*, 116.
103. *The Case of Civilization against Hitlerism*, 115.
104. *The Case of Civilization against Hitlerism*, 122–35.
105. *The Case of Civilization against Hitlerism*, 137.
106. *The Case of Civilization against Hitlerism*, 142.
107. "Protest on Nazis at Garden Tonight," *New York Times*, March 7, 1934. The article concluded with a list of about fifty supporting organizations drawn from labor unions, Zionist and other Jewish groups, sympathetic German associations, and the ecumenical Fellowship of Faiths.
108. "Nazis 'Convicted' of World 'Crime' by 20,000 in Rally."
109. "Nazis 'Convicted' of World 'Crime' by 20,000 in Rally."
110. "Nazis 'Convicted' of World 'Crime' by 20,000 in Rally."
111. "Nazis 'Convicted' of World 'Crime' by 20,000 in Rally."
112. "Leaders See Peril to Civilization," *New York Times*, March 8, 1934.
113. "Ohio Group Protests," *New York Times*, March 8, 1934.
114. "Mayor, Smith Predict Nazi Downfall," *New York Evening Journal*, March 8, 1934.
115. "Garden Rally Indicts Hitler; Asks Boycott," *New York Herald Tribune*, March 8, 1934.
116. "'Great Peoples'—Trial against Hitler Tomorrow Evening at Madison Square Garden," *Forverts*, March 6, 1934.
117. "Hitler Trial Today in Madison Square Garden," *Forverts*, March 7, 1934.
118. "'Socialists Fight for Human Freedom,' Declares Ab Cahan," *Forverts*, March 7, 1934.
119. "'Socialists Fight for Human Freedom,' Declares Ab Cahan."
120. "Hitler Stands Today before the Judgment of the Entire Civilized World," *Der Tog*, March 7, 1934.
121. "Sharp Sword of Boycott Must Be Wielded—Demands Seabury, Prosecutor of Trial," *Der Tog*, March 8, 1934.
122. "American Jewish Congress Greets Hitler with Verses from the New Testament," *Morgn Frayhayt*, March 6, 1934.
123. "Garden Filled for Trial over Hitlerism," *Morgn Frayhayt*, March 8, 1934.
124. Dorothy V. Jones, *Toward a Just World: The Critical Years in the Search for International Justice* (Chicago: Univ. of Chicago Press, 2002), 145.

125. Anthes, "Publicly Deliberative Drama," 394.

126. "Convict Hitler by Providence Jury in Temple," *Jewish Telegraphic Agency*, March 23, 1934.

3. Differing Jewish Responses to the Final Solution in 1943 and Their Effects

1. John M. Efron, *The Jews: A History* (Upper Saddle River, NJ: Pearson Prentice Hall, 2009), 360.

2. Efron, *The Jews*, 361.

3. Efron, *The Jews*, 361.

4. Anita Shapira, *Land and Power: The Zionist Resort to Force, 1881–1948* (New York: Oxford Univ. Press, 1992), 161.

5. Efron, *The Jews*, 361.

6. Mitchell Cohen, *Zion and State: Nation, Class, and the Shaping of Modern Israel* (New York: B. Blackwell, 1987), 154.

7. Louis Rapoport, *Shake Heaven & Earth: Peter Bergson and the Struggle to Rescue the Jews of Europe* (Jerusalem: Gefen Publishing House, 1999), 15–17.

8. Rapoport, *Shake Heaven & Earth*, 35.

9. Monty Noam Penkower, "Vladimir (Ze'ev) Jabotinsky, Hillel Kook-Peter Bergson, and the Campaign for a Jewish Army," *Modern Judaism* 31, no. 3 (October 2011), 339.

10. Penkower, "Vladimir (Ze'ev) Jabotinsky," 341.

11. In a letter to Willem Visser 't Hooft, Secretary General of the World Council of Churches, Riegner recalls that the first report of the Final Solution reached him at the end of July 1942 and he communicated the information to Wise at the beginning of August. According to Wise's recollection, the information originated from a highly placed anti-Nazi German industrialist whom he left unnamed. Johan M. Snoek, *The Grey Book: A Collection of Protests against Anti-Semitism and the Persecution of Jews Issued by Non-Roman Catholic Churches and Church Leaders during Hitler's Rule* (Assen, Netherlands: Van Corcum, 1969), 274; and Wise, *Challenging Years*, 274.

12. Yehuda Bauer, "The Holocaust, America, and American Jewry," *Israel Journal of Foreign Affairs* 6, no. 1 (2012): 65.

13. The sardonic tone of the ad is that of its author, Ben Hecht. Wise's sympathetic biographer Melvin Urofsky complains, "Bergson and Hecht, under no discipline, could issue the most outrageous statements, well aware that they would face no reprisals." Urofsky, *A Voice That Spoke for Justice*, 336.

14. Haskel Lookstein, *Were We Our Brothers' Keepers?: The Public Response of American Jews to the Holocaust, 1938–1944* (New York: Hartmore House, 1985), 137, 138.

15. Lookstein, *Were We Our Brothers' Keepers?*, 138.

16. Bergson's close colleague, Samuel Merlin, has a different recollection of how the March 1 rally came about. Responding to Lucy Dawidowicz's article "Indicting American Jews," *Commentary*, June 1, 1983, Merlin asserts that Wise, aware of Bergson's plans for the March 8 pageant, felt compelled to push ahead with plans for "Stop Hitler Now." As proof, he cites the official minutes of a meeting of the Planning Committee of the American Jewish Congress, held on December 29, 1942: "The matter of holding a Madison Square Garden meeting was revived, in view of the information that the Jewish Army Committee is planning a similar meeting." Merlin also cites David Wyman's assertion: "Apprised of the army committee's plan to hold a demonstration at Madison Square Garden on March 9, Wise and the American Jewish Congress quickly decided to schedule a March 1st meeting at the same location." Merlin, "Letter to the Editor," *Commentary*, September 1, 1983.

17. Lookstein, *Were We Our Brothers' Keepers?*, 139.

18. Nonetheless, a meeting of its Joint Emergency Committee, the American Jewish Committee adopted all eleven points of the resolution of the March 1 rally, objecting only, in light of its anti-Zionist position, to the phrase "Jewish Homeland" in paragraph 6. "Joint Emergency Committee Minutes," March 4, 1943, American Jewish Committee Archives.

19. "Huge Rally Demands Rescue of Doomed Jews," *New York Times*, March 2, 1943.

20. "Huge Rally Demands Rescue."

21. "Huge Rally Demands Rescue."

22. "Huge Rally Demands Rescue."

23. "Huge Rally Demands Rescue."

24. "Church Peace Union Charter," in Charles S. Macfarland and the Council on Religion and International Affairs, *Pioneers for Peace through Religion, Based on the Records of the Church Peace Union (founded by Andrew Carnegie) 1914–1945* (New York: Fleming H. Revell, 1946), 192ff.

25. Karen Kennedy Sinclair, *The Church Peace Union: Visions of Peace in Troubled Times* (New York: Garland, 1993), 129.

26. The Church Peace Union would enthusiastically support the establishment of the United Nations. Sinclair, *The Church Peace Union*, 130–33.

27. Sinclair, *The Church Peace Union*, 130–31.

28. "Huge Rally Demands Rescue."

29. "75,000 Sought Entrance to New York Meeting Protesting Nazi Massacres of Jews," Jewish Telegraphic Agency, March 3, 1943.

30. "Proposals for Aiding Jews," *New York Times*, March 2, 1943.

31. "Huge Rally Demands Rescue."

32. "Help Save the Remnant of Jews in Europe," *Morgn Zhurnal*, February 28, 1943.

33. "Help Save the Remnant of Jews in Europe."

34. "To All Jewish Storekeepers in New York," *Morgn Zhurnal*, March 1, 1943.

35. "Mourning and Protest Meeting Today in Madison Square Garden," *Forverts*, March 1, 1943.

36. "Come to the Garden Today to Save the Millions of Nazi Victims," *Morgn Frayhayt*, March 1, 1943.

37. Moshe Duchovny, "Lament of Jews Carries Over on to New York Streets," *Morgn Zhurnal*, March 2, 1943.

38. Meyer Nuremburger, "The Eternal Light Has Lit the Darkened Jewish Faces," *Morgn Zhurnal*, March 2, 1943.

39. Robert N. Rosen, *Saving the Jews: Franklin D. Roosevelt and the Holocaust* (New York: Thunder's Mouth Press), 267.

40. "Joint Emergency Committee Minutes," March 15, 1943, American Jewish Committee Archives.

41. "Memo on Instructions for How to Coordinate Mass Demonstrations," March 22, 1943, American Jewish Committee Archives.

42. "Our Churches and the Jews in Europe," *Federal Council Bulletin*, April 1943, 15.

43. "Our Churches and the Jews in Europe."

44. "Christians' Concern Found to Be Rising," *New York Times*, May 2, 1943, 40.

45. "Christians' Concern Found to Be Rising."

46. "Federal Council of Churches Proclaims 'Day of Compassion' for Persecuted Jews," Jewish Telegraphic Agency, April 26, 1943.

47. In the same letter to Willem Visser 't Hooft from Riegner, cited above, Wise asked Cavert to use the occasion of Cavert's visit to Geneva at the beginning of September 1942 to clarify for him that it was truly the extermination of the Jewish people that the Nazis had determined, which Cavert was able to ascertain. Snoek, *The Grey Book*, 274.

48. "Federal Council of Churches Proclaims 'Day of Compassion.'"

49. "Day of Compassion Praised By Rabbis," *New York Times*, May 2, 1943.

50. "Day of Compassion Praised By Rabbis."

51. M. Todd Bennett, *One World, Big Screen: Hollywood, the Allies, and World War II* (Chapel Hill: The Univ. of North Carolina Press, 2012), 97–98.

52. James J. Kimble, *Mobilizing the Home Front: War Bonds and Domestic Propaganda* (College Station: Texas A&M Univ. Press, 2006), 5.

53. Ben Hecht, *A Child of the Century* (New York: Simon and Schuster, 1954), 518.

54. "Guide to the Fight for Freedom Committee Records 1941–1947," Fight for Freedom Committee, Special Collections Research Center, University of Chicago Library.

55. Ichiro Takayoshi, *American Writers and the Approach of World War II, 1935–1941* (New York: Cambridge Univ. Press, 2015), 1–3.

56. It is difficult to take Hecht seriously on this point, considering the numerous rallies and publications I have already touched on. One might ask, where had he been for the last ten years? Hecht, *A Child of the Century*, 519.

57. Hecht, *A Child of the Century*, 520–21.

58. Hecht, *A Child of the Century*, 520.

59. Hecht, *A Child of the Century*, 552.

60. Rafael Medoff, "The Pageant That Alerted America about the Holocaust," in *The Jews Should Keep Quiet: Franklin D. Roosevelt, Rabbi Stephen S. Wise, and the Holocaust* (Philadelphia and Lincoln: The Jewish Publication Society of America and the University of Nebraska Press, 2019), 148–50.

61. Medoff, "The Pageant That Alerted America."

62. Hecht, *A Child of the Century*, 564. According to Medoff, Wise strenuously resisted Jewish groups acting apart from his sphere of influence, characterizing those with whom he disagreed as dissidents who had no right to speak on behalf of Jewish people. Wise also lamented the fact that Bergson and Hecht had such success recruiting Hollywood celebrities to join them. Doubtlessly this sense of competition was heightened by the fact that Wise was busy organizing "Stop Hitler Now." Seymour Rossel, *The Holocaust: The World and the Jews, 1933–1945* (Millburn, NJ: Behrman House, 1992), 136.

63. One ought not ignore Hecht's loyalty to Bergson personally and to his group as factors contributing to his sour view of American Jewish leadership generally, and particularly that of Stephen Wise, of whom he speaks quite disparagingly. For alternative views of Bergson's activities, the degree of his importance, and the impact of his allies on the ongoing critique of Wise's leadership in these crucial years, see Dawidowicz, "Indicting American Jews"; and J. J. Goldberg, "Debunking a Libelous Myth of American Jewish Indifference to Looming Holocaust," *Jewish Daily Forward*, December 20, 2013.

64. According to her biographer, Stella Adler served on the show's production committee and played a prominent role in securing the services of her brother, Luther, and his wife, Sylvia Sidney. Sheana Ochoa, *Stella!: Mother of Modern Acting* (Milwaukee, WI: Applause Theatre & Cinema Books, 2014), 170.

65. "'We Will Never Die' Stirs Packed Garden," *Daily Mirror*, March 10, 1943.

66. According to Hecht, Stephen Wise brought a delegation to Dewey in an attempt to call off "The Day of Mourning," characterizing Hecht and his cohorts as

"dangerous racketeers who are bringing terrible disgrace on our already harassed people." Hecht, *A Child of the Century*, 575, 576.

67. Ben Hecht, *We Will Never Die: A Memorial Dedicated to the 2,000,000 Jewish Dead of Europe* (New York: Committee for a Jewish Army of Stateless and Palestinian Jews, 1943).

68. Gerold Frank, "'We'll Never Die' Seen by 40,000," *New York Journal-American*, March 10, 1943.

69. Frank, "'We'll Never Die' Seen by 40,000."

70. "'We Will Never Die' Stirs Packed Garden."

71. "'We Will Never Die' Stirs Packed Garden."

72. Michael Williams, "40,000 Jam Garden, Mourn Martyred Jews," *Brooklyn Daily Eagle*, March 10, 1943.

73. Arthur Pollock, "Jews Whom Hitler Put to Death Remembered at the Garden," *Brooklyn Daily Eagle*, March 10, 1943.

74. "Huge Audience in Madison Square Garden Expresses Grief and Distress Over Nazi Slaughters," *Forverts*, March 10, 1943.

75. "More Than 40 Thousand People at Pageant in Garden about Slaughter of Jews," *Morgn Frayhayt*, March 11, 1943.

76. "Thousands of Jews at the Mass Memorial," *Morgn Zhurnal*, March 10, 1943.

77. John F. Sears, *Refuge Must Be Given: Eleanor Roosevelt, the Jewish Plight, and the Founding of Israel* (West Lafayette, IN: Purdue Univ. Press, 2021), 4, 5. Sears paints a detailed picture of her lengthy participation in Jewish causes, which extended beyond the war to her committed advocacy for Jewish statehood.

78. Eleanor Roosevelt, "My Day, April 14, 1943," *The Eleanor Roosevelt Papers Digital Edition* (2017), https://www2.gwu.edu/~erpapers/myday/displaydoc.cfm?_y=1943&_f=md056470.

79. Medoff, "The Pageant That Alerted America."

80. Sears, *Refuge Must Be Given*, 131–32.

81. Quoted in Sears, *Refuge Must Be Given*, 131–32.

82. Robert Skloot, "We Will Never Die: The Success and Failure of a Holocaust Pageant," *Theatre Journal* 37, no. 2 (1985), 179.

83. Skloot, "We Will Never Die," 179.

84. Hecht, *A Child of the Century*, 576.

85. Hecht brought back many members of the previous company, including Luther Adler, who directed; Kurt Weill; and Paul Muni, who, along with Adler's half sister, Celia, a major star in Yiddish theater, played the leads. The cast of veterans was also joined by the newcomer Marlon Brando, who played the part of David, a distraught Holocaust survivor who delivers an impassioned, pro-Zionist speech at the end of the play.

86. *"We Will Never Die,"* Official Souvenir Program (Los Angeles: Hollywood Bowl, 1943).

87. *"We Will Never Die,"* Official Souvenir Program.

88. Jacques Maritain, *A Christian Looks at the Jewish Question* (New York: Longmans, Green and Co., 1939), 42.

89. The anti-Christian tone of this piece shocked the American Jewish Congress so much that it begged Hecht to delay its publication because of possible anti-Jewish backlash. Colin Shindler, *The Rise of the Israeli Right: From Odessa to Hebron* (Cambridge: Cambridge Univ. Press, 2015), 220.

90. Richard Breitman and Allan J. Lichtman, *FDR and the Jews* (Cambridge, MA: The Belknap Press of Harvard Univ. Press, 2013), 170.

91. Later that month, on November 24, Bergson's groups ran another ad in the *Times*, again written by Hecht, "HOW WELL ARE YOU SLEEPING?" in which he asks, "Is There Something You Could Have Done to Save Millions of Innocent People—Men, Women and Children—From Torture and Death?" Marc Lee Raphael, *The Columbia History of Jews and Judaism in America* (New York: Columbia Univ. Press, 2009), 304.

92. Breitman and Lichtman, *FDR and the Jews*, 218.

4. Jewish and Christian Zionists

1. Hutchison, *Between the Times*, xii.

2. Robert A. Schneider, "Voice of Many Waters: Church Federation in the Twentieth Century," in Hutchison, *Between the Times*, 97.

3. Schneider, "Voice of Many Waters," 102.

4. Robert Schneider notes that although fewer than one-third of the thirty-three denominations that formed the FCC in 1908 were mainline, nine establishment churches accounted for 61 percent of the FCC's 413 official delegates. Schneider, "Voice of Many Waters," 103.

5. Schneider, "Voice of Many Waters," 102.

6. George M. Marsden, *Fundamentalism and American Culture: The Shaping of Twentieth Century Evangelicalism, 1870–1925* (New York: Oxford Univ. Press, 1980), 91.

7. A thoroughly dismissive view of the role of dispensationalist Christians in the American Zionist movement that also tars them with the broad brush of antisemitism may be found in Göran Gunner and Robert O. Smith, eds., *Comprehending Christian Zionism: Perspectives in Comparison* (Minneapolis: Fortress Press, 2014), 242.

8. As Stephen Spector notes, the term "Christian Zionist" does not seem to have appeared before 1903 and was used sparingly until it achieved wide usage in

the 1990s. Stephen Spector, *Evangelicals and Israel: The Story of American Christian Zionism* (New York: Oxford Univ. Press, 2009), 2.

9. Yaakov S. Ariel, *An Unusual Relationship: Evangelical Christians and Jews* (New York: New York Univ. Press), 2013, 83.

10. David A. Rausch, *Zionism within Early American Fundamentalism, 1878–1918: A Convergence of Two Traditions* (New York: E. Mellen Press, 1979), 264.

11. Ariel, *An Unusual Relationship*, 85.

12. Ariel, *An Unusual Relationship*, 86.

13. Quoted in Yaakov S. Ariel, *On Behalf of Israel: American Fundamentalist Attitudes toward Jews, Judaism, and Zionism, 1865–1945* (Brooklyn, NY: Carlson Publishing, 1991), 70–71.

14. Ariel, *On Behalf of Israel*, 55.

15. Shalom Goldman, *Zeal for Zion: Christians, Jews, & the Idea of the Promised Land* (Chapel Hill: The Univ. of North Carolina Press, 2009), 25.

16. Ariel, *On Behalf of Israel*, 78–79.

17. Ariel, *On Behalf of Israel*, 72.

18. "Jews in America: Chicago as Incubator of American Zionism," Jewish Virtual Library, https://www.jewishvirtuallibrary.org/chicago-as-incubator-of-american-zionism.

19. "Jews in America."

20. "Stephen Wise to Rev. William E. Blackstone," June 30, 1917, Blackstone Correspondence, Collection 540, Box 7, Folder 6, Billy Graham Center Archives.

21. Wise, in his own account of meetings with President Wilson during this period to press for the Zionist cause, makes no mention whatsoever of either Blackstone or the Memorial. Wise, *Challenging Years*, 186–89.

22. Wise, *Challenging Years*, 186–87, quoted in Ariel, *On Behalf of Israel*, 90.

23. Paul Merkley notes that both Brandeis and Wise later made their thinking known that "what guaranteed the victory for the Zionists was not their greater skill in playing the political and diplomatic game, but their success in appealing to Woodrow Wilson's biblically based Christian faith." Merkley, *The Politics of Christian Zionism*, 88–89.

24. "Nathan Straus to Rev. William E. Blackstone," May 26, 1916, Blackstone Correspondence, Collection 540, Box 7, Folder 6, Billy Graham Center Archives.

25. Quoted in Rausch, *Zionism within Early American Fundamentalism*, 267–68.

26. Louis D. Brandeis, *Letters of Louis D. Brandeis, Volume IV, 1916–1921, Mr. Justice Brandeis*, ed. Melvin I. Urofsky and David W. Levy (Albany: State Univ. of New York Press, 1975), 278.

27. In the course of lengthy correspondence with Jewish leaders, including Brandeis, Straus, and Jacob de Haas, that is replete with verses from both the Hebrew Bible and the New Testament, Blackstone wrote ardently of his devotion

to Zionism and urged his Jewish correspondents to accept Jesus. Blackstone Correspondence, Collection 540, Box 7–8, Billy Graham Center Archives.

28. Ariel, *On Behalf of Israel*, 86.

29. Shapira, *Land and Power*, 188–89.

30. Merkley, *The Politics of Christian Zionism*, 99.

31. Emanuel Neumann, *In the Arena: An Autobiographical Memoir* (New York: Herzl Press, 1976), 110–11.

32. Neumann, *In the Arena*, 113–14.

33. Neumann, *In the Arena*, 114.

34. Merkley, *The Politics of Christian Zionism*, 102.

35. Merkley, *The Politics of Christian Zionism*, 102.

36. Merkeley assigns more Machiavellian motives to the ZOA's failure to build on Neumann's success. He posits that political machinations—namely, the alignment of Zionist leaders with the Roosevelt candidacy and a desire, therefore, to distance themselves from the Republican support they had so lately sought to cultivate—were the most significant factors in the APC's sudden abandonment. Merkley, *The Politics of Christian Zionism*, 105.

37. Cohen, *Not Free to Desist*, 160.

38. Melvin I. Urofsky, *American Zionism from Herzl to the Holocaust* (Lincoln: Univ. of Nebraska Press, 1995), 422.

39. Doreen Bierbrier, "The American Zionist Emergency Council: An Analysis of a Pressure Group," *American Jewish Historical Quarterly* 60, no. 1 (1970), 83, http://www.jstor.org/stable/23877930.

40. Melvin Urofsky gives Neumann high marks for his efforts: "Neumann's genius soon turned what had been a defunct propaganda piece into an impressive group of men and women who reached into areas hitherto untouched by Zionism." Urofsky, *American Zionism from Herzl to the Holocaust*, 422.

41. Neumann, *In the Arena*, 152.

42. Alben William Barkley, *That Reminds Me: The Autobiography of the Veep* (Garden City, NY: Doubleday, 1954), 96.

43. In May 1942, over six hundred mostly American Zionists met at the Biltmore Hotel in New York City for the Extraordinary Zionist Conference, where, following Rabbi Abba Hillel Silver's strongly worded address on behalf of Jewish statehood, a unanimous vote was taken to make the establishment of a Jewish "commonwealth" the American Zionists' most pressing goal. Aaron Berman notes that the use of the more ambiguous word "commonwealth" rather than "state" reveals the divisions in the movement regarding the nature of Jewish nationhood, and in particular, what political expression it would find. Aaron Berman, *Nazism, the Jews, and American Zionism, 1933–1948* (Detroit, MI: Wayne State Univ. Press, 1990), 86–88.

44. Neumann, *In the Arena*, 152.

45. Neumann, *In the Arena*, 152–53.
46. Neumann, *In the Arena*, 153.
47. Neumann, *In the Arena*, 153.
48. Neumann, *In the Arena*, 153.
49. Neumann, *In the Arena*, 155.
50. Samuel Halperin, *The Political World of American Zionism* (Detroit, MI: Wayne State Univ. Press, 1961), 183.
51. Bierbrier, "The American Zionist Emergency Council," 89.
52. Halperin, *The Political World of American Zionism*, 183.
53. Gurock, *America, American Jews, and the Holocaust*, 401.
54. Neumann, *In the Arena*, 155.
55. Reinhold Niebuhr, "The Crisis," *Christianity and Crisis* 1, no. 1 (1941), 1.
56. Reinhold Niebuhr, "The Christian Faith and the World Crisis," *Christianity and Crisis* 1, no. 1 (1941), 6.
57. Reinhold Niebuhr, "Jews after the War, Part 1," *The Nation*, February 21, 1942, 215.
58. Niebuhr, "Jews after the War," 215.
59. Niebuhr, "Jews after the War," 216.
60. Neumann, *In the Arena*, 156.
61. "Conference of Christian Leaders Urges Free Immigration of Jews to Palestine," Jewish Telegraphic Agency, December 16, 1942.
62. Merkley, *The Politics of Christian Zionism*, 142.
63. Carl Hermann Voss and David A. Rausch, "American Christians and Israel, 1948–1988," *American Jewish Archives* 40, no. 1 (1988), 42.
64. Voss and Rausch, "American Christians and Israel," 42.
65. Voss and Rausch, "American Christians and Israel," 46.
66. Caitlan Carenen quotes Carl Voss in a lecture given in Jerusalem in 1966 regarding the question of Jewish statehood at its most pressing moment during the Truman presidency: "I would say that Dan Poling had more influence on President Harry Truman, and whatever pro-Zionist moves Truman made, than anybody else." Caitlin Carenen, *The Fervent Embrace: Liberal Protestants, Evangelicals, and Israel* (New York: New York Univ. Press, 2012), 124.
67. When called on to testify before the Anglo-American Committee of Inquiry in 1946, Poling asserted: "Christians believe overwhelmingly that Palestine was divinely selected as the site of the Jewish nation. I am trying as the representative of the Christian groups to present what is, we believe, the Christian viewpoint." Untitled testimony, undated, Reinhold Niebuhr Papers, Box 63, Library of Congress.
68. These resolutions never came to the floor because they could have embarrassed the president in his negotiations with Britain, and because there was no consensus among American Jews about the Zionist agenda. Henry L. Feingold, *A Time*

for Searching: Entering the Mainstream, 1920–1945, vol. 4 of *The Jewish People in America* (Baltimore, MD: Johns Hopkins Univ. Press, 1992), 247; Merkley, *The Politics of Christian Zionism*, 152–53.

69. "Resolutions by the Executive Committee of the Christian Council on Palestine," 1943, cited in Caitlin Carenen, "The American Christian Palestine Committee, the Holocaust, and Mainstream Protestant Zionism, 1938–1948," *Holocaust and Genocide Studies* 24, no. 2 (2010), 278.

70. Voss and Rausch, "American Christians and Israel," 42.

71. Voss and Rausch, "American Christians and Israel," 43.

72. Bierbrier, "The American Zionist Emergency Council," 97.

73. The immigration provisions of the 1939 White Paper expired in March 1944. Bending its statutes to play for time, the British were still issuing a small number of immigration certificates to Jewish immigrants, but even these were set to run out by fall 1945. The new government was faced with the decision to either continue the policy or to abandon it. Michael J. Cohen, "The British White Paper on Palestine, May 1939. Part II: The Testing of a Policy, 1942–1945," *The Historical Journal* 19, no. 3 (1976), 751–53.

74. Cohen, "The British White Paper," 750.

75. Bierbrier, "The American Zionist Emergency Council," 97.

76. Judith Tydor Baumel, *The "Bergson Boys" and the Origins of Contemporary Zionist Militancy* (Syracuse, NY: Syracuse Univ. Press, 2005), 148.

77. "Jewish Leaders Hail Hearst Papers for Espousing Rally of Palestine," *New York Journal-American*, October 1, 1945.

78. "Asks Britain to Open Door to Palestine," *New York Journal-American*, September 30, 1945.

79. "Asks Britain to Open Door to Palestine."

80. "Truman's Letter to Eisenhower and Part of Harrison's Report," *New York Herald Tribune*, September 30, 1945.

81. "Dewey Leads Huge Rally in Appeal for Palestine," *New York Journal-American*, October 1, 1945.

82. "Dewey Leads Huge Rally in Appeal for Palestine."

83. "Dewey Leads Huge Rally in Appeal for Palestine."

84. "Dewey Leads Huge Rally in Appeal for Palestine."

85. "Dewey Exhorts Britain to Open Palestine 'Now,'" *Herald Tribune*, October 1, 1945.

86. "Dewey Backs Plea for Jewish State at Big Rally Here," *New York Times*, October 1, 1945.

87. "Dewey Backs Plea for Jewish State at Big Rally Here."

88. The *Journal-American* and the *Herald Tribune* ran similar stories about the statement of the Council's president on October 1.

89. "Council for Judaism Objects to Implication That All American Jews Back Zionist Aims," *New York Times*, October 1, 1945.

90. "Truman Asked to Aid Jewish Immigration," *New York Times*, September 30, 1945.

91. "Truman Asked to Aid Jewish Immigration."

92. "Jewish State Opposed," *New York Times*, September 30, 1945.

93. "Jewish State Opposed."

94. Bierbrier, "The American Zionist Emergency Council," 105.

95. "An Open Letter to Prime Minister Attlee," *Morgn Frayhayt*, September 28, 1945, 3.

96. "50,000 at People's Demonstration Demand Only That Britain Open the Doors of Israel to Jews," *Morgn Frayhayt*, October 1, 1945.

97. "Demonstration Sunday Evening," *Morgn Zhurnal*, September 28, 1945.

98. "Our Right to Israel," *Morgn Zhurnal*, September 28, 1945.

99. "England Bears Great Guilt for the Murder of Six Million Jews," *Morgn Zhurnal*, October 1, 1945.

100. "Only Many Thousands on the Streets Will Make an Impression," *Forverts*, September 30, 1945, 1, 9.

101. "Storm of Protest Against 'White Paper' at Zionist Meeting," *Forverts*, October 1, 1945.

102. "After the Protest Demonstration at Madison Square Garden," *Forverts*, October 2, 1945.

103. Bierbrier, "The American Zionist Emergency Council," 404.

104. "Three-Day Conference of Christian Ministers Demands Opening of Palestine for Jews," Jewish Telegraphic Agency, November 16, 1945.

105. "Mass Demonstration of 250,000 New Yorkers Backs Jewish Demands for Palestine," Jewish Telegraphic Agency, October 25, 1945.

106. "International Christian Conference Opposes Anglo-U.S. Inquiry on Displaced Jews," Jewish Telegraphic Agency, November 4, 1945. The Commission was nonetheless formed, and the following year it recommended that the Jewish immigration restrictions be dropped.

Conclusion

1. Hutchison, *Between the Times*, 196.

2. "Stuttgart Declaration of Guilt (Council of the Protestant Church in Germany, 1945," in *Bridges: Documents of the Christian-Jewish Dialogue, Volume One, The Road to Reconciliation (1945–1985)*, ed. Franklin Sherman (New York: Paulist Press, 2011), 41.

3. "Declaration of Guilt toward the Jewish People (Evangelical Lutheran Church of Saxony, 1948," in Sherman, *Bridges, Volume One*, 45.

4. "The Christian Approach to the Jews (World Council of Churches, 1948)" in Sherman, *Bridges, Volume One*, 48.

5. Reinhold Niebuhr, "The Relations of Christians and Jews in Western Civilization," in *The Essential Reinhold Niebuhr: Selected Essays and Addresses*, ed. Robert McAfee Brown (New Haven, CT: Yale Univ. Press, 1987), 198.

6. Niebuhr, "The Relations of Christians and Jews in Western Civilization," 184.

7. "*Dabru Emet* (Speak the Truth): A Jewish Statement on Christians and Christianity," in *Bridges: Documents of the Christian-Jewish Dialogue, Volume Two, Building a New Relationship (1986–2013)*, ed. Franklin Sherman (New York: Paulist Press, 2011), 511–14.

8. "Declaration on the Relation of the Church with Non-Christian Religions," in Sherman, *Bridges, Volume Two*, 168.

9. "Orthodox Rabbinic Statement on Christianity," The Center for Jewish-Christian Understanding and Cooperation, https://ccjr.us/dialogika-resources/documents-and-statements/jewish/orthodox-2015dec4 (accessed December 31, 2015).

10. "Orthodox Rabbinic Statement on Christianity."

11. Carenen, "The American Christian Palestine Committee," 290.

12. Patrick Henry, "'And I Don't Care What It Is': The Tradition-History of a Civil Religion Proof-Text," *The Journal of the American Academy of Religion* 49, no. 1 (1981), 41.

13. Mark Silk, "Notes on the Judeo-Christian Tradition in America," *American Quarterly* 36, no. 1 (1984), 66.

14. K. Healan Gaston, *Imagining Judeo-Christian America: Religion, Secularism, and the Redefinition of Democracy* (Chicago: Univ. of Chicago Press, 2019), 80–82.

15. Will Herberg, *Protestant, Catholic, Jew: An Essay in American Religious Sociology* (Garden City, NY: Doubleday, 1955), 98. Silk directs the reader to the critique of Herberg's viewpoint offered in Patrick Henry's "'And I Don't Care What It Is.'"

16. Herberg, *Protestant, Catholic, Jew*, 98.

17. Anita Norich, *Discovering Exile: Yiddish and Jewish American Culture during the Holocaust* (Stanford, CA: Stanford Univ. Press, 2007), 79.

Bibliography

Archives

American Jewish Committee Archives, New York, NY
Blackstone Correspondence. Billy Graham Center Archives, Wheaton College, Wheaton, IL
Fight for Freedom Committee Records, 1941–1947. University of Chicago Library, Chicago, IL
Keesing's Contemporary Archives, London Ltd., 1933
Lazaron, Morris S., Papers. American Jewish Archives, Cincinnati, OH
Niebuhr, Reinhold, Papers. Library of Congress, Washington, DC
Tuttle, Charles S., Papers, 1926–1970. New York State Library, Albany, NY

Referenced Sources

American Jewish Committee. *The Jews in Nazi Germany: The Factual Record of Their Persecution by the National Socialists.* New York: American Jewish Committee, 1933.

———. *The Voice of Religion: The Views of Christian Religious Leaders on the Persecution of the Jews in Germany by the National Socialists.* New York: American Jewish Committee, 1933.

American Jewish Congress. *Hitlerism and the American Jewish Congress: A Confidential Record of Activities, March–December.* New York: American Jewish Congress, 1934.

American Jewish Congress and Bainbridge Colby. *The Case of Civilization against Hitlerism, Presented under the Auspices of the American Jewish Congress at Madison Square Garden, New York, March 7, 1934: The Pleaders, Bainbridge Colby, Bernard S. Deutsch, Arthur R. Brown . . . [et al.].* New York: R. O. Ballou, 1934.

Anthes, Louis. "Publicly Deliberative Drama: The 1934 Mock Trial of Adolf Hitler for 'Crimes against Civilization.'" *The American Journal of Legal History* 42, no. 4 (1998): 391–410.

Ariel, Yaakov S. *On Behalf of Israel: American Fundamentalist Attitudes toward Jews, Judaism, and Zionism, 1865–1945*. Chicago Studies in the History of American Religion 1. Brooklyn, NY: Carlson Publishing, 1991.

———. *Evangelizing the Chosen People: Missions to the Jews in America, 1880–2000*. Chapel Hill: Univ. of North Carolina Press, 2000.

———. *An Unusual Relationship: Evangelical Christians and Jews*. New York: New York Univ. Press, 2013.

Asch, Sholem. *One Destiny: An Epistle to the Christians*. New York: G. P. Putnam's Sons, 1945.

Barkley, Alben William. *That Reminds Me: The Autobiography of the Veep*. Garden City, NY: Doubleday, 1954.

Bauer, Yehuda. "The Holocaust, America, and American Jewry." *Israel Journal of Foreign Affairs* 6, no. 1 (2012): 65–68.

———. *Jews for Sale?: Nazi-Jewish Negotiations, 1933–1945*. New Haven, CT: Yale Univ. Press, 1994.

———. *My Brother's Keeper: A History of the American Jewish Joint Distribution Committee, 1929–1939*. Philadelphia: Jewish Publication Society of America, 1974.

Baumel, Judith Tydor. *The "Bergson Boys" and the Origins of Contemporary Zionist Militancy*. Syracuse, NY: Syracuse Univ. Press, 2005.

Beizer, Michael, and Mikhail Mitsell. *The American Brother: The "Joint" in Russia, the USSR and the CIS*. New York: American Jewish Joint Distribution Committee, 2004.

Belloc, Hilaire. *The Jews*. Boston: Houghton Mifflin, 1922.

Bennett, M. Todd. *One World, Big Screen Hollywood, the Allies, and World War II*. Chapel Hill: The Univ. of North Carolina Press, 2012.

Berman, Aaron. *Nazism, the Jews, and American Zionism, 1933–1948*. Detroit, MI: Wayne State Univ. Press, 1990.

Bernstein, Arnie. *Swastika Nation: Fritz Kuhn and the Rise and Fall of the German-American Bund*. New York: St. Martin's Press, 2013.

Bernstein, Mark I., and Laurence R. Milstein. "Trial as Theater." *Trial* 33, no. 10 (1997): 64–69. https://www.scribd.com/doc/294172086/Trial-Magazine-Trial-as-Theatre.

Bierbrier, Doreen. "The American Zionist Emergency Council: An Analysis of a Pressure Group." *American Jewish Historical Quarterly* 60, no. 1 (1970): 82–105. http://www.jstor.org/stable/23877930.
Brandeis, Louis D. *Letters of Louis D. Brandeis, Volume IV, 1916–1921, Mr. Justice Brandeis.* Albany: State Univ. of New York Press, 1975.
Breitman, Richard, and Alan M. Kraut. *American Refugee Policy and European Jewry, 1933–1945.* Bloomington: Indiana Univ. Press, 1987.
Breitman, Richard, and Allan J. Lichtman. *FDR and the Jews.* Cambridge, MA: The Belknap Press of Harvard Univ. Press, 2013.
Brenner, Michael. *Zionism: A Brief History.* Princeton, NJ: M. Wiener, 2003.
Brown, Robert McAfee, ed. *The Essential Reinhold Niebuhr: Selected Essays and Addresses.* New Haven, CT: Yale Univ. Press, 1987.
Carenen, Caitlin. "The American Christian Palestine Committee, the Holocaust, and Mainstream Protestant Zionism, 1938–1948." *Holocaust and Genocide Studies* 24, no. 2 (2010): 273–96.
———. *The Fervent Embrace: Liberal Protestants, Evangelicals, and Israel.* New York: New York Univ. Press, 2012.
Coffman, Elesha J. *"The Christian Century" and the Rise of the Protestant Mainline.* New York: Oxford Univ. Press, 2013.
Cohen, Michael J. "The British White Paper on Palestine, May 1939. Part II: The Testing of a Policy, 1942–1945." *The Historical Journal* 19, no. 3 (1976): 727–57.
Cohen, Mitchell. *Zion and State: Nation, Class, and the Shaping of Modern Israel.* New York: B. Blackwell, 1987.
Cohen, Naomi Wiener. *Not Free to Desist: The American Jewish Committee, 1906–1966.* Philadelphia: Jewish Publication Society of America, 1972.
Curtis, Susan. *A Consuming Faith: The Social Gospel and Modern American Culture.* Baltimore, MD: Johns Hopkins Univ. Press, 1991.
Cypkin, Diane. "Mayor Fiorello H. LaGuardia and His Rhetoric vis-à-vis the Jews, 1934–1945." *Proceedings of the New York State Communication Association* 2010, article 5 (April 16, 2012): 1–87. https://docs.rwu.edu/cgi/viewcontent.cgi?article=1013&context=nyscaproceedings.
Dawidowicz, Lucy S. "American Jews and the Holocaust." *Commentary*, June 1983.
———. "Indicting American Jews." *Commentary*, June 1, 1983.

———. *The War against the Jews: 1933–1945*. New York: Bantam Books, 1986.

Dinnerstein, Leonard. "Antisemitism in Crisis Times in the United States: The 1920s and 1930s." In Gilman and Katz, *Anti-Semitism in Times of Crisis*, 212–26.

Efron, John M. *The Jews: A History*. Upper Saddle River, NJ: Pearson Prentice Hall, 2009.

Estraikh, Gennady. "Professing Leninist Yiddishkayt: The Decline of American Yiddish Communism." *American Jewish History* 96, no. 1 (2010): 33–60.

Feingold, Henry L. *Bearing Witness: How America and Its Jews Responded to the Holocaust*. Syracuse, NY: Syracuse Univ. Press, 1995.

———. *The Politics of Rescue: The Roosevelt Administration and the Holocaust, 1938–1945*. New Brunswick, NJ: Rutgers Univ. Press, 1970.

———. *A Time for Searching: Entering the Mainstream, 1920–1945*, vol. 4 of *The Jewish People in America*. Baltimore, MD: Johns Hopkins Univ. Press, 1992.

Fischel, Jack R., and Susan M. Ortmann. *The Holocaust and Its Religious Impact: A Critical Assessment and Annotated Bibliography*. Westport, CT: Praeger, 2004.

Fischer, Klaus P. *Hitler & America*. Philadelphia: Univ. of Pennsylvania Press, 2011.

Friedman, Saul S. *No Haven for the Oppressed: United States Policy toward Jewish Refugees, 1938–1945*. Detroit, MI: Wayne State Univ. Press, 1973.

Gaston, K. Healan. *Imagining Judeo-Christian America: Religion, Secularism, and the Redefinition of Democracy*. Chicago: Univ. of Chicago Press, 2019.

Gilman, Sander L., and Steven T Katz, eds. *Anti-Semitism in Times of Crisis*. New York: New York Univ. Press, 1991.

Golden, Jonathan J. "From Cooperation to Confrontation: The Rise and Fall of the Synagogue Council of America." PhD diss., Brandeis Univ., 2008.

Goldman, Shalom. *Zeal for Zion: Christians, Jews, & the Idea of the Promised Land*. Chapel Hill: Univ. of North Carolina Press, 2009.

Gorny, Yosef. *The Jewish Press and the Holocaust, 1939–1945: Palestine, Britain, the United States, and the Soviet Union*. New York: Cambridge Univ. Press, 2012.

Gunner, Göran, and Robert O. Smith, eds. *Comprehending Christian Zionism: Perspectives in Comparison*. Minneapolis, MN: Fortress Press, 2014.

Gurock, Jeffrey S., ed. *America, American Jews, and the Holocaust*, vol. 7 of *American Jewish History: A Eight-Volume Series*. New York: Routledge, 1998.

———, ed. *American Zionism: Mission and Politics*, vol. 8 of *American Jewish History: A Eight-Volume Series*. New York: Routledge, 1998.

Guttman, Allen. "Berlin 1936: The Most Controversial Olympics." In *National Identity and Global Sports Events: Culture, Politics, and Spectacle in the Olympics and the Football World Cup*, edited by Alan Tomlinson and Christopher Young, 65–82. Albany: State Univ. of New York Press, 2006.

Halperin, Samuel. *The Political World of American Zionism*. Detroit, MI: Wayne State Univ. Press, 1961.

Hecht, Ben. *A Child of the Century*. New York: Simon and Schuster, 1954.

———. *We Will Never Die: A Memorial Dedicated to the 2,000,000 Jewish Dead of Europe*. New York: Committee for a Jewish Army of Stateless and Palestinian Jews, 1943.

Hedstrom, Matthew S. *The Rise of Liberal Religion: Book Culture and American Spirituality in the Twentieth Century*. New York: Oxford Univ. Press, 2012.

Henry, Patrick. "'And I Don't Care What It Is': The Tradition-History of a Civil Religion Proof-Text." *The Journal of the American Academy of Religion* 49, no. 1 (1981): 35–49.

Herberg, Will. *Protestant, Catholic, Jew: An Essay in American Religious Sociology*. Garden City, NY: Doubleday, 1955.

Hertzberg, Arthur. *The Zionist Idea: A Historical Analysis and Reader*. Garden City, NY: Doubleday, 1959.

Hoffman, Conrad. *The Jews Today: A Call to Christian Action*. New York: Friendship Press, 1900.

Hutchison, William R., ed. *Between the Times: The Travail of the Protestant Establishment in America, 1900–1960*. New York: Cambridge Univ. Press, 1989.

Jones, Dorothy V. *Toward a Just World: The Critical Years in the Search for International Justice*. Chicago: Univ. of Chicago Press, 2002.

Katz, Dovid. *Words on Fire: The Unfinished Story of Yiddish*. New York: Basic Books, 2004.

Kimble, James J. *Mobilizing the Home Front: War Bonds and Domestic Propaganda*. College Station: Texas A&M Univ. Press, 2006.

Kraut, Benny. "A Wary Collaboration: Jews, Catholics, and the Goodwill Movement." In Hutchinson, *Between the Times*, 193–230.

Lincoln, Bruce. *Discourse and the Construction of Society: Comparative Studies of Myth, Ritual, and Classification*. New York: Oxford Univ. Press, 1989.

Lipstadt, Deborah E. *Beyond Belief: The American Press and the Coming of the Holocaust, 1933–1945*. New York: Free Press, 1986.

Lookstein, Haskel. *Were We Our Brothers' Keepers?: The Public Response of American Jews to the Holocaust, 1938–1944*. New York: Hartmore House, 1985.

Macfarland, Charles S., and the Council on Religion and International Affairs. *Pioneers for Peace through Religion, Based on the Records of the Church Peace Union (founded by Andrew Carnegie) 1914–1945*. New York: Fleming H. Revell, 1946.

Maritain, Jacques. *A Christian Looks at the Jewish Question*. New York: Longmans, Green and Co., 1939.

Marsden, George M. *Fundamentalism and American Culture: The Shaping of Twentieth-Century Evangelicalism, 1870–1925*. New York: Oxford Univ. Press, 1980.

Mazzenga, Maria. *American Religious Responses to Kristallnacht*. New York: Palgrave Macmillan, 2009.

Medoff, Rafael. "The Pageant That Alerted America about the Holocaust." In *The Jews Should Keep Quiet: Franklin D. Roosevelt, Rabbi Stephen S. Wise, and the Holocaust*, 148–50. Philadelphia and Lincoln: The Jewish Publication Society of America and the University of Nebraska Press, 2019.

Merkley, Paul Charles. *The Politics of Christian Zionism, 1891–1948*. Portland, OR: Frank Cass, 1998.

Merlin, Samuel. "Letter to the Editor." *Commentary*, September 1, 1983.

Michels, Tony. *A Fire in Their Hearts: Yiddish Socialists in New York*. Cambridge, MA: Harvard Univ. Press, 2005.

National Conference on Palestine, American Palestine Committee, and Christian Council on Palestine, eds. *The Voice of Christian America: Proceedings of the National Conference on Palestine, Washington,*

D.C., *March 9, 1944*. New York: American Palestine Committee and Christian Council on Palestine, 1944.

Nawyn, William E. *American Protestantism's Response to Germany's Jews and Refugees, 1933–1941.* Ann Arbor, MI: UMI Research Press, 1981.

Neumann, Emanuel. *In the Arena: An Autobiographical Memoir.* New York: Herzl Press, 1976.

Niebuhr, Reinhold. "The Christian Faith and the World Crisis." *Christianity and Crisis* 1, no. 1 (1941): 6.

———. *Christianity and Power Politics.* New York: C. Scribner's Sons, 1940.

———. "The Crisis." *Christianity and Crisis* 1, no. 1 (1941): 1.

———. "Jews after the War, Part 1." *The Nation*, February 21, 1942.

———. "The Relations of Christians and Jews in Western Civilization." In Brown, *The Essential Reinhold Niebuhr*, 182–204.

Norich, Anita. *Discovering Exile: Yiddish and Jewish American Culture during the Holocaust.* Stanford, CA: Stanford Univ. Press, 2007.

Ochoa, Sheana. *Stella!: Mother of Modern Acting.* Milwaukee, WI: Applause Theatre & Cinema Books, 2014.

"Orthodox Rabbinic Statement on Christianity." The Center for Jewish-Christian Understanding and Cooperation. http://cjcuc.com/site/2015/12/03/orthodox-rabbinic-statement-on-christianity/.

Passow, David. *The Prime of Yiddish.* Hewlett, NY: Gefen, 1996.

Peck, Abraham J., and American Jewish Archives. *American Jewish Archives, Cincinnati: The Papers of the World Jewish Congress, 1939–1945.* New York: Garland, 1990.

Peck, Abraham J., Mazal Holocaust Collection, and Jewish Institute of Religion, Hebrew Union College, eds. *Jews and Christians after the Holocaust.* Philadelphia: Fortress Press, 1982.

Penkower, Monty Noam. "Vladimir (Ze'ev) Jabotinsky, Hillel Kook-Peter Bergson, and the Campaign for a Jewish Army." *Modern Judaism* 31, no. 3 (October 2011): 332–74. doi:10.1093/mj/kjr017.

Raphael, Marc Lee. *The Columbia History of Jews and Judaism in America.* New York: Columbia Univ. Press, 2009.

Rapoport, Louis. *Shake Heaven & Earth: Peter Bergson and the Struggle to Rescue the Jews of Europe.* Jerusalem: Gefen Publishing House, 1999.

Rausch, David A. *Zionism within Early American Fundamentalism, 1878–1918: A Convergence of Two Traditions.* New York: E. Mellen Press, 1979.

"Resolutions Passed by The Church Peace Union [now Carnegie Council], at Its First Meeting, February 10th, 1914." http://www.carnegiecouncil.org/about/history/church_peace_union.html.

Rittner, Carol, and John K. Roth, eds. *From the Unthinkable to the Unavoidable: American Christian and Jewish Scholars Encounter the Holocaust.* Westport, CT: Praeger, 1997.

Robinson, John Bunyan. *The Epworth League: Its Place in Methodism: A Manual.* Cincinnati, OH: Cranston and Stowe, 1890.

Rosen, Robert N. *Saving the Jews: Franklin D. Roosevelt and the Holocaust.* New York: Thunder's Mouth Press, 2006.

Rosenbaum, Robert A. *Waking to Danger: Americans and Nazi Germany, 1933–1941.* Santa Barbara, CA: Praeger, 2010.

Rosenthal, Michael. *Nicholas Miraculous: The Amazing Career of the Redoubtable Dr. Nicholas Murray Butler.* New York: Farrar, Straus and Giroux, 2006.

Rossel, Seymour. *The Holocaust: The World and the Jews, 1933–1945.* Millburn, NJ: Behrman House, 1992.

Sarna, Jonathan D. *The American Jewish Experience.* New York: Holmes & Meier Publishers, 1997.

———. *American Judaism: A History.* New Haven, CT: Yale Univ. Press, 2004.

Schneider, Robert A. "Voice of Many Waters: Church Federation in the Twentieth Century." In Hutchison, *Between the Times*, 95–121.

Sears, John F. *Refuge Must Be Given: Eleanor Roosevelt, the Jewish Plight, and the Founding of Israel.* West Lafayette, IN: Purdue Univ. Press, 2021.

Shafir, Shlomo. "American Jewish Leaders and the Emerging Nazi Threat (1928–January 1933)." 1979. https://sites.americanjewisharchives.org/publications/journal/PDF/1979_31_02_00_shafir.pdf.

Shapira, Anita. *Land and Power: The Zionist Resort to Force, 1881–1948.* New York: Oxford Univ. Press, 1992.

Sherman, Franklin, ed. *Bridges: Documents of the Christian-Jewish Dialogue, Volume One, The Road to Reconciliation (1945–1985).* New York: Paulist Press, 2011.

———, ed. *Bridges: Documents of the Christian-Jewish Dialogue, Volume Two, Building a New Relationship (1986–2013)*. New York: Paulist Press, 2011.

Shindler, Colin. *The Rise of the Israeli Right: From Odessa to Hebron*. Cambridge: Cambridge Univ. Press, 2015.

Silk, Mark. "Notes on the Judeo-Christian Tradition in America." *American Quarterly* 36, no. 1 (1984): 65–85.

Sinclair, Karen Kennedy. *The Church Peace Union: Visions of Peace in Troubled Times*. New York: Garland, 1993.

Sittser, Gerald Lawson. *A Cautious Patriotism: The American Churches & the Second World War*. Chapel Hill: Univ. of North Carolina Press, 1997.

Skloot, Robert. "'We Will Never Die': The Success and Failure of a Holocaust Pageant." *Theatre Journal* 37, no. 2 (1985): 167–80.

Snoek, Johan M. *The Grey Book: A Collection of Protests against Antisemitism and the Persecution of Jews Issued by Non-Roman Catholic Churches and Church Leaders during Hitler's Rule*. Assen, Netherlands: Van Corcum, 1969.

Spear, Sheldon. "The United States and the Persecution of the Jews in Germany, 1933–39." In Gurock, *America, American Jews, and the Holocaust*, 71–98.

Spector, Stephen. *Evangelicals and Israel: The Story of American Christian Zionism*. New York: Oxford Univ. Press, 2009.

Steinacher, Gerald, and Brian Barmettler. "The University in Exile and the Garden of Eden." In *Reassessing History from Two Continents: Festschrift Günter Bischof*, edited by Martin Eichtinger, Stefan Karner, Mark Kramer, and Peter Ruggenthaler, 49–68. Innsbruck: Innsbruck University Press, 2013.

Sussman, Lance J. "'Toward Better Understanding': The Rise of the Interfaith Movement in America and the Role of Rabbi Isaac Landman." *The American Jewish Archives Journal* 34, no. 1 (1982): 35–51.

Takayoshi, Ichiro. *American Writers and the Approach of World War II, 1935–1941*. New York: Cambridge Univ. Press, 2015.

Tent, James F. *In the Shadow of the Holocaust: Nazi Persecution of Jewish-Christian Germans*. Lawrence: Univ. Press of Kansas, 2003.

Urofsky, Melvin I. *American Zionism from Herzl to the Holocaust*. Lincoln: Univ. of Nebraska Press, 1995.

———. *A Voice That Spoke for Justice: The Life and Times of Stephen S. Wise.* Albany: State Univ. of New York Press, 1982.

Voss, Carl Hermann, and David A. Rausch. "American Christians and Israel, 1948–1988." *American Jewish Archives* 40, no. 1 (1988): 41–82. https://sites.americanjewisharchives.org/publications/journal/PDF/1988_40_01_00.pdf.

Waite, Robert G. "'Raise My Voice against Intolerance.' The Anti-Nazi Rally in Madison Square Garden, March 27, 1933, and the American Public's Outrage over the Nazi Persecution of Jews." *New York History Review*, October 20, 2013. https://newyorkhistoryreviewarticles.blogspot.com/2013/.

Wise, Stephen S. *As I See It.* New York: Jewish Opinion Publishing Corporation, 1944.

———. *Challenging Years: The Autobiography of Stephen Wise.* New York: Putnam's Sons, 1949.

Wise, Stephen S., Justine Wise Polier, and James Waterman Wise. *The Personal Letters of Stephen Wise.* Boston: Beacon Press, 1956.

World Jewish Congress. *Unity in Dispersion: A History of the World Jewish Congress.* New York: Institute of Jewish Affairs of the World Jewish Congress, 1948.

Wyman, David S. *The Abandonment of the Jews: America and the Holocaust, 1941–1945.* New York: Pantheon Books, 1984.

———. *Paper Walls: America and the Refugee Crisis 1938–1941.* Amherst: University of Massachusetts Press, 1968.

Wyschogrod, Michael. "Orthodox Judaism and Jewish-Christian Dialogue." Unpublished essay, January 28, 1986. https://www.bc.edu/content/dam/files/research_sites/cjl/texts/center/conferences/soloveitchik/sol_wyscho.htm.

Youngs, J. William T. *The Congregationalists.* Westport, CT: Greenwood Publishing Group, 1998.

Index

Italic page number denotes illustration.

Abend Blat, Dos, 47
Adler, Celia, 234n85
Adler, Cyrus, 22, 219n35; of AJC, 78, 82; *The Voice of Religion* and, 82
Adler, Luther, 136; Hecht and, 234n85
Adler, Stella, 136, 233n64
AECZA. *See* American Emergency Committee for Zionist Affairs
AFL. *See* American Federation of Labor
AJC. *See* American Jewish Committee
Aleichem, Sholem, 51
Alexander II (Czar), 168
Alexander III (Czar), 168
America, 145
American Board of Missions to the Jews, 88
American Board of Rabbis, 25
American Christian Palestine Committee, 197; American Zionist Emergency Council and, 198; Lazaron of, 207; United Nations Special Committee on Palestine and, 206–7
American Citizens League of Ohio, 109
American Civil Liberties Union, 98, 102
American Committee of Jewish Artists, Writers, and Scientists, 222n109
American Council for Judaism, 193
American Emergency Committee for Zionist Affairs (AECZA), 127, 178, 182
American Federation of Labor (AFL), 108, 109, 120
American Hebrew, 68
American Jewish Committee (AJC), 18, 34, 162; Cyrus Adler of, 78, 82; American Jewish Congress and, 216, 224n20; *The Baptist Courier* and, 85–86; B'nai B'rith and, 76–77; *The Christian Century* and, 82–84; Clinchy and, 75; "Confidential Bulletin" of, 79–80; FCC and, 77; Final Solution and, 115–16, 131, 132–33; on Hitler, 218n33; in JEC, 127, 231n16; *The Jews in Nazi Germany* by, 10–11, 76–81, 114; Kishinev pogroms and, 216n4; League of Nations and, 79; Irving Lehman of, 24; Marshall of, 219n35; Proskauer

253

American Jewish Committee (AJC) (*cont.*)
  of, 72, 76–77; reluctance of, 20–21; Franklin D. Roosevelt and, 54; "Stop Hitler Now" and, 120, 131; Roger Straus of, 74, 75, 77; Truman and, 193; *The Voice of Religion* by, 10–11, 62, 77, 81–83, 88–91, 114, 162; Wise and, 24, 25, 26, 28–29, 75–76
American Jewish Congress, 16, 18, 20, 21, 29, 162; AJC and, 216, 224n20; Central Association of German Citizens of Jewish Faith and, 28; Deutsch of, 38, 96; Final Solution and, 115–16; in JEC, 127; Madison Square Garden and, 161–62; Franklin D. Roosevelt and, 54; "Stop Hitler Now" and, 126; Tenenbaum of, 38; Wise of, 117. *See also The Case of Civilization against Hitlerism*
American Jewish Joint Distribution Committee, 194
American Legion, 26
American Palestine Committee (APC), 100, 164, 174–77, 190; AZEC and, 177, 189; Brandeis at, 175–76; CCP and, 197; Emanuel Neumann and, 206, 228
American Zionist Emergency Committee (AZEC), 164, 198, 199; "An Open Letter to Mr. Attlee" and, 194–95; APC and, 177; *Journal-American* and, 190
American Zionist Emergency Council, 182–83; American Christian Palestine Committee and, 198; APC and, 188, 189, 197; CCP and, 188, 189, 197; Jewish Agency and, 189–90; Silver of, 186
Anglo-American Commission of Inquiry, 197; Poling at, 238n67
Anthes, Louis, 112–13
Anthony, Alfred Williams, 68
Anti-Defamation League, 128
antisemitism, 19, 22, 26, 35, 161, 209, 211; American organizations for, 216n2; Atkinson on, 124; Cadman on, 90; Cahan on, 49; Curran on, 219n40; *Dabru Emet* on, 205; FCC on, 149; of Hitler, 30, 55, 124, 146, 202; Hoffman on, 72–73; Information and Service Associates on, 76; Jewish Telegraphic Agency and, 226n65; Judeo-Christian tradition and, 210; LaGuardia and, 227n78; National Conference of Christians and Jews on, 201; *New York Times* on, 59, 220n47; Franklin D. Roosevelt and, 219n43; Wise on, 40, 219n36; World Council of Churches and, 203
APC. *See* American Palestine Committee
Arbiter Tsaytung, Di, 47
Ariel, Yaakov, 173
Arnold, Edward, 142
Asch, Sholem, 1–2, 73, 149, 212; in *Forverts*, 47; Hoffman and, 223n12
Atkinson, Henry, 123, 124
Attlee, Clement, 189, 192; "An Open Letter to Mr. Attlee," 194–95; AZEC and, 197
Ayers, Lemuel, 137
AZEC. *See* American Zionist Emergency Committee

Baker, Newton D., 74
Baldwin, Roger, 98
Balfour, David, 167
Balfour Declaration, 117, 169–70, 173; Daniel Poling on, 192
"Ballad of the Doomed Jews of Europe" (Hecht), 147
Bankhead, Tallulah, 134
Baptist Courier, The, 85–86, 89
Barker, Lewellys, 109
Barkley, Alben W., 179–81
"Battle of Warsaw, The," 143
Beard, Charles A., 98
Beard, Mary Ritter, 66; in *The Case of Civilization against Hitlerism*, 98–99
Belloc, Hilaire, 226n65; in *The Voice of Religion*, 89–90
Ben-Ami, Jacob, 136
Ben-Ami, Yitzhak, 133
Benny, Jack, 134
Bergson, Peter: Hecht and, 118, 133–48, 230n13, 233nn62–63; Wise and, 116, 119–20, 136, 148, 231n16, 233nn62–63
Bergson boys, 118–19
Berlin, Irvin, 134
Berlin Localanzeiger, 26
Berlin Summer Olympics, 99–100, 228n89
Bermuda Conference, 145
Bernstein, Herman, 49
Bernstein, Mark, 92
Bernstein, Philip, 174
Betar, 117, 118
Bierbrier, Doreen, 195
Blackstone, William, 167–73
Blackstone Memorials, 168, 169, 170, 171, 172
Blackwood, I. C., 94

Blaustein, Jacob, 193
B'nai B'rith, 20, 29; AJC and, 76–77; on Christian evangelism, 223n10; FCC and, 70; on Hitler, 218n33; in JEC, 127; "Stop Hitler Now" and, 120
Board of Foreign Missions, of Presbyterian Church, 100, 170
Board of Home Missions, of Presbyterian Church, 88
Board of National Missions, of Presbyterian Church, 72
Borah, William, 177
Boston Globe, , 33
Bowron, Fletcher, 143
Brandeis, Louis, 169, 171–72; American Jewish Congress and, 216n3; at APC, 175–76; Blackstone and, 236n27; Wilson and, 236n23
Brando, Marlon, 234n85
Brooklyn Daily Eagle, 139, 140
Brown, Arthur Judson, 100–101, 109
Brundage, Avery, 228n89
Butler, Nicolas Murray, 77, 224n23

Cadman, S. Parkes, 69; in *The Christian Century*, 83; in *The New York Herald Tribune*, 90; in NCJC, 75; in *The Voice of Religion*, 89–90
Cahan, Abraham, 39, 46–49; in *The Case of Civilization against Hitlerism*, 102, 103, 109, 111, 112
Cantor, Eddie, 134
Cantwell, John, 142
Capital Journal, 81
Cardozo, Benjamin, 41; in NCJC, 75
Carenen, Caitlan, 207, 238n66
Carnegie, Andrew, 123

Case of Civilization against Hitlerism, The, 11, 92–116, 143, 228n96; Holmes in, 105–6, 109, 112; LaGuardia in, 96–97, 108–9; *New York Times* and, 106–8, 109, 110; Wise in, 94–96, 102, 103–5, 109, 112
Catt, Carrie Chapman, 94
Cavert, Samuel McCrea, 75, 128–29, 232n47; in *The Christian Century*, 82, 83
CCP. *See* Christian Council on Palestine
Celler, Emanuel, 144–45
Central Association of German Citizens of Jewish Faith: American Jewish Congress and, 28; Deutsch and, 28; Wise and, 27–28
Central Conference of American Rabbis, 31; Franklin of, 68
Chagall, Marc, 149
Chesterton, G. K., 226n65
Chicago Hebrew Mission, 88, 167
Chicago Tribune, 33
Chosen People Ministries, 209
Christian Advocate, The, 86–87, 89
Christian Century, The, 82–84, 89, 226n51
Christian Council on Palestine (CCP), 123, 164, 174–75, 199, 206; APC and, 197; AZEC and, 189
Christian evangelism, 71–74, 88, 162–63, 166; Blackstone and, 172; B'nai B'rith on, 223n10; FCC and, 201–2; Hoffman and, 223n12, 223n18; by London Society of Promoting Christianity, 167; Restorationism and, 209; revival of, 208
Christian Front, 210, 216n2

Christian Looks at the Jewish Question, A (Maritain), 145
Christian realists, 199
Christian Science Monitor, The, 33–34
Christian Zionism, 12–13, 68, 70, 161–99, 235n8. *See also specific individuals and organizations*
Church Peace Union, 123–24, 130, 149, 199
CIO. *See* Congress of Industrial Organizations
Clinchy, Everett R.: in *The Christian Century*, 82; of National Conference of Christians and Jews, 54; in NCJC, 75
Coffin, Henry Sloan, 75, 207; in *The Christian Century*, 83
Cohen, Alfred M., 20
Cohen, Harry, 143
Cohen, Naomi, 177
Colby, Bainbridge, 95, 109
Cold War, 200
Commission on International Justice and Goodwill, 41
Committee for a Jewish Army of Stateless and Palestinian Jews, 120, 133; *We Will Never Die* and, 137, 139
Committee for Peace and Justice in the Holy Land, 207
Committee on Good Will between Jews and Christians, 70, 74, 75
Committee on the Christian Approach to the Jews, 72, 203
Commonweal, 145; Williams of, 77, 79, 154
Communist Party, *Morgn Frayhayt* and, 46, 51–53
Communists, 21; in Cold War, 200

Conboy, Martin, 69
"Confidential Bulletin," 79–80
Congregationalist and Herald of Gospel Liberty, The, 84–85, 89
Congregation Rodelph Sholom, 34
Congress of Industrial Organizations (CIO), 120
Conway, Edward A., 124
Cooper, Ashley, 167
Coughlin, Charles, 210
Council for Protestant Churches, 202
Council of Orthodox Rabbis, 25
Cross, Wilbur, 94
Curran, Edward Lodge, 30; on anti-semitism, 219n40
Curtis, Charles, 175, 176

Dabru Emet (Speak the Truth), 204–5
Daily Mirror, The: on Truman, 191; on *We Will Never Die*, 139, 140
Darby, Charles Nelson, 167
Dawidowicz, Lucy, 231n16
"Declaration of Guilt toward the Jewish People," 202
Declaration on the Relation of the Church to Non-Christian Religions (*Nostra Aetate*), 205–6
Department of Jewish Evangelization, of Presbyterian Church, 88
Detroit Free Press, 33
Deutsch, Bernard S., 22; of American Jewish Congress, 38, 96; in The Case of Civilization against Hitlerism, 95–96, 102, 109, 112; Central Association of German Citizens of Jewish Faith and, 28; JWV and, 25; of New York City Board of Aldermen, 96
Dewey, John, 93

Dewey, Thomas, 122–23, 126, 130, 149, 196; *Journal-American* on, 191–92; *New York Times* on, 192–93; *We Will Never Die* and, 136, 139, 140; Wise and, 233n66
Dinnerstein, Leonard, 216n2
"Diplomatic Mockery" (Celler), 144–45
Discourse and the Construction of Society (Lincoln), 5
Douglas, William O., 122
Dowling, Victor, 69
dual-covenant theology, 204
Duchovny, Moshe, 126
Duffy, Francis, 69
Dunn, John J., 45

ECZA. *See* Emergency Committee for Zionist Affairs
Einstein, Albert, 51, 218n26
Eisenhower, Dwight D., 210, 211; *New York Herald Tribune* on, 191
Emergency Committee for Zionist Affairs (ECZA), 178
Emergency Committee to Save the Jewish People of Europe, 148
emeth (truth), 56
Epshteyn, Shakhne, 52
Epworth Herald, The, 87–88, 89
Epworth League, The, 87
Estraikh, Gennady, 222n105
evangelism. *See* Christian evangelism
Evian Conference, 145
Extraordinary Zionist Conference, 237n43

Faunce, W. H. P., 69
FCC. *See* Federal Council of Churches

Index

Feathering, Doug, 143
Federal Council of Churches (FCC), 10, 199; AJC and, 77; Anthony of, 68; on antisemitism, 149; Brown of, 100; Cadman of, 69; in *The Christian Century*, 82; Christian evangelism of, 71–74, 201–2; Commission on International Justice and Goodwill of, 41; Committee on Good Will between Jews and Christians of, 70, 74, 75; "day of compassion" of, 149; Great Commission and, 165; Hoffman of, 72–73; International Missionary Council of, 72, 73; in JEC, 127, 128, 130; Landman and, 201; mainline churches in, 235n4; McConnell and, 70; Niebuhr and, 70; North of, 170; O'Connell of, 43–44; Franklin D. Roosevelt and, 70; "Stop Hitler Now" and, 127–30; Tucker of, 125; Wise and, 201
Federation of American Zionists, 169
Federation of Churches, 40
Feffer, Itzik, 222n109
Feingold, Henry L., 238n68
Fichel, Jack R., 3
Final Solution, 11–12; AJC and, 115–16, 131, 132–33; American Jewish Congress and, 115–16; Jewish responses to, 113–50; Jewish Telegraphic Agency and, 128–29; Franklin D. Roosevelt and, 131; Wise and, 119, 230n11; World Jewish Congress and, 131
First Zionist Congress, 169
Fischer, Klaus, 95, 227n72
Fish, Hamilton, Jr., 175
Flag Is Born, A, 144

Ford, Henry, 19, 217n7
Forverts, 39, 61, 63, 196; on *The Case of Civilization against Hitlerism*, 110–11; on Hitler, 47–48, 64; Margoshes in, 49; *Morgn Frayhayt* and, 52, 222n105; *New York Times* and, 53; sensational journalism in, 52; Socialist Labor Party and, 46–47; on "Stop Hitler Now," 126; on *We Will Never Die*, 140; on Wise, 48
Forverts Association, 52
Fosdick, Harry Emerson: of Committee for Peace and Justice in the Holy Land, 207; in *New York Times*, 54–55
Four Freedoms Foundation, 210
Franklin, Leo, 68
Fredman, J. George, 25–26
Free Synagogue, 16, 29–30, 70–71
From the Unthinkable to the Unavoidable (Rittner and Roth), 3
Front Page, The, 133
Fun to Be Free, 133, 135, 138

Garfield, John, 136
Gaston, K. Healan, 210
German American Bund, 15, 215n1, 216n2
German Council of Rabbis, 27
Gibbons, James Cardinal, 123
Goebbels, Joseph, 46
Goldberg, Ben-Zion, 51
Goldstein, Israel, 129
Goldwyn, Samuel, 143
Gorny, Yosef, 221n95
Gospels, the: antisemitism and, 73; Christian Zionists and, 167; *The Epworth Herald* and, 88; FCC

and, 72; London Society of Promoting Christianity and, 167
Great Commission, 73, 74; FCC and, 165
Greater New York Federation of Churches, The, 30–31
Great Reversal, 165
Green, Theodore A., 30
Greenberg, Chaim, 135
Gunga Din, 133

Haas, Jacob de, 236n27
Habakkuk 1:12, 136
Harrison, Benjamin, 168
Harrison, Earl G., 191
Hart, Moss, 135
Hayes, Carlton J. H., 74
Hays, Arthur Garfield, 228n96; in *The Case of Civilization against Hitlerism*, 102
Hearst, William Randolph, 80–81, 109–10, 190
Hecht, Ben, *155*, 190; Luther Adler and, 234n85; Bergson and, 118, 133–48, 230n13, 233nn62–63; Wise and, 136, 233n66. *See also We Will Never Die*
Heine, Heinrich, 51
Henreid, Paul, 136
Herberg, Will, 211
Herring, Clyde L., 94
Hertz, Joseph Herman, 121
Herzl, Theodor, 117, 171
High, Stanley, 98
Hinsley, Arthur, 121
Hirsch, Emil G., 123, 124
Hitler, Adolf, 4, 5, 11–12, 16, 17, 198, 206; AJC and, 21; American indignation of, 32–33; in "An Open Letter to Mr. Attlee," 195; antisemitism of, 30, 55, 124, 146, 202; boycott by, 46, 54; Cadman on, 90; *The Christian Advocate* on, 86; complaints of, 26; *The Congregationalist and Herald of Gospel Liberty* on, 85; dictatorial power of, 93; early regime days of, 31; Einstein on, 218n26; *Forverts* on, 47–48, 64; Hecht and, 133; Holmes on, 45; *The Jews of Nazi Germany* on, 80–81; Margoshes on, 49, 50; Marshall on, 217n10; *New York Times* on, 65; political control of, 18; Franklin D. Roosevelt and, 21–22; Smith on, 35–36; *Der Tog* on, 50; Treaty of Versailles and, 100–101, 103; Wise on, 218n33. *See also Case of Civilization against Hitlerism, The*; "Stop Hitler Now;" We Will Never Die
Hoffman, Conrad: Asch and, 223n12; of FCC, 72–73; Lazaron and, 223n18; Presbyterian Church Board of Home Missions and, 88
Hofman, Ben-Tsien, 52
Hollywood Bowl: Waxman at, *159*; We Will Never Die at, 142–43
Holmes, John Haynes, *153*; in *The Case of Civilization against Hitlerism*, 105–6, 109, 112; in *The Christian Century*, 82; Goldberg and, 51; Wise and, 45
Holocaust and Its Religious Impact, The (Fichel and Ortmann), 3
Hoover, Herbert, 176
Hope-Simpson, John, 174
Hopkins, William, 175, 176–77

Hovevei Zion (Lovers of Zion), 169, 175
Hull, Cordell, 22–23, 25; Dunn and, 45; Green and, 30; O'Brian and, 37, 43; Smith and, 36
Hutchison, William, 5, 164–65, 201

Imagining Judeo-Christian America (Gaston), 210
Independent Order of B'rith Abraham, 25
Information and Service Associates, 76
Interfaith Committee, 30–31; Tuttle of, 40
Intergovernmental Committee on Refugees, 191
International Catholic Truth Society, 30
International Christian Conference for Palestine, 197
International Conference of Christians and Jews, 204
International Missionary Council, 72, 73
Irgun Tzvai Le'umi (The National Military Organization), 117, 118, 133

Jabotinsky, Vladimir, 117–18
JEC. *See* Joint Emergency Committee on European Affairs
Jesus of Nazareth (Klausner), 70–71
Jewish Agency: American Zionist Emergency Council and, 189–90; Jabotinsky and, 117
Jewish Anti-Fascist Committee, 222n109

Jewish Army, 118
Jewish Labor Committee, 127
Jewish Labor Federation, 120
Jewish Legion, 117
Jewish Telegraphic Agency, 40, 93–94, 226n65; on *The Case of Civilization against Hitlerism*, 107; Final Solution and, 128–29
Jewish War Veterans (JWV), 24–26; *The Case of Civilization against Hitlerism and*, 108; O'Brian and, 36–37; Wise and, 25, 29
Jews, The (Belloc), 90
Jews and Christians after the Holocaust (Peck), 3
Jews in Nazi Germany, The, 10–11, 76–81, 114
"Jews in the War," 137
"Jews Today, The" (Hoffman), 73
Johnson, Alvin, 94, 226n70; Mary Beard and, 98
Joint Emergency Committee on European Affairs (JEC), 127, 128, 130, 231n16
Jones, Dorothy, 112
Journal-American, The: AZEC and, 190; on Thomas Dewey, 191–92; on LaGuardia, 192; on "Stop Hitler Now," 121; on Truman, 191; on *We Will Never Die*, 139, 140; on Wise, 192
Judeo-Christian tradition, 14, 210–12; antisemitism and, 210; Wise on, 95
JWV. *See* Jewish War Veterans

Kahn, Alexander, 39
Kaplan, Mordechai, 75
Kaufman, Beatrice, 135

Kaufman, George S., 135
Kennedy, Joseph, 134
King, William, 175
Kirby, Gustavus, 100, 109
Kishinev pogroms, 216n4
Klausner, Joseph, 70–71
Kohut, Rebecca: in *Der Tog*, 50–51; of World Congress of Jewish Women, 39, 49
Kook, Avraham Yitzhak Hacohen, 118
Kook, Dov, 118
Kook, Hillel. *See* Bergson, Peter
Krants, Philip, 47
Kristallnacht, 177
Ku Klux Klan, 35–36

LaFollette, Robert, Jr., 175
LaGuardia, Fiorello, *151*, 196, 227n77; antisemitism and, 227n78; in *The Case of Civilization against Hitlerism*, 96–97, 108–9; *Journal-American* on, 192; Margoshes and, 222n101
Landman, Isaac, 10; of *American Hebrew*, 68; Permanent Commission for Better Understanding Between Protestants, Catholics, and Jews, and, 68–69, 74; Wise and, 201
Lazaron, Morris, 193–94, 196; of American Christian Palestine Committee, 207; Hoffman and, 223n18
League of Nations: AJC and, 79; *The Congregationalist and Herald of Gospel Liberty* and, 85
Lehman, Herbert H., 37–38; Jewish Telegraph agency and, 94;
Proskauer and, 77; Wise and, 220n57
Lehman, Irving, 24; on Permanent Commission for Better Understanding Between Protestants, Catholics, and Jews, 69
Lenya, Lotte, *156*
Le'umi, Irgun, 117
Levenson, Edward, 228n96
Lincoln, Bruce, 5, 6
Lipstadt, Deborah, 220n47, 226n51
Literary Digest, The, 80
London Society of Promoting Christianity, 167
Lookstein, Haskel, 120
Lovejoy, Arthur O., 94
Lovers of Zion (Hovevei Zion), 169, 175
Lowel Courrier-Citizen, 81

MacFarland, Charles S., 123
Mack, Julian, 216n3
Madison Square Garden, 164; American Jewish Congress and, 161–62; March 27,1933, 6–7, 9, 15–56, 186; September 30, 1945, 13, 189–97. *See also Case of Civilization against Hitlerism, The*; "Stop Hitler Now;" *We Will Never Die*
Magnes, Judah L., 49, 170
Maharal of Prague, 55–56
mainline churches, 164–65; in FCC, 235n4
Mann, Louis, 124
Manning, William T., 31, 40, 41–43, 46, *152*, 221n72; *in The Voice of Religion*, 89
Margolies, Moses Z., 47

Margoshes, Samuel, 31, 38–39; in *The Case of Civilization against Hitlerism*, 102–3, 111; in *Forverts*, 49; LaGuardia and, 222n101; in *Der Tog*, 50
Maritain, Jacques, 145–46, 149, *159*, 210
Marshall, Louis, 217n10; of AJC, 219n35
Mayer, Louis B., 143
McAlister, Hill, 94
McConnell, Francis J., 70
Medoff, Rafael, 142, 144, 233n62
"Mercy—Which We May Need One Day for Ourselves," 145
Meredith, Burgess, 134
Merkley, Paul, 236b23, 237n36
Merlin, Samuel, 133, 231n16
Merman, Ethel, 134
Michels, Tony, 52
Mikhoels, Solomon, 222n109
Millar, William B., 30–31; of Federation of Churches, 40
Miller, Leslie A., 94
Milstein, Laurence, 92
Moley, Raymond, 98
Moody Bible Institute, 167
Morgan, J. P., 168
Morgenthau, Henry, 69
Morgn Frayhayt, 222n109; on *The Case of Civilization against Hitlerism*, 111–12; Communist Party and, 46, 51–53; *Forverts* and, 52, 222n105; Socialist Party and, 52; on "Stop Hitler Now," 125, 126; on *We Will Never Die*, 140–41; on Wise, 71
Morgn Zhurnal, 195–96; on "Stop Hitler Now," 126; on *We Will Never Die*, 140, 141

Moscow Declaration, 148
Mott, John, 123, 223n10, 223n12
Muni, Paul, 136, 234n85
Murray, William H., 94

Nashville Tennessean, The, 81
National Conference of Christians and Jews, 41; on antisemitism, 201; Clichy of, 54; Lazaron of, 194, 223n18
National Conference of Jews and Christians (NCJC): Cadman of, 90; in *The Christian Century*, 82; FCC and, 74; leadership of, 74–75; Permanent Commission for Better Understanding Between Protestants, Catholics, and Jews, and, 70; Proskauer and, 82; Roger Straus of, 77, 82
National Federation of Orthodox Congregations, 25
National Jewish Scholars Project, 204–5
National Military Organization, The (Irgun Tzvai Le'umi), 117, 118, 133
National Union for Social Justice, 216n2
National War Veterans, 26
NCJC. *See* National Conference of Jews and Christians
Neilson, William T., 93
Neumann, Emanuel, 174, 175, 176, 237n40; APC and, 206, 228; ZOA and, 237n36
Neumann, Sundel, 175
Newman, Lewis, 34
New Palestine, 120

New York City Board of Aldermen: Deutsch of, 96; Franklin D. Roosevelt and, 54
New York Evening Journal, The: on *The Case of Civilization against Hitlerism,* 109–10; on *The Jews in Nazi Germany,* 80–81
New York Herald Tribune, 30–31, 33; Cadman in, 90; on *The Case of Civilization against Hitlerism,* 110; on Eisenhower, 191; on *The Jews in Nazi Germany,* 80; on "Stop Hitler Now," 121
New York Times, 15–16, 34–35, 38–39, 58; on American Council of Judaism, 193; on antisemitism, 59, 220n47; "Ballad of the Doomed Jews of Europe" in, 147; on *The Case of Civilization against Hitlerism,* 106–8, 109, 110; on Thomas Dewey, 192–93; on Dunn, 45; *Forverts* and, 53; Fosdick in, 54–55; on Green, 30; on Hitler, 65; on *The Jews in Nazi Germany,* 80; Kohut and, 49; Lazaron in, 193–94; on Herbert Lehman, 37–38; on O'Brian, 26; on Prodnitz, 27; on "Stop Hitler Now," 121, 125, 128; *Der Tog* and, 53; on Truman, 191; "Uncle Abraham Reports" in, 148; on Weizmann, 121–22; on *We Will Never Die,* 139–40; Wise and, 23, 24, 39–40, 48; on Wise and Bergson, 119–20
Nicolas II (Czar), 32
Niebuhr, Reinhold, 210; in *The Christian Century,* 82, 83; of Christian realists, 199; dual-covenant theology and, 204; FCC and, 70; in NCJC, 75; "The Relations of Christians and Jews in Western Civilization" by, 203
Niger, Shmuel, 49
Night of January 16th (Rand), *The,* 92–93
Norich, Anita, 212
North, F. M., 170
Nostra Aetate (Declaration on the Relation of the Church to Non-Christian Religions), 205–6
Nuremburg Laws, 54, 177
Nurenburger, Meyer, 126

O'Brien, John Patrick, 26; Goldberg and, 51; Hull and, 37, 43; JWV and, 36–37
O'Connell, Francis John, 46, 47; of FCC, 43–44
Office of War Information, 132
Olympics, 99–100, 228n89
One Destiny (Asch), 1–2, 212
"Open Letter to Mr. Attlee, An," 194–95
Opinion, 29
Order of St. Gregory the Great, 69
"Orthodox Judaism and Jewish-Christian Dialogue" (Wyschogrod), 2–3
Ortmann, Susan M., 3

Palmerston, Lord, 167
Passfield White Paper, 174, 175, 177
Pattern for Peace (Conway, Oldham, and Mann), 124
Paul VI (Pope), 205
Peace Church Union, 120
Peck, Abraham J., 3

People's Relief, 39
Permanent Commission for Better Understanding Between Protestants, Catholics, and Jews, 69–70, 74
Pfulf, Toni, 99
Philadelphia Jewish Exponent, 142
Pinchot, Gifford, 94
Poling, Daniel, 192, 196; at Anglo-American Commission of Inquiry, 238n67; Truman and, 238n66
Pound, Roscoe, 69
Presbyterian Church: Board of Foreign Missions of, 100, 170; Board of Home Missions of, 88; Board of National Missions of, 72; Department of Jewish Evangelization of, 88
Prodnitz, Julius, 27
Proskauer, Joseph, 24, 193; of AJC, 72, 76–77; NCJC and, 82
Protestant-Catholic-Jew (Herberg), 211
Protocols of the Elders of Zion, 80
Provisional Executive Committee for General Zionist Affairs, 175

Rabbinical Council of America, 2
Rains, Claude, 134, 142
Rand, Ayn, 92–93
Rapture, the, 172
Reader's Digest, 135
Red Scare, 19
"Relations of Christians and Jews in Western Civilization, The," 203
"Religion in a Post-Holocaust World," 3
"Remember Us," 135, 137, 139, 143

Restorationism: Blackstone and, 167–73; Christian evangelism and, 209; London Society of Promoting Christianity of, 167
Riegner, Gerhard, 120, 230n11, 232n47; of World Jewish Congress, 119
Rise of American Civilization (Beard, M., and Beard, C.), *The*, 98
Rittner, Carol, 3
Robinson, Bill "Bojangles," 134
Robinson, Edward G., 136
Rockefeller, John D., 168
Rogers, James, 175
"Roll Call," 137
Roosevelt, Eleanor, 141–42, 234n78
Roosevelt, Franklin D., 20, 30, 31; AJC and, 54; American Jewish Congress and, 54; antisemitism and, 219n43; *The Case of Civilization against Hitlerism* and, 97, 108; FCC and, 70; Final Solution and, 131; in *Fun to Be Free*, 134; Hitler and, 21–22; New York City Board of Aldermen and, 54; Rose and, 135; "Stop Hitler Now" and, 131; War Refugee Board and, 144; Wise and, 29, 119, 148
Rose, Billy, 133–34, 135
Rosenbaum, Robert, 227n77
Rosenberg, Adam, 169
Rosenberg, James N., 24; *The Voice of Religion* and, 82
Rosenfeld, Jonah, 47
Rosenthal, Michael, 224n23
Rosenwald, Lessing J., 193
Roth, John K., 3
Rothenberg, Morris, 39
Rudley, Herbert, 136

Saginaw Daily News, The, 81
Salutski, Yankev, 52
Scarface, 133
Schapiro, David, 49
Schneider, Robert, 165, 235n4
Schwabacher, Wolfgang, 76
Seabury, Samuel, 105, 109, 111
Sears, John F., 142, 234n80
Second Coming, 167
Selznick, David O., 143
Shafir, Shlomo, 21, 216n5
Shaw, Walter, 174
shem, 56
Sidney, Sylvia, 136
Silk, Mark, 210
Silver, Abba Hillel, 188, 237n43; of American Zionist Emergency Council, 186
Silver Abba Hillel, 192; Hearst and, 190; on *New York Times*, 193; "An Open Letter to Mr. Attlee" by, 194–95
Silver Shirts, 98, 216n2; at *The Case of Civilization against Hitlerism*, 108
Singer, Isaac Bashevis, 47
Singer, Israel Joshua, 47
Skloot, Robert, 143–44
Smith, Alfred E., 30–31, 40; in *The Case of Civilization against Hitlerism*, 96, 108–9; on Ku Klux Klan, 35; in *Time*, 60; Wise and, 41
Social Democrats: *Di Arbiter Tsaytung* and, 47; Mary Beard on, 99; Cahan on, 103
Social Gospel movement, 43, 166
Socialist Labor Party, 46–47
Socialist Party, 52

Socialists, 21; *Forverts* and, 196
Sola Pool, David de, 129
Speak the Truth (*Dabru Emet*), 204–5
Spector, Stephen, 235n8
Speer, Robert, 170
Steinberg, Milton, 174
"Stop Hitler Now," 11–12, 116, 120–31; *We Will Never Die* and, 141, 146–47; Wise and, 146–47
Straus, Nathan, 171; Blackstone and, 236n27
Straus, Roger Williams, 74, 75; of AJC, 77; of NCJC, 77, 82
Sturmer, Der, 221n72
"Stuttgart Declaration of Guilt," 202
Synagogue Council of America, 129, 190
Synod of the Evangelical Lutheran Church of Saxony, 202
Syzk, Arthur, 157

Tageblatt, 71
Tampa Morning Tribune, 81
Tears of Rage (Syzk), 157
Temple, William, 121
Tenenbaum, Joseph, 38
Thompson, Dorothy, 210
Tillich, Paul, 210
Time, 60
Today, 98
Tog, Der, 31, 38–39, 46; on *The Case of Civilization against Hitlerism*, 111; circulation of, 221n95; establishment of, 49; on Hitler, 50; Kohut in, 50–51; Margoshes in, 50; *New York Times* and, 53
totalitarianism, 210

Treaty of Versailles, 100–101, 103
"Trial as Theater" (Bernstein, M., and Milstein), 92
Truman, Harry S, 190; AJC and, 193; AZEC and, 197; *Journal-American* on, 191; Poling and, 238n66
truth (*emeth*), 56
Tucker, Henry St. George, 125, 127, 128
Tuttle, Charles H., 40, 41, 42–43
Tydings, Millard, 97, 109, 112

"Uncle Abraham Reports" (Hecht), 148
Union of Orthodox Jewish Congregations, 25
Union of Orthodox Rabbis, 25; Margolies of, 47
United Nations, 121, 122; International Christian Conference for Palestine and, 197
United Nations Special Committee on Palestine, American Christian Palestine Committee and, 206–7
United Palestine Appeal, 71
United Presbyterian, The, 88, 89
Urofsky, Melvin, 218n33, 219n36, 220n57, 230n13, 237n40

Veterans of Foreign Wars, 26
Visser 't Hooft, Willem, 230n11, 232n47
Voice of Religion, The, 10–11, 62, 77, 81–83, 88–91, 114, 162
Voss, Carl, 238n66

Wagner, C. Everett, 31
Wagner, Robert F., 36–37, 149; Goldberg and, 51; Emanuel Neumann and, 179; on United Nations, 122
Wakeman, Seth, 98
Waldman, Morris, 79
Wallace, Ernest, 27
Warburg, Felix, 82
War Refugee Board, 144
Warren, Earl, 143
Waxman, Franz, 158
Weill, Kurt, 134, 144, 156, 234n85
Weinstein, Albert, 51
Weizmann, Chaim, 117, 121–22
Welles, Sumner, 119
We Will Never Die (Hecht), 12, 116, 131–41, 157; at Hollywood Bowl, 142–43; Eleanor Roosevelt at, 141–42; "Stop Hitler Now" and, 141, 146–47; Wise and, 142
What I Believe (Asch), 73
"When That Man Is Dead and Gone," 134
"White Book." See *Jews in Nazi Germany, The*
White Knights of the Camellia, 216n2
White Paper, Passfield, 174, 175, 177
White Paper of 1939, 13, 188, 189, 239n73
Wiesel, Elie, 3
Wilkie, Wendell, 122
Williams, Michael: in *The Case of Civilization against Hitlerism*, 102, 109; of *Commonweal*, 77, 79, 154; League of Nations and, 79
Wilson, Woodrow, 169, 170–71; Brandeis and, 236n23; Wise and, 236n21, 236n23

"Win the War—Win the Peace," 124
Wise, Stephen S., 6, 9, 11, 18, 31, 32, 57, 67–68; AJC and, 24, 25, 26, 28–29, 75–76; of American Jewish Congress, 117; American Jewish Congress and, 216n3; "An Open Letter to Mr. Attlee" by, 194–95; on antisemitism, 40, 219n36; Bergson and, 119–20, 136, 148, 231n16, 233nn62–63; Berlin Summer Olympics and, 99–100, 228n89; Blackstone and, 169, 170, 171; in *The Case of Civilization against Hitlerism*, 94–96, 102, 103–5, 109, 112; Central Association of German Citizens of Jewish Faith and, 27–28; Christian Zionists and, 173; Clinchy and, 55; Thomas Dewey and, 233n66; Final Solution and, 119, 230n11; *Forverts* on, 48; at Free Synagogue, 16, 29–30, 70–71; Green and, 30; Hearst and, 190; Hecht and, 136, 233n66; on Hitler, 218n33; Holmes and, 45; Hull and, 22; *Journal-American* on, 192; on Judeo-Christian tradition, 95; JWV and, 25, 29; Klausner and, 70–71; Kook and, 116; Landman and, 201; Herbert Lehman and, 220n57; Maharal of Prague and, 55–56; *Morgn Frayhayt* on, 71; in NCJC, 75; *New York Times* and, 16, 23, 24, 39–40, 48; on Permanent Commission for Better Understanding Between Protestants, Catholics, and Jews, 69; Prodnitz and, 27; Franklin D. Roosevelt and, 29, 119, 148; Smith and, 41; at "Stop Hitler Now," 120–31, 146–47; United Palestine Appeal and, 71; *We Will Never Die* and, 142; Wilson and, 236b23, 236n21; of ZOA, 117
Woll, Matthew, 109
Woman on Trial (Rand), 92–93
World Congress of Jewish Women, 39, 49
World Council of Churches, 230n11; antisemitism and, 203
World Jewish Congress: Final Solution and, 131; Riegner of, 119; "Stop Hitler Now" and, 131
World Union of Zionist Revisionists, 117
World Zionist Congress, 163
World Zionist Organization, 117
Wyman, David, 231n16
Wyschogrod, Michael, 2–3, 4

Yeshiva College, 25
YMCA, 72

Zhitlovsky, Chaim, 49
Zionism. *See specific topics*
Zionist Organization of America (ZOA), 11–12, 164, 169, 174, 206; Emanuel Neumann and, 237n36; *New Palestine of*, 120; Rothenberg of, 39; Wise of, 117

A native New Yorker, **Alan M. Shore** holds a doctorate in Modern Jewish History and Culture from the Graduate Theological Union in Berkeley. He contributed an entry on the work of Sholem Asch to the *Encyclopedia of Jewish History and Culture* and wrote the foreword to *A Hebraic Inkling: C. S. Lewis on Judaism and the Jews* by P. H. Brazier.

www.ingramcontent.com/pod-product-compliance
Lightning Source LLC
Chambersburg PA
CBHW031939230426
43672CB00010B/1971